BECOMING
A SAILOR

by
Paul Trammell

ISBN: 9781973478836

Table of Contents

The Search   3

Childhood Memories of Sailing   20

Maiden Voyage   25

The Okefenokee   30

St Petersburg   43

Departure   96

St Lucia to Puerto Rico   140

Dry Tortugas to Miami   196

St Augustine to The Bahamas and Back   222

Miami to St Augustine   289

Epilogue   329

Acknowledgements   331

The Search

I can see civilization and perhaps it can see me, but it can't reach me, and I can't reach it. All the noise and activity of the city lie beyond the horizon; out here, tranquility reigns. The only sounds are the faint rumble of the wind in my sails, the creaking of the rig, and the gentle lapping of the water as it slides across the hull of my little ship. Clean air fills my chest and smells of nothing. The city skyline fades and then disappears below the horizon. The sea and the sky are all that surround me, and the movement of the water and the stillness of the clouds captivate my mind.

There is nothing to do but steer.

I focus on a stationary cloud in front of the bow while gently moving the tiller, just enough to counteract the motion of the waves over which we ride, cloud-steering all day long. There are no distractions, no artificial noises, sounds or smells. This is the home of nature, and I feel welcomed here.

The ocean is an enormous wilderness on which I am confined to the surface. It is all-powerful. It is indifferent to my presence. Man lives in awe of the ocean, rarely venturing beyond its edge or penetrating its depth. Most of it is a vast unexplored mystery. Its waters contain countless creatures of all shapes and sizes, some beautiful beyond explanation, others hideous, most benign, while others strike an instinctive fear in our hearts.

A hiss and a splash reveal dolphins riding in my wake, rolling, twisting, breathing the same air I might have exhaled moments ago, while I breathe in the air they exhale. I smile at the thought of these intelligent creatures taking notice of my little sailboat. I think I make eye-contact with one. It is smiling too.

As quickly as they come, the dolphin disappear, and the ocean is again silent. The invisible wind continues to push and pull us forward, towards a destination that is days away. I look aft and take note of the angle at which the waves approach. I steer by maintaining this angle. This way I can look somewhere besides forward for a while, taking in a different view. I watch the bubbles rise in our wake. I see a bird gliding on the same wind that propels *Sobrius*. The bird slows, folds its wings in, and dives straight down into the ocean, disappearing beneath its surface. Moments later it emerges - head pointing skyward, mouth open, swallowing an unlucky fish. The bird fades into the distance, this time disappearing behind the waves. But it reappears soon after, back in the sky, gliding.

There is nothing to do but steer.

Peace has settled over me, and I don't want it to end. There is no greater peace than that which comes from a fine day of sailing on the ocean, beyond the reach of all the responsibilities of land, where options are so limited that there is nothing to do but sail – steer the boat, trim the sails – one need not make too many decisions. I can't simply step off the boat and go do something productive. I have to sail, there is no other option, so my mind settles into an extraordinary state of relaxation, peace, solitude, and harmony.

But nothing is permanent. Contrast always looms, yet without contrast, all is grey, neither good nor bad. Peace, solitude, and harmony can quickly give way to chaos out on the ocean, and sailing brings tranquility, terror, and everything in between.

Contrast allows us to deeply appreciate what is good; contrast strengthens us like the wind strengthens a tree. Nature is the master of contrast, and exposure to nature and its myriad faces, moods, and extremes, empowers us, balances us, and cleanses our soul. Out on the ocean in a small sailboat, exposure to nature is absolute.

Nature is as close to God as we can get with our physical bodies; to live with nature is to live with God, to live without nature is to live without God, and is the definition of sin: without. We must commune with nature to be whole; we must commune with nature to purify our souls.

I must have done more good than bad in my life, because the ocean has allowed me safe and pleasant passage so far. My boat has stayed on the surface, and the wind has carried us to our destinations. I've explored sailing alone, and I have fallen in love with it. Challenges have come my way, and I've managed to get through them. Peace and wonder have come my way, and I've enjoyed them fully.

Nature is the greatest gift we have, and I want to experience all it has to offer during my life here on Earth, in this time. Nature is forever changing, and man is currently altering nature. So now is the time to explore, to experience, and to preserve what we can of the natural world.

When the time comes, and it will come for all of us, to pass on to the next world, what will we remember? What will we most value from the time we spent here? It will not be the time we wasted in frivolous activities; it will not be the time we spent chasing money; it will not be the time we spent servicing our egos. We will remember and cherish our good deeds, our adventures, and our time deep in nature, when we were closest to God. We will remember when Heaven and Earth were one, when nothing else mattered but the here and now. In the end, all we have are our memories, all we leave behind are our deeds, and all we take with us are our experiences.

~~~

I'm happiest when on adventure, a nomad submerged in nature, experiencing the real world, wild, untamed and unspoiled. I seek this out whenever I can get away from my normal life in a house, with a truck and a job, and all the amenities that make our lives easy and homogenous, one day blending into the next with a sameness that dulls the senses. The common man mistakes comfort for happiness, and falls into a routine promoting the former over the latter. Occasional discomfort brings about resistance to discomfort, new appreciation for the good things in life; it helps us redefine what is good and eliminate unnecessary trappings.

In the year 2016, I began to design a new life for myself, one that would focus on adventure and require discipline, endurance to discomfort, resistance to cravings, education, and learning new skills. My goal was to sail on the open ocean, by myself, singlehanded, cut off from society. I craved adventure at its greatest, and nature spoke to me and reminded me of the ocean and sailboats. I didn't have a boat, but I began training and preparing for what I knew would come.

I identified everything that had so far prevented me from becoming a sailor, and I set out to overcome all obstacles in my path. I lacked knowledge, so I read and studied all I could about sailing, devouring books and taking notes as if I was back in school. I lacked experience, so took a one-week sailing class and crewed on offshore passages and in local races. I feared being cold at sea, so I tried to become more cold-tolerant, by taking cold showers and long walks on the beach in cold and windy weather. I feared drowning, so I took up ocean swimming. I knew I could never be a sailor if I was a drunk, so I stayed sober.

I chose a name for my sailboat long before I found her: *Sobrius*, Latin for sobriety. I wrote this name, with a smiley face underneath, on a sticky note and stuck it to a map of the world which is tacked to the wall in front of my desk, where I would see it every day, like a talisman that would make my dream more real, while the map was a daily reminder of where I wanted to take the sailboat that I didn't yet have.

Sailing on the ocean, no land in sight, clean air, nature, silence, adventure, these are the things I dreamed about, not at night, but when sitting quietly at my desk or walking on the beach in the morning. I wanted to sail to far-away places and see parts of the world that I had not yet seen. I wanted to experience the ocean in all its moods (not literally *all* of them). I wanted to dive beneath the surface, see the underwater worlds, the fish, the coral, the depths. I wanted to escape.

I needed a new life; I had ditched my old one. In the past life I had traded nature and adventure for intoxication in a long slow barter that I was somewhat unaware of. In my new life I was going to take back adventure. I craved it like a drug, like the drugs from my past. I needed a sailboat, and nothing was going to stop me from getting one, it was just a matter of time. And as so often happens to the determined, eventually I got what I wanted.

~~~

I became obsessed with looking at and researching sailboats online well before I had any money saved or any real plan to get one. I wanted to be ready when the time came to buy a sailboat, so I took in all the information I could that might enable me to choose the right boat. I poured over the online listings and researched all the boats that looked interesting. I read articles and online forums, looked at statistics, studied the pros and cons of different designs. It was overwhelming at times, but slowly I began forming opinions about what I wanted in a sailboat.

I knew that a new life waited for me, and a sailboat would bring me there. It wasn't long before I picked up the phone and began calling the numbers listed on the sailboat advertisements and talking to the sellers, and of course, this eventually led to seeing boats in person.

I looked at many sailboats in 2016. The first was an old Irwin 44 (44 feet long) ketch. It wasn't the right boat for me, and I felt this before I looked at it, but it was close to home and I needed to get started. After spending an inordinate amount of time devouring the pictures and descriptions of boats for sale online, I determined that I needed to go and see one in person, in order to make my mission to get a sailboat more real. In order for dream to become reality, one must get the dream off the ground, and looking at this first boat signified my dream taking off, going from the purely mental stage to the concrete stage of action.

Through much study of sailboat design and singlehanding, I determined that I wanted a boat steered by a tiller as opposed to a wheel so as to facilitate singlehand sailing. The tiller allows the skipper more mobility while steering, and can be controlled with the legs or knees to free up the hands for trimming the sails. An autopilot for a tiller is simpler and less expensive than one for a wheel, and the tiller is also more easily adaptable to sheet-to-tiller steering or windvane-steering compared to a wheel

At first I wanted a boat with a full keel, which runs the full length of the hull, as opposed to a fin keel, which is shorter but deeper. The fin keel offers more speed, maneuverability, and windward performance, while the full keel offers more stability and safety. But then I discovered a compromise: the fin keel with skeg-hung rudder. The skeg is like a miniature keel which supports and protects the rudder and provides some directional stability while retaining most of the performance of a strictly fin-keeled boat.

I continued, and the next two boats I looked at were more suited to my intended purposes: a Camper-Nicholson 31, then a Southern Cross 31, both full-keeled, heavily-built, double-ended (pointed on the bow and the stern, like a canoe) ocean-crossing sailboats. Both of these boats were recommended in John Vigor's book *Twenty Small Sailboats to Take You Anywhere* and would have been good choices, yet I had no idea how to come up with the money to purchase either at the time. But I needed to see them, to sit in their cockpits and put my hand on the tiller. I needed to visualize myself spending weeks at a time in a sailboat and see how this made me feel. I needed to learn all I could about sailboats in order to make an informed and educated decision when the time came to buy one, and I knew the time would come.

I became interested in the Sadler line of unsinkable sailboats (the 29 and the 34) after reading about them. Unsinkability seemed like a great idea to me. They essentially have two hulls, one smaller than the other and fit inside the larger one. The space between them is filled with foam. I found one for a very reasonable price up in Maryland, so I drove all the way there from Florida and back over a weekend to see it. I reasoned that if I was going to be a singlehanded ocean-crossing sailor, then a drive to Maryland and back, over a weekend, should be no problem. The marathon drive further reinforced the reality of my mission to become a sailor.

The green Sadler 29, which sat in a dry-dock by the Chesapeake Bay, was a very stout-looking boat, and I was tempted to make an offer on the spot. But the boat did not have a working engine, and so instead I returned home and waited until the owner fixed the engine, after which I hired a marine surveyor to inspect the boat.

He stopped his inspection early and only charged me half the agreed-upon price. He found some major issues right away, including diesel fuel, as well as water, all over the inside of the boat, and his instruments picked up water-intrusion in the floatation built into the hull. If water had permeated the built-in floatation, I reasoned that the boat was no longer unsinkable and heavier than it should be. I lost interest.

Next I found a Dufour Arpege in St Petersburg, and I went to see it and two other boats in one trip through south Florida. The first boat I visited, in Indiantown, was an Ocean Voyager 26. It was a full-keeled double-ender that looked like a miniature version of a Westsail 32, a classic ocean-crossing sailboat. But it had been long-neglected and also had no standing headroom inside. Further south, in Pompano Beach, I looked at a beautiful Cape Dory 28 that looked like it needed no work at all. I was very interested in this boat, and the owner was extremely eager to sell. In fact he was so eager that

I became suspicious of him. I kept on driving, all the way to St Petersburg to see the Dufour Arpege.

The Arpege attracted me right away, even though it looked a bit neglected, with no varnish on the teak, and a tarp covering its main hatch. I liked its aggressive looks, and I had read nothing but positive reviews about them. At least one had even circumnavigated the globe. I liked it enough that I made an offer and scheduled an inspection, and I returned a few days later for the inspection and sea-trial. The marine surveyor looked all over the boat, finding a couple of soft spots on the deck, but nothing catastrophic. We took it out into Tampa Bay for a sail, which seemed fine to me, and around the corner for a haul-out at Salt Creek Marina, where the boat was lifted out of the water so the we could inspect the hull.

The keel was a cast-iron fin with a bulb at the bottom, way ahead of its time for a boat from 1972. The iron was very pitted, and the keel had oysters and barnacles all over it. The rudder was supported by a long thin skeg, which I liked. I was warming up to the fin-keel and skeg-hung rudder idea. The surveyor walked around the boat while tapping on the hull with a rubber hammer and listening for hollow sounds that would indicate delamination of the hull. None was found. However, little flakes of bronze fell to the ground as the surveyor tapped on a blade of the propeller with the back of his pocketknife. Galvanic corrosion (preferential corrosion of dissimilar metals when in contact with an electrolyte (seawater)) had taken its toll and the propeller was ruined. There was no sacrificial zinc anode attached. Apparently, the diver who had been paid to regularly clean the bottom and inspect the zinc had not been doing his job.

But overall, the boat looked fine to me, and the surveyor seemed to like it too. After an hour of inspection, the yard lowered the Arpege back into Salt Creek and the four of us climbed onboard for the return trip to the St Petersburg Municipal Marina.

As we motored out of Salt Creek we were all startled by the loud beeping of an alarm. The engine was overheating and the engine-temperature alarm was assaulting the otherwise tranquil afternoon. We had to stop the engine, right when we really needed it to turn to starboard and motor upwind and away from a seawall. Al, the broker, was at the helm.

"Get a sail up!" he shouted at us as we slowly drifted downwind.

The owner of the boat and I went to the main and tried to hoist it, but the hard and inflexible battens in the mainsail were getting caught in the rope network of the lazyjacks, preventing the mainsail from rising. I alternately pulled and lowered the halyard, trying to work the sail around the lazyjacks, but my inexperience won the day, and the sail remained only halfway up and ineffective at providing forward thrust.

"At least get the jib up" Al yelled as we drifted towards the corrugated-steel seawall and certain destruction.

The owner of the boat, a young man with large round glasses and a calm demeanor, went to the headsail halyard and raised it while I struggled with the main. We began moving forward instead of sideways. He then released the lazyjacks, freeing the battens of the mainsail, which I was then able to raise. The main immediately caught wind and added to our forward motion.

We barely missed the seawall as we slowly began moving parallel to it, and then away from it upwind. Al tacked us into deeper water away from the seawall, and then turned us around and back into Salt Creek. We returned to the Salt-Creek Marina, where he sailed us into a slip. The secretary at the marina was kind enough to give the four of us a ride back to the St Petersburg Municipal Marina where I discussed the findings with the surveyor before driving home.

~~~

The Arpege's engine, a clean and modern Yanmar YGM10, was one of its main attractions to me, and since it had problems, I backed out of the deal. Soon after I found another Arpege in Miami and drove there to see it. This one was beautiful and had been meticulously maintained. Its hull was bright blue, all the stainless steel was polished and shining in the sunlight, and it was clean and looked ready to go. The owner had passed away, but had sailed this boat on long ocean voyages to the Azores and the Caribbean. It was loaded with electronics, had roller furling, a 28 horsepower Yanmar diesel, and lots of spare parts and tools. This little sailboat was eager for adventure and had an air of wonder to it. I made an offer on the spot. The seller gave a verbal acceptance, and I agreed to set up an inspection and wire a deposit after I returned to St Augustine.

Since I was in Coconut Grove, I decided to meet my high-school sweetheart Cristina, who lived there. We met at a café and reminisced. Little did we know that I would be here again on another Arpege in January.

After returning to St Augustine, wiring a deposit, and setting up a survey of the Arpege, I was informed that the seller had legal problems and could not proceed with the sale.

The next boat I looked at was a big, majestic, and classic Alberg 35. I loved it. But it was, by comparison to the Arpege, an enormous sailboat, and the entire bow area of the deck was severely delaminated. My father cautioned against a boat this big, saying it would be a difficult boat on which to learn to sail, and that I would be reluctant to sail it on account of its size and lack of maneuverability due to its full-keel. Days before I looked at the Alberg, I watched a man try to turn his full-keeled Bristol 44 around in a marina. The boat simply would not turn in such a small space and he actually collided with another boat that was sitting peacefully in its slip. I think my father was right, and I didn't follow up on this one. Maybe in the future I'll look at another Alberg; they are beautiful boats with a reputation of seaworthiness.

I found another Cape Dory, this one a 30′ cutter, and quickly went to see it. I loved it. I scheduled a survey and a return trip. But during the survey, the inspector took an oil sample from the engine, sent it to a lab for analysis, and it was found by the lab to have major saltwater intrusion. This was enough to make me back out of the deal.

In the meantime, the owner of the first Arpege had the water pump rebuilt and the engine was running again. I decided to go ahead with this one. The price was right, and it was the right boat, just big enough to live on if I needed to, and well-suited for a singlehander. In November of 2016, I went to St. Petersburg with an envelope full of cash, and purchased the Arpege. It was mine!

~~~

After the seller and the broker left, I was alone with my sailboat. I stood on the dock gazing lovingly at her. The hull was the dark blue of deep clean water, with a faded gold stripe at the waterline. The bow and transom gracefully overhung the water giving her the classic look of sailboats from the 60′s and 70′s. The neglected teak of the toe rail, handholds, and tiller was a silver-grey, like the color of weathered aluminum, and looked like it had not been varnished since the turn of the century. The deck was off-white with two hatches, one facing forward and one facing aft. Long horizontal windows, dropping to a point at the front, ran down the sides of the low coachroof and gave the vessel the look of an animal with its eyebrows furrowed. The acrylic of the hatches and windows was bright blue, but crazed from many years of exposure to the sun. The lifelines were not the usual steel cable, but instead thin white line which did not give an impression of safety. A blue tarp, the kind you buy at a hardware store, covered the main hatch and the area between it and the mast, an obvious sign of leaks. Although it looked neglected, the little sailboat gave the impression of seaworthiness and speed. It looked like it was made to venture out into the ocean and make the best of the wind. I sensed that she wanted a new owner and still had some life in her.

Sobrius (formerly Galadriel) on the day I bought her

The Arpege is a 30' sloop and was designed for fast offshore cruising. It was the boat that launched the Dufour brand. Revolutionary at its time, but common now, it has an iron fin-keel with a bulb at the bottom, shaped like a torpedo, which increases the boat's stability and speed, and a skeg supports and protects the rudder. The cockpit is small and allows water to flow back out into the ocean through two large drains. A small well-drained cockpit is necessary for ocean sailing, preventing the boat from being overwhelmed by the breaking of a wave over the rear of the vessel and filling the cockpit with seawater. The steering is accomplished with a tiller.

The mainsheet and the two winches which control the jib-sheets are both accessible from the tiller, facilitating singlehand sailing. The headsail (also called a jib) "hanks" onto the headstay (the steel cable that connects the bow to the top of the mast). This is the old-fashioned way of attaching a sail to the headstay with spring-loaded clips called "hanks." This is opposed to the more modern and convenient (and expensive) roller-furling, in which the headsail is wrapped around the headstay when not in use.

Inside are two quarter-berths underneath the cockpit benches. In front of the starboard berth is a navigation table; in front of the port berth is a small two-burner alcohol stove and a tiny sink. Two more berths are in the main salon, with storage above and below them, and a removable table attaches to the steel mast-compression post. Further forward is a head (toilet) opposite some shelves and a hanger for clothes, and in the bow is a small storage area.

There is no refrigerator or air conditioner. It is a simple boat and I figured it would be a good choice for singlehanding, as I intended to do.

~~~

Immediately after buying her, I spent two months in St Petersburg, docked at the Municipal Marina in the slip that I took over from the previous owner, living in and working on *Sobrius*. The surveyor provided me with a long list of tasks to be completed before sailing home to St. Augustine, and I added many of my own chores to the list. The marina was right in the center of downtown and surrounded by greenspace on the bayfront, walking paths, and upscale shopping and dining.

Luckily, St Petersburg was a sailing city, with many resources for the sailor renovating a boat. There were chandleries, a sail loft, a store specializing in selling sails, another that sold only hoses, one that sold only fasteners, another that specialized in fiberglass and epoxy, and even a solar panel dealer. I was never in need of a part or product that was not available.

The first thing I did was replace the exhaust hose, which was followed by the cockpit drain-hoses and the sink drain-hose. Hoses seemed like something easy to replace and I wanted to start with something at which I knew I would succeed. Next I replaced all the interior and exterior lights with LED lights. This was in order to save electricity while sailing and to reduce my need to run the engine to charge the batteries, which I also replaced. My reliance on the engine was drastically further reduced by the installation of two 55-watt solar panels.

Much of the wiring inside the boat I replaced, and I added some outlets for USB and car-lighter-type DC electrical chargers, which I use to charge my iPhone, Kindle, two handheld VHF radios, my video camera, a flashlight, and one powers a small fan.

In order to prevent myself from falling overboard and watching the sailboat sail off without me, I installed three padeyes in the cockpit to which I could clip tethers from my safety harness and thus be firmly attached to the boat. One padeye I mounted to the floor to be used while in the cockpit, and the other two I mounted to the cockpit bulkhead and from these I can lead flat nylon strap to two cleats that I installed at the bow. These straps are known as jacklines and to them I clip a tether from my safety harness when I need to go on deck while sailing. My lifejacket is built like a climber's harness and has two short tethers tied to it with carabiners on the ends. It is these carabiners that I clip to the padeyes and jacklines. I have two so that if I am moving forward and need to cross an obstacle, like a jib-sheet, I can clip one past the obstacle before unclipping the other one. When I am working outside the cockpit I clip one tether to a shroud (a steel cable that supports the mast) while the other is clipped to a jackline so that I am clipped to two different things. I really don't want to fall off the boat!

The Arpege's deck had many leaks, so I spent a lot of time tracking these down and sealing them. I also painted non-skid paint on the deck to give me better grip while walking outside the cockpit, crucial for keeping firm footing and staying aboard. All of the woodwork on deck got sanded, epoxied and varnished. All deck hardware got rebedded (removed, cleaned and bolted back to the deck with new caulk). I put a lot of time and effort into these projects, working all day every day, and my background as a carpenter was invaluable in the restoration process. I would never have been able to afford to pay someone else to do all the work that I did to my beloved little sailboat. I could barely afford to do it myself!

The repairs went on for a full two months of ten-hour days. During this time, I sailed in Tampa Bay to get used to the boat and to learn how to singlehand (sail by myself). This was a wonderful part of my life that I will always remember and cherish, working hard, but strictly for myself and for my dream, to become a singlehand sailor.

Each morning I would wake before the sun, make coffee, and walk along the beautiful bayfront of St Petersburg, strolling along the sidewalk that fronts the water, looking at boats and trying to meditate while watching the sunrise. I figured that I needed to learn to meditate in order to sleep in twenty-minute increments while sailing, and to just keep my sanity and clarity of mind during the long periods of solitude. Sleeping in short increments, while the boat is sailing via an autopilot, was suggested by more than one author as a safety precaution, and while suggested lengths of time varied between authors, twenty minutes was the most conservative number, so I made it my goal.

~~~

St Petersburg sunrise

Even though many are superstitious about changing the name of a boat and strongly advise against doing so, I changed the name of my sailboat from *Galadriel* to *Sobrius* (which I pronounce SOH-bree-us). Sobriety brought me to sailing, and the name *Sobrius*, Latin for sobriety, would forever remind me of my commitment to stay sober. The previous February 3rd marked my first year of sobriety, and I had bought myself a one-week sailing class as a reward for my efforts. This led to an obsession with sailing that brought me to *Sobrius* and St. Petersburg. I reasoned that if I named my sailboat *Sobrius*, I would be further disinclined to start drinking again. So far, this strategy has been successful.

This is the story of becoming a singlehand sailor, and my solo journey from St Petersburg to my home in St Augustine. This was my first singlehand journey, and my previous sailing experience was minimal. I had read many books on sailing, sailed on friends' boats and sailed offshore a few times. But I had never owned a sailboat besides a dinghy that I restored and then sold after only sailing a handful of times (I bought an electric guitar with the money). I had never planned a sailing journey and had never been responsible for knowing how to skipper a sailboat. But I had confidence that I could pull it off with a lot of studying, the right vessel, and some practice before embarking on the journey.

Childhood Memories of Sailing

Childhood adventures teach us that life has much more to offer than what our houses and neighborhoods contain. They teach us new skills. They teach us to overcome obstacles. They teach us to manage our fear and rise above it.

When I was very young, we lived in New Orleans, and my father had a 30′ wooden sailboat, without an engine, that he kept on Lake Pontchartrain. I only have vague memories of this boat, a Knarr, but this was my first exposure to sailing.

In my earliest memory of sailing I am with my father, my brother, our friend Satoshi, and his father, sailing on Tampa Bay. I remember being nervous thinking the boat was going to tip over when it heeled. But my father reassured me that, like a Weeble, the boat could lean over but would never capsize. And since the adults weren't worried, my fears subsided.

I've always loved swimming, and I wanted to get in the water at every opportunity. So, after persuading my father, he put life jackets on us, tied us to a line, and let us float around in the bay. In the water, attached to the boat only by a thin line, floating in the unknown, is perhaps my first memory of adventure. The world became much bigger that day.

When I was eleven and twelve years old, at summer camp, we sailed Sunfish on a lake in North Carolina. We were a pack of crazy young boys with minimal instruction, two per boat, sailing into each other and causing a general ruckus on the water. I distinctly remember seeing one boat completely capsize and another run right over it. I think we all spent a considerable amount of time *in* the water.

As a child, I spent all of my free time in the woods when we lived in West Virginia, or on the bayou when we lived in Louisiana. I just wanted to be out in nature, so sailing with my father was always a treat. I loved being on a boat, and rough seas or bad weather didn't bother me much.

As a young teenager, my father let me join him and his friends on a sail in the Chesapeake Bay, and then another to The Bahamas from Ft Lauderdale. Sailing offshore, with no land in sight, was a wonderful and new experience. I was awed by the way we used the wind to propel us forward, even when the wind came from ahead of us. I sat on the foredeck and tried to figure out this mystery, straddling the bow and letting my feet dip in the water between waves. I loved manning the helm when the adults would give me the opportunity, but the bow was my favorite place to ride, staring down at the occasional odd sea creature drifting by.

I remember a huge pod of dolphin following us on the way to The Bahamas, riding our bow-wake and leaping into the air. It seemed like a wild circus act to me. I couldn't believe how many of them there were, and was astonished at how high they jumped and how fast they swam. The ocean was proving to be a place of wonder and magic.

My father took me on another trip that was to be from Sarasota, Florida, to the Dry Tortugas. On this trip we had to avoid bad weather and ended up in Charlotte Harbor instead. While we didn't have nice weather or see any beautiful islands, I still enjoyed the sailing and being exposed to nature.

The whole family, my mother and father, younger sister and older brother, sailed from Marco Island to the Dry Tortugas when I was sixteen. We were part of a flotilla of ten sailboats, which made us all feel safer. It was nice having the family all together on an adventure, confined to the small space of a sailboat. This was surely a bonding experience for all of us.

I remember we were all incredulous that no water would be available in the Dry Tortugas. Drinking water was rationed, and we could not shower at all. This was a great surprise to me on the first day, but caused no problems overall. We ate lots of potatoes boiled in seawater, which sounds odd but is actually quite good.

In the anchorage at Garden Key, next to Fort Jefferson, we dropped two anchors in a "V" pattern, and I dove to set them firmly in the sand, which made me feel useful. One night there was a thunderstorm with strong winds all night and all the other boats drug their anchors, some bumping into others. But I was proud that our anchors held firm and our boat stayed put. I was proud that I had pleased my father with my diving ability. I've set anchors like this ever since.

Another family in the flotilla had children and an inner-tube. We had a grand time being pulled across the water behind their dinghy, and rolling each other in the tube down a sand-dune and into the water.

Lobster were plentiful and easy to catch. My parents were very encouraging of my lobster hunting, and I had five in a bucket before another adult in our flotilla realized what I was doing. He informed us that catching lobster was illegal within the national park, and each one could bring a $500 fine. They all went back into the water immediately.

I snorkeled on the healthy reefs and saw a huge expanse of live elkhorn coral, like a marine forest. Fish swam all through it, while I swam around the edges. A large barracuda followed me around and made me nervous. I got out of the water on a beach before swimming back to the sailboat after I gave the big toothy fish time to lose interest in me. Another time someone dropped a plate overboard and I jumped in with mask and snorkel to retrieve it. But I was scared out of the water by two huge stingrays swimming along the bottom. Little did I know they would have caused me no harm. I was also scared out of the water by ctenophores (also known as comb jellies). I was snorkeling around the boat and suddenly noticed hundreds of them all around me. I thought they were jellyfish and would sting me (they don't sting). So I swam under and around them back to the boat and got out as fast as I could. I now understand that there is almost nothing in the ocean that a swimmer should fear. The animals all just go about their business and rarely interact with humans.

On the way back to the mainland, sailing across the Gulf of Mexico, I was taking a shift at the helm in the middle of the night. The stars were out and we sailed peacefully in light winds. My mother was asleep on the bench beside me.

The wind increased and the stars faded away as clouds blocked their light. Waves seemed to grow out of nowhere, and the wind continued to strengthen. The sailboat heeled further and further, until the port rail was in the water. At this point I was being assaulted by heavy spray from the waves that we crashed through, like someone was throwing buckets of water at me. Luckily it wasn't cold.

I looked below deck and called for my father, who had been sleeping. He was now putting on foul-weather gear and emerged with two harnesses. He put on one and I put on the other, tethering myself to the binnacle (the supporting structure for the steering wheel). My mother was below handing out lifejackets and hand-held lights to my brother and sister. She was 10 at the time, and I remember her saying "we're all going to die!"

My father got up on deck and made his way to the mast to reef the mainsail, telling me to steer us into the wind. But even though I turned the wheel all the way to the right, we could not point into the wind. The boat heeled further and further, and finally it seemed as though we were about to capsize. I was standing on the normally vertical part of the cockpit bench when I looked to my left at the dark water and was sure that I would soon be in it. The boat heeled so much that the rudder came out of the water and we just slid sideways with the wind holding the boat so the mast was nearly parallel to the water. We had broached.

Although I never swore in front of my parents, I yelled "Get the damn sail down!" at my father, who was still calmly working at the mast. I really didn't know what was going on. Eventually he got the sails reefed and the boat settled into a more comfortable position. As a sailor, I don't think he was ever worried, but the rest of us certainly were.

This experience, I think, was formative and set the scale for me. In the future, if something wasn't as scary as that, I could certainly handle it.

Maiden Voyage
November, 2016

I had been working on *Sobrius* for about two weeks when I asked myself why I hadn't sailed her yet. Every morning I just wanted to work on her, perhaps because, as a carpenter, this was something I understood. But sailing by myself, out of a slip and past other boats, out a harbor, around the bay and back, docking without crashing into anything, was not a series of events with which I was familiar. Specifically, I determined that it was a fear of docking back in my slip without crashing into the neighboring boats or the wooden dock with its pilings and barnacles that really worried me and was delaying my maiden voyage. I needed a method of docking that would guarantee that I didn't hit anything, and I was having trouble visualizing this, but I knew there must be a solution.

I slept on the idea, and a vision came to me in the middle of the night. As I lay in the starboard bunk, I imagined tying two lines (ropes) making a large X horizontally across my slip, from the pilings at the entrance of the slip to a cleat on the dock, about a foot or two above the water. These lines would catch *Sobrius* upon return and bring us to a stop in the center of my slip without the risk of hitting anything. I would only need to grab a stern line hanging from the piling on the way in and we would be safe. The X lines would also hold the bow in place after I untied the bowlines before departing. I loved the idea and was eager to try it out.

On the morning of November 23rd, 2016, I tied mooring lines in an X across my slip and started the one-cylinder diesel engine inside *Sobrius*. I then walked around the boat looking for last-minute chores. I had already chosen a headsail and hanked it to the headstay, tied sheets to its clew and led them back through the jib-cars to the two winches in the cockpit.

The jib-halyard was shackled to the head of the headsail. Jacklines were in place. The mainsail cover was off and stowed; the main halyard was shackled to the mainsail, ready to hoist. A handheld VHF radio was in the cockpit, clipped to the jackline, turned on, and ready to use. The stern-anchor was in place on the stern rail, ready to deploy in an emergency. I put on my lifejacket, gloves, and my black leather hat.

I checked the wind direction, looking at the wind vane on the top of the mast, and chose which dock-lines to untie fist. The bow was held in place by the X, so I untied the bow-lines first and coiled them on the dock. Next I untied the stern-lines and hung them on the pilings, ready to catch on the way back in. I reached down to the shift-lever in the cockpit and put *Sobrius* in reverse for the first time.

The RPM's slowly increased, raising the pitch of the rumbling engine as *Sobrius* slowly backed out of her slip. Carefully I watched the oyster-encrusted pilings as *Sobrius* passed by them, steering with the tiller to avoid contact. I backed her out of the slip and pulled the tiller to port, turning my little ship into the channel, avoiding backing into all the sailboats across from us. Again I reached down to the shift-lever and put *Sobrius* in forward gear. Our backward momentum kept us moving astern for a moment, and I briefly wondered if we were in forward gear, but then we came to a stop and magically began moving forward. I turned and looked ahead. I was the captain of my own vessel. I stood proud with the tiller in one hand and the taut main-sheet in the other; I steered *Sobrius* through the marina and towards Tampa Bay, master of my universe. My dream was becoming reality.

~~~

As we motored through the marina, we passed all manner of boats tied up in their slips: sailboats large and small, then on the outside catamarans, shiny and fast-looking, a big racing monohull with the names of sponsors covering the hull sides, trawlers – one on which sat a man smoking a cigar. I waved to the man, and he waved back, relaxed and comfortable on his large motor-yacht, me nervous and proud on my humble sailboat. A bright orange ketch with the hard angles of a steel hull stood out among the white sailboats. A brightly-painted mural decorated the side of a houseboat that looked like it never left the dock. There was the faint smell of diesel fumes and sea creatures in the air as I passed the marina office and its sea wall. I waved to a fisherman standing under a palm tree on the wall; he smiled and waved back. The sun was rising. A white heron was also fishing on the rocks opposite the man. Seagulls called; the bay beckoned; *Sobrius* motored on.

I pulled the tiller to port and *Sobrius* responded by turning to starboard, following the channel to the bay. We began to encounter small waves and I pushed the shift-lever further down to increase our speed. I turned us to port and we faced the bay for the first time as a team – *Sobrius* and me. A red channel-marker on our left indicated our entrance into Tampa Bay, and as we entered, I felt a change beginning in me. I was slowly becoming a sailor.

~~~

Everything was new: the feel of the sailboat under my feet; the sounds of the engine, the wind and the water moving past the hull; the sight of Tampa Bay; the blue-grey color of the water; the maritime smell of the air; the emotion that sailing alone brings, self-confidence mixed with serenity. I relished in the moment, it was one that I could never repeat, my first solo sail in a boat bigger than my old 14-foot dinghy from many years prior.

We motored into the bay until I felt it was safe to hoist the sails, whereupon I turned *Sobrius* into the wind and used a bungee to tie off the tiller amidships while I went forward to raise the mainsail. I clipped in to the jackline with the carabiner tethered to my lifejacket and moved to the mast. I crept in a hunched-over manner to avoid being hit in the head by the boom should it come swinging at me unexpectedly. At the mast I uncleated the main halyard from the black mast-cleat and pulled downward. The sail rose. I had to raise it a bit, lower it and raise it again a few times to work the battens around the lazyjacks (a series of lines that support the mainsail when it is down), and after a minute or two the white sail was all the way up.

I looked around to make sure we weren't about to hit anything, then I used the winch to tighten the halyard, and the mainsail responded by becoming tight and flat. I tied the halyard back to the cleat on the mast and moved the winch-handle to the winch on the opposite side of the mast which I would use to raise the headsail. I pulled it up quickly with its green and white halyard and the winch sang its metallic song as I used it to tighten the halyard and make the headsail taut. After cleating off the jib-halyard, I carefully made my way back to the cockpit, trimmed the jib, untied the tiller and steered us to port and onto a broad reach, with the wind coming directly from starboard.

I let out the mainsheet so the sail would catch the wind and propel us forward, and when all looked right, I reached down to the engine-kill knob by the shift-lever (a knob which I had installed) and pulled. The rumbling of the engine stopped, and the low-oil-pressure alarm sounded (as it is supposed to when you kill the engine). I turned off the key and tossed it in the cockpit pocket, quieting the alarm. Silence. As I looked up and forward, my right hand on the tiller, the only sounds were the wind in the sails and the water moving across the hull, rising and falling as we moved through the small waves on Tampa Bay. The feeling of elation that came over me during this first sail was compounded by the fact that this was literally a dream-come-true. After a full year of preparation, study, and daydreaming, I was finally sailing singlehanded on my own sailboat!

A door to the entire world opened up to me. On this little ship, I could sail anywhere I wished. My life expanded in this instant of realization. I was no longer bound to the land. I was no longer stuck in one place. *Sobrius* was big enough to live in, and I could take her anywhere that the wind blew, and I intended to take her far.

The Okefenokee
Christmas, 2015

Adventure is what gives my life meaning, and it comes in many forms. Seeing natural places that few humans get to see is like unwrapping presents. Venturing deep into nature, in the forest, on the water, or under the water, not knowing what's around each bend, behind the next wave, or beneath the surface, brings about a euphoria that reminds us that we are alive, fully appreciating God's creation, feeling the heightened senses one experiences when completely aware. Nature bestows gifts on those who seek out her depths, dark corners and hidden kingdoms.

My ambition to become a sailor was reawakened while paddling my canoe through the silent and pristine swamps of the Okefenokee.

It all started when I quit drinking on February 3rd in the auspicious year of 2015. I had reasoned that part of my therapy would come from doing things that drinking had prevented me from doing in the past. Adventure was on the top of my list, and after researching where I could go to be deepest in nature and the furthest from roads, I discovered the Okefenokee National Wildlife Reserve, a 650-square-mile swamp in southern Georgia which makes up the headwaters of the Suwanee river. Canoe trails wind around the reserve in a great circle and lead to nine camping platforms. Each of these platforms is no less than eight miles from any other platform. All are completely secluded and deep in wilderness, providing a quiet place to be alone and contemplate nature.

I booked a five-day canoe trip over Christmas of 2015 and ventured into the swamp alone. It was out in this water-dominated wilderness, while paddling on my second day, that I realized how much I liked being in a boat, deep within nature – nomadic, immersed in wilderness. I looked about me, across miles of swamp and low vegetation in all directions, and I remembered how much I had liked sailing with my father when I was a child. It was that moment in the Okefenokee, looking out across the vast wetland prairie from my canoe, that I decided to become a sailor.

~~~

The Okefenokee Wildlife Refuge is all wilderness, mostly swamp, and mostly inaccessible to humans. Cut through the refuge is the Suwannee canal, the only deep water in the reserve, and various shallow canoe trails lead through vast prairies of shallow water and emergent vegetation. Islands dot the landscape, inhabited by densely-clumped trees and bushes, all trying to squeeze onto the tiny bits of "land". Huge floating mats of peat on which grass and other plants grow drift about, mimicking land, but give way when pushed with a paddle. There is nowhere to stand. One's boat is the only means of ingress or egress, and there are no other people to lend a hand should one be needed. Self-reliance is paramount, enhancing the feeling of being one with nature, exposed to all of its elements, beautiful and dangerous.

This feeling has always appealed to me, no other humans around, no civilization, no one on which to rely besides myself, exposed to raw nature, one with nature. I used to feel this way when riding my mountain-bike on long loops in the forest, when I knew I was so deep that mistakes could be fatal, and that I simply must keep riding in order to get out of the woods. Inaction is not an option, nor is giving up. Surfing can feel this way too, especially on days when the surf is big, or when far from shore, or if the ocean is particularly unruly. SCUBA diving, freediving, and ocean swimming all elicit the same emotional response. The more one can be exposed to nature, the more one lives.

The immediate reward for extreme exposure to the forces of nature is a feeling of deep peace and satisfaction, the opposite of anxiety, oneness with something big and divine, perhaps a small taste of enlightenment. The more permanent and longer-lasting rewards include an increased self-confidence, loss of fears that might otherwise prevent one from accomplishment, and wonderful memories that can be recalled and relived at any time. This can be a useful tool when one needs to mentally escape to a "happy place". I sometimes need to go, in my mind, to the reefs of The Virgin Islands, colorful and teeming with life, where I dove as a teenager. The sense of accomplishment from such events is long-lasting and can put a stop to any thoughts of failure or mediocrity in life. Indeed, adventure and exploration give life meaning.

~~~

Preparing for an adventure is certainly part of the fun. I discovered the Okefenokee via Facebook after posting a query requesting deep-wilderness-adventure suggestions. A high-school classmate suggested an Okefenokee canoe trip. After a bit of research, I discovered the system of camping platforms spread out across the refuge, accessible only by canoe or kayak, which must be reserved in advance. Aside from some photos, a crude map, and legends of alien-abductions and families of Bigfoot living in the swamp, I found little other information. I called the reserve office and was pleased to find the woman who answered very friendly and helpful, and she assisted me in booking a four-night trip.

The Okefenokee has a reputation for an abundance of alligators, of which I have always had a deep fear. Alligators come up in dreams on a regular basis. Usually the scene ends with me in a canoe or a car that is slowly sinking at night in dark water with alligators around. Sometimes I'm swimming and come to realize that alligators surround me. In other dreams the alligators are ridiculously large, and in some dreams people get eaten. Yes, these dreams sometimes got ugly.

one of the 363 alligators I saw

One intention of this trip was to overcome my fear of these animals. In order to feel safe enough in my canoe to do this trip, I improvised a float-bag using my inflatable mattress, making the boat unsinkable. I also brought, and kept close-at-hand, a rifle and a machete. All of my gear was packed in water-tight storage bins and I tied everything to the boat.

Soon after pushing off from shore on the first day, I saw an alligator with something in its mouth that looked like a partially-decayed body part of some mammal, a deer's leg perhaps, and certainly an ominous sight at the beginning of my adventure. It was the first of 363 alligators that I saw during my 5-day trip. I counted them all; it gave me something to do while paddling, and I was certainly obsessed with these prehistoric dinosaur-like creatures.

The alligators were an almost constant presence, and I

kept getting the sensation that my canoe was sinking whenever I saw one. Many, many times I looked down at the floor of the boat to reassure myself that it was not taking on water, but there was always a little water in the bottom of my canoe which had dripped off my kayak paddle, and I stared at it to see if it was getting deeper; it never was. My subconscious was confusing my recurring dreams with reality, but reality was also communicating with my subconscious, slowly easing my deep-seated fear of alligators.

Most of the alligators I saw were sitting on the bank or a peat-island, or just an emergence of mud. When they saw me they mainly did one of three things. About a third remained still as I passed, calmly looking at me while lying on the bank. The other two-thirds of them rushed into the water as I approached. While some slipped into the dark water slowly and quietly, others sprinted into the water with a great splash. Half of these would disappear underwater before I got to them, and the others would swim away.

However, most of the time I was navigating narrow canoe trails which were only about 10-20 feet wide and three feet deep. When alligators went underwater out in front of me, I would have to pass over them. This terrified me every time, and it was a common occurrence, generating a physical manifestation of fear in my chest like a swelling of the heart and a tightening of the skin around the chest.

I was reminded of the feeling I get when surfing, sitting on my board waiting for a wave, and I see a shark near me. After its fin goes under and I can't see it anymore I have a very uncomfortable anticipation of immanent disaster, thinking it could bite me at any moment, without seeing it coming. Luckily I see a shark less than once a year.

As I drifted across the spot where a gator was lying on the bottom, I either paddled with very shallow strokes (if I was going upstream) or I kept my paddle out of the water and my arms up and let my momentum carry me across. I was afraid I would bump the alligator with my paddle causing it to bolt and unintentionally capsize my canoe, and of course it would then eat me. Sometimes I looked back after passing over one, to see if it was following me, but these alligators never resurfaced while I was watching; they can hold their breath for a very long time.

A few alligators swam out in front of my canoe, as if leading me, swimming point, I have no idea why. The one that did this for the longest time approached me from shore, and then swam about ten feet in front of me for about 100 yards, watching me with one eye. While it was doing this, we came upon a smaller alligator floating and seemingly preoccupied with its alligator thoughts. The gator swimming in front of me swam straight into the other one, there was a big splash, and both went underwater. As I passed over the place where they collided, I feared they were fighting underwater and would capsize my canoe, and then eat me. Another time one went under and then led my canoe underwater, either crawling on the bottom or exhaling. I was aware of this because of the bubbles that led my canoe for about fifty yards, which I found bizarre at the time.

Aside from the ubiquitous alligators, I also saw a lot of sandhill cranes, always in groups of two or more walking through the tall grass that dominated most of the scenery. These birds stand about four feet tall and they walk about as if looking for something. When they fly they are loud, croaking their crackling calls as if warning anyone in their landing area to look out – they are not graceful landers, but rather look like they will crash-land instead. White Ibis fed in the shallow areas in large flocks, and occasionally I spotted a white heron standing solo and keeping watch over the endless marsh. I took a lot of video during this trip, and I later edited it all into a short video, which I posted on YouTube (Okefenokee Christmas 2015, https://youtu.be/RltgVWZ6dTk).

~~~

One of the things I really appreciated about the

Okefenokee was that it was not overly-safe, as most organized things in America are. The refuge management is clearly not concerned with lawsuits from under-prepared campers. I found this refreshing. I was reminded of Latin America in this respect. However, there was ample, if primitive, signage along the trails, as long as you paid attention (close attention). I also bought a good topographical map before departing. Getting lost out there would be disastrous and would surely end in becoming the meal of an alligator.

The platforms were all different, but were generally about 30′ x 15′ with a roof over about half the structure. One was made of plastic floating-dock sections, and the rest were built like wooden decks. They all had a picnic table and a clean outhouse, and they all had expansive views. All but one allowed easy-access to any alligator that might want to climb aboard and lay on a nice hard, flat, and dry surface. There was no railing around the platforms, which would have significantly lessened the adventure-level. There was only one platform of the four on which I slept that had dry land around it, and thus the only one that I stepped off of. It was also the only one with an alligator on it when I arrived.

It was my third day in the reserve, and I was paddling along the headwaters of the Suwanee River looking for the platform where I would spend the night. Dark forest on both sides shaded the black water, and I had just passed alligator number 199. I was wondering what number 200 would be like. Would it be really big? Would it be aggressive? No, I was thinking as I paddled along, it'll just be another alligator. Just as this thought was fading from my mind, I saw a wooden platform on the left, and sitting still on it was a full-sized alligator. This is exactly what I had feared the most. Before I decided to take this trip, I imagined this scenario and wondered what one should do in this situation. How do you get an alligator off the platform? How do you know it won't come back? How could you sleep at night knowing that the alligators can and will come onto the platform?

As I faced the platform, which was about thirty by fifteen feet, from the water, the alligator was on the left side. The front of the deck was over the water and the back was sitting on dry land. I paddled my canoe to the side of the platform opposite the alligator and came up with a plan. I decided that the gator was an opportunity for me to finally get over my fear of these creatures and that I should try to coexist with it.

While still sitting in my canoe, I began unloading what I could, and placing my gear between me and the gator, which hadn't moved yet and was about twenty feet away. I had a cooler and two large plastic bins that made a rudimentary barrier between us. I also got out my rifle, a Marlin 30-30, which was already loaded.

my little friend, alligator number 200 (the boards it is lying across are 8 inches wide)

Not sure what to do next, I took the rifle and sat on a railing on the back of the platform, between it and the forest (there was no railing elsewhere). I pondered my situation. I thought about firing the gun to scare the alligator, but I was pretty sure that I was not even supposed to have a gun in here and I didn't want the noise to attract any unwanted attention. I got off the railing and set up my chair with my wall of bins and my cooler between me and the alligator. I got a root-beer out of the cooler and relaxed, just hanging out with an alligator. I took some video. After about three hours, the alligator slid itself into the water. I slept that night with both ears up and in a state of semi-awareness.

~~~

As with many of my favorite adventures, I did not want to leave. On the fifth day, I wanted to go on to the next platform. Instead I had 11 miles to paddle, upstream, with my truck and all of the world's civilization waiting for me. Back to the rat-race. I didn't want to go. How can I make this lifestyle more permanent, I thought. What is it about this that makes me feel so good? What do I really want out of life? What do I value most from my past? What other wonderful things has fear prevented me from doing? What should come next? I suppose sobriety brings about thoughts like these.

I shall try to answer these questions in order. To make this lifestyle more permanent, I need to work hard when there is work to be done and money to be made, and then travel long and deep when work slows. This would be instead of taking it easy and working occasional short days and taking numerous small vacations. In the long term, I will need to set myself up to be able to work while travelling, either by writing or by doing carpentry on boats.

What makes canoeing through the wilderness alone so enjoyable is the exposure to and communion with nature, the silence, the beauty, the tranquility, and the simplicity. I like being alone in the wilderness. It makes me feel capable, self-reliant. There is no one with whom to bargain and negotiate about where or when to go or what to do. Nobody chatters in my ear disrupting the silence and peace.

What I want out of life is adventure, a variety of experiences, education, knowledge, enlightenment. These are also the things I value most from my past. I value all the camping, skiing, canoeing, rafting, mountain-biking, diving, swimming, spelunking, travelling, and certainly surfing. I value all the things I have learned, both from life lessons and from book-reading and school. I value the time with family, and the girlfriends. I value all that I have created: the houses I built, the paintings I have painted, the songs I have written and performed. Creativity and adventure rise to the top of the list, and this is what I want for the future.

What has fear prevented me from doing? This is a difficult question to answer, because I fear the answers. Reproduction and marriage are certainly on the list, but I still feel like I have made the right choices here. Without intending to offend any of my past girlfriends who may be reading this, I feel lucky that I never married any of them, or anyone else for that matter, and I am certainly glad that I don't have any children. I'm beginning to think I was meant to be alone in my adult life. Fear of heights has prevented me from skydiving and rock-climbing. Fear of women has prevented me from talking to hundreds or perhaps thousands of beautiful women. Fear of sailing prevented me from becoming a sailor, but I am determined to overcome this one. The others I'm not so sure about. Perhaps I will skydive someday.

~~~

the final evening of my Okefenokee adventure

The Okefenokee was the largest roadless wilderness area I could find in my vicinity, and it was big enough that the entire time there I could not hear cars or trucks, which is rare in the eastern United States. Instead I heard only the sounds of birds, the songs of frogs, and the occasional bellowing of an alligator, the falling of rain, and the gentle sound of my canoe moving through the water. Tranquility reigned and nature bestowed her gifts all day and all night. This search for roadless areas reminded me of the biggest roadless wilderness of all, one that I live right next to - the ocean.

While paddling the canoe through the silent wilderness, I was reminded of sailing with my father when I was a child. I remembered emerging from the interior of the boat in the early morning and looking out at the blue ocean beneath the blue sky, no land in sight. I remembered the deep feeling of peace. I remembered the thrill of being so far from land and civilization. I craved adventure, and sailing seemed like the biggest adventure available. It was at this point that I determined to become a sailor.

St Petersburg
November 2016

Sailing books have been my constant companion since my time in the Okefenokee, and while working on *Sobrius* in St Petersburg I continued reading about and studying sailing. Some of the books I read were essentially textbooks, while others were non-fiction sailing adventures. I read all of Bernard Moitessier's books, and I even read his classic, *The Long Way,* twice. Moitessier was not only a great adventurer, but, in my opinion, a great writer. His prose transports the reader to the ocean and conveys the emotions that he felt in the scene. When reading Moitessier, I feel like I am out there on his boat, experiencing what only a veteran singlehand sailor can experience, the true essence of the sea, nature in all her glory and power, tranquility, anxiety, joy, fear, the sky and the sea. He is the sort of man who, after sailing all the way around the world in the first ever singlehand non-stop circumnavigation race, decided not to return to England to finish and probably win the race, but instead continued on almost completely around the world again, sailing for a second time around the Cape of Good Hope, across the Indian Ocean, around Cape Leeuwin and all the way to Tahiti, just because he wanted to.

The Self-Sufficient Sailor and *Storm Tactics* by Lin and Larry Pardey began my obsession with studying heavy weather techniques, followed soon by *Fastnet Force 10* by John Rousmaniere and the classic *Heavy Weather Sailing* by K Adlard Coles. *How to Sail Around the World* by Hal Roth furthered my dream. I love reading about sailing in bad weather because the more I read and learn about it the less I fear it. Preparation is the key to not only survival at sea, but also to enjoying the time spent sailing offshore. What is terrifying becomes fun when the fear is managed and proper technique is known and executed.

Singlehanding techniques are still a favorite subject, and I read *A World of My Own* by Robin Knox Jonhnston, *One Hand for Yourself, One for the Ship* by Tristan Jones, *Singlehand Sailing, Thoughts, Tips, Techniques and Tactics* by Andrew Evans, *Mingming* by Roger D Taylor, *Trekka* by John Guzzwill, *Storm Passage, Open Boat Across the Pacific,* and *The Ocean Waits* by Webb Chiles. Singlehand sailing is primarily what I am interested in, and in order to sail alone on long passages and adventures, one must learn various techniques and one must set up the boat accordingly. The singlehand sailor also must have the confidence that comes from knowing how to handle whatever situation arises. Much of this knowledge can be found in books. Of course it must all be practiced as well, but the first step, in my opinion, especially when one does not have a sailboat, is reading. This way we will at least know what we are supposed to do when a bad situation arises. We might not do everything right, but we will at least have a store of knowledge to sift through.

I also read a handful of books that discussed sailboat structure and qualities. By John Vigor I read *The Seaworthy Offshore Sailboat* and *Twenty Small sailboats to Take You Anywhere. Buy Outfit & Sail* by Cap'n Fatty Goodlander provided loads of good advice. John Kretschmer was a favorite author, supplying me with *Sailing a Serious Ocean, At the Mercy of the Sea,* and *Flirting with Mermaids.* There were many more books, and sailing books still dominate my reading.

From a good book, one can learn a lifetime of accumulated knowledge. When faced with a situation at sea, the avid reader will have stores of relevant information to help solve the problem at hand.

I also look for common themes within my readings. If multiple authors say the same thing about a particular subject, then I figure it is probably true. Common themes I can recall include keeping the sailboat simple – the fewer systems upon which the captain must rely the better. A sailboat should be comfortable, well organized, and efficient. Learn how to heave-to and practice this on your boat. Controlling boat speed when sailing downwind in heavy weather is essential, and can be achieved by towing drogues, or a variety of things that provide resistance, like long lnes. Give hard things wide berth. Keep your electrical budget to a minimum. Reef (decrease sail-area) early. Use paper charts in addition to a chartplotter. Have multiple GPS units. Concerning safety, prioritize staying aboard. Equip your boat with a reliable engine, but don't rely on the engine any more than absolutely necessary; sail as if you don't have one. Don't put sails away when motoring into a harbor, rather keep them ready to hoist should the engine quit. A tiller is a better choice than a wheel for a singlehander. A boat is never ready to leave port, but eventually you must go. Don't wait until you are old to buy a boat and cruise, do it now.

~~~

Armed with the knowledge of my studies and minimal sailing experience, on Wednesday November 23rd, 2016, I was out on Tampa Bay sailing my thirty-foot sailboat by myself, and feeling like the king of the world. It was a sunny day and the wind was light, creating small wavelets on the water. The wind wasn't strong enough to produce whitecaps, so instead each wavelet was topped with little bright yellow reflections of the sun. I put *Sobrius* on a close reach, tightened the sheets, tied off the tiller with a bungee cord, clipped my tether to a jackline, and crept forward along the windward deck.

I stood at the bow wearing my black leather hat, my left hand holding firmly to the stainless-steel forestay, and looked out ahead as we silently moved forward at about three knots. My dream was becoming reality. I had progressed from dreamer to doer. Much like my sobriety, I had crossed a line from which I would never regress. I was a sailor now. This was clearly the beginning of a lifelong journey among the fishes and birds, the whales, the gales, the wind and the waves of the world's oceans.

Back in the cockpit, I steered *Sobrius* on multiple points of sail (upwind, downwind, across the wind), and we ghosted along at about three knots, as told by the chartplotter. Way up above the Earth's atmosphere, GPS satellites monitored our position and calculated *Sobrius'* speed. Another Satellite relayed our position to the SPOT headquarters somewhere in Texas, where our ever-changing location was downloaded to the internet. This site was being monitored by my father, who vicariously sailed along with me. He had helped me buy *Sobrius*, and the SPOT was one way for me to include him in the adventure. I am a lucky man to have been born into his family, in fact, I am the luckiest person I know.

As I became more comfortable with my vessel I craved more speed. A larger sail was stowed below in a black sailbag. I pulled the tiller to me and hove-to. With *Sobrius* sitting still, I went below and retrieved the genoa (the largest headsail).

Clipped in to the jacklines, I went forward to the mast and lowered the headsail's halyard and pulled on the downhaul. The sail came down on the deck with no problem, rewarding me with a feeling of success since I installed the downhaul according to the instructions in one of the books I read. I unhanked the sail, untied the sheets, carefully rolled up the sail, bagged it and tossed it in the cabin, then I unrolled the genoa, hanked it to the forestay, tied on the sheets, connected the halyard, and went to the mast. I looked around to confirm that we were not about to hit anything.

The skyline of St. Petersburg rose above the horizon. A large commercial tanker moved slowly far away. We were safe, and I pulled on the green and white halyard. The genoa rose from the deck, but it was upside down. Back to the deck came the genoa, and back to the bow went I to unhank and flip the sail over, reconnect the halyard, and raise it again, right-side-up this time. This is why we practice, so we can make all the mistakes during sea-trials instead of when it really counts, out on the open ocean, perhaps at night in bad weather.

We sailed until it was time to go back to shore and I hove-to again so I could lower the sails. I left the genoa on deck and both sails ready to hoist again should the motor fail. We slowly motored back to the St. Petersburg Municipal Marina, past the channel markers, the marina office, the brightly-colored house-boat, catamarans and white sailboats. The orange sailboat marked my dock, where I turned right, then left, moving slowly, nervously. This would be the first time I pulled *Sobrius*, or any boat, into a slip. I tried to proceed as slowly and safely as possible, but this was all new to me, and I was quite nervous about the very real possibility of running my boat into someone else's.

I had the boat-hook ready at hand to grab the line I left dangling from the piling on the way in. I turned *Sobrius* to the left and began entering the slip, then quickly reached down to the shift-lever to put her in reverse. But the lever stuck and I couldn't get it past neutral. Into the slip we proceeded, and at too great a speed. In the future, I would enter the slip much more slowly, but not this time. We entered with way too much momentum and I let go of the shift-lever and instead caught a line from the piling on the left, I pulled on this with all my might, trying to slow down my 8,000-lb ship before we crashed into the dock. Thankfully, my X-lines caught the bow and between them and my straining back, we came to a stop before crash-landing. My dignity was left intact, however my back was not so lucky, as later that night it seized up and left me with a few days of misery and immobility. However, I was very thankful for a successful maiden voyage and a safe return to the slip. I tied the X-lines every time thereafter, and was always happy to come to an easy stop in my slip after a sail.

Singlehand miles: 3

~~~

On Sunday, November 27^{th,} I got back to work. First, I used gelcoat to repair many small cracks in the deck, the coachroof, and around the cockpit. Next, I sanded the toerails (a strip of teak all the way around the top of the hull) with 120-grit sandpaper, then applied a coat of clear West-System epoxy. This took most of the day, but I also installed wire-cleats to some of the wires leading to the interior lights. Most days involved ten hours of outside work, followed by some easy interior work after dinner, which I thought of as mini-projects. I was committed to *Sobrius* and all I wanted to do was work on her and prepare for the journey home. I had originally guessed that it would take about two weeks of work to get her ready to sail home, but this was indeed a gross underestimate.

For this evening's mini-project I applied for an operator's license through the FCC by first getting an FRN number and then filling out form 605. This was all necessary in order to get an MMSI number, which positively identifies the ship with the Coast Guard. The operator's license was necessary in order to legally contact foreign ports on the VHF radio. It has other advantages, like increasing the chances of rescue by foreign entities, and allowing the use of single-sideband radio (useful for long-distance communication), should I ever get one. I debated with myself quite a bit over this long and arduous process, because one can obtain an MMSI number quite easily without obtaining an operator's license, but I decided to follow maritime law, and since I intended to sail to foreign countries, I opted for the operator's license.

~~~

The renovation of *Sobrius* quickly became an obsession.

During these first eight days I literally did nothing besides work on the boat and shop for supplies. Some days I would realize at 7:00pm that I hadn't eaten all day. Even after I called it quits and stopped working I immediately started thinking of other non-physical chores that I could do inside the cabin, like researching parts online, or setting up the SPOT, or reading Don Casey's *Sailboat Maintenance Manual*.

I was beginning to feel as if I had finally found the new life I had been seeking. I was becoming a sailor. I had found an obsession that could yield positive results. Some of us, myself included, are predisposed to dive all the way into whatever interests us and push it to its limits. Thus it is essential to dive into constructive behaviors, otherwise we destroy ourselves in hedonistic pursuits. Sailing was my savior as I had been searching for a new form of satisfaction after achieving sobriety. This was my new life, and I was running with it.

~~~

On November 28th, I woke with a stiff back, as I had expected from the previous day's sanding marathon and the injury I sustained during my first docking attempt. I left the marina and walked through downtown St. Petersburg as the sun rose, sipping coffee I had made in my French press, as the city came to life. A large crew of construction workers assembled for their morning briefing behind a tall chain-link fence at the base of a building in progress. Women walked their dogs, joggers jogged. Smartly-dressed people walked briskly to work with coffee in one hand and a phone in the other, typing with their thumbs. I strolled casually, sipping my coffee and thinking about the tasks I wanted to dive into upon returning to my sailboat. Everyone in the city had different chores ahead of them, and yet we were all walking on the sidewalks together this morning, living our own lives in our own worlds, but walking the same morning walk.

Back aboard *Sobrius* and with a stiff back, I made a list of supplies I needed, then went shopping. I navigated with my phone propped up horizontally in my black Chevy Suburban and went to Home Depot first. Here I got sandpaper. At west Marine I purchased two blocks (pulleys), a rigging knife, and a short length of line, and a 12Volt receptacle. The blocks and line were for a sheet-to-tiller self-steering rig I intended to set up.

Next I drove an hour to Tarpon Springs to SV Hotwire Enterprises (a solar-panel supplier). I was driving around the neighborhood where my all-knowing phone told me the store was located, looking for a commercial building. I had a picture in my head of a large glass store-front displaying solar panels and electrical gizmos. But all I saw was a modest residential neighborhood. However, one of the houses had solar panels on the roof, and an odd-looking car in the driveway, which seemed to have solar panels on its roof as well. I called the "store" and confirmed the location. This was it.

I parked in the driveway and found the proprietor around back in his workshop. Outside in the grass an apprentice was making propeller blades, out of fiberglass resin, for a wind-generator. Solar panels were stacked in various places in the yard, and the shop was full of wires, odd parts and electricians' tools. John greeted me and we discussed my project at length. I ended up ordering two 50-watt solar panels, articulating arms, wires, connectors, and a charge controller – a complete kit. The price was very reasonable and the service impeccable. I don't know how I would have installed solar panels without his help designing the project.

Back at the boat, I worked for the remainder of the day sanding and epoxying the tiller, two handrails and two cockpit rails. It was a very productive day indeed.

~~~

December 3, ship's log:

"22 months sober today!"

"Today, like yesterday and the day before, was spent sanding, epoxying, and varnishing. My goal was to apply two coats of clear epoxy followed by four coats of varnish. Each coat takes a day to dry before it can be lightly sanded and the next coat applied. I discovered that I had totally missed the teak supporting the traveler – it was the same color as the aluminum track and blended right in with it. So I sanded this teak and put a coat of epoxy on it. I also put a coat of epoxy on a teak box that covers the engine-starting electronics."

"While epoxying, I backed out two screws on each of the two backstay chainplates [the backstays are long steel wires that attach to the top of the mast at one end and to the rear of the boat at the other, the chainplates are stainless steel plates that connect the wires to the boat] and filled the holes with epoxy before buttering the screws with epoxy and reinserting them."

"Later I attacked a leak in the deck by carefully scraping the caulk off the electrical wires that protrude from the deck and then enter the mast (these wires supply electricity to the running lights on the mast). I then chipped away any bad fiberglass gel-coat around the wires, sanded the area, poured on a new layer of gel-coat (liquid fiberglass). I then applied new caulk around the wires. This stopped another of many leaks, helping me keep the interior dry."

"I also wire-brushed the CQR anchor and applied Ospho to it. This, with the magic of chemistry, attacks rust and stops it from getting worse."

"For my evening mini-project, I researched acrylic for hatch replacements." As I write these words, I still haven't replaced these, and they are still blue and crazed [plastic is said to be "crazed" when it has countless cracks within it –

caused by long exposure to the sun].

~~~

On the night of December 4th, I practiced polyphasic sleep, or sleeping in short intervals. This is necessary for the singlehand sailor as sleeping for longer that 20 minutes at a time would put the boat in danger of being run down by another vessel. Twenty minutes is the time it might take to collide with another ship just past the horizon and moving towards my sailboat. That is, if the sailor looks to the horizon and sees no ship, then takes a nap, yet there was a fast-moving ship just out of view over the horizon on a collision course, it would take about twenty minutes for a collision to occur. This I had read and this I practiced on this night.

I set my alarm for 20 minutes and tried to go to sleep. Knowing that you only have twenty minutes to sleep makes it considerably harder to fall asleep, and thinking about falling asleep is a sure way to prevent sleep. Clearing the mind helps. On this night, I lasted from 8:30 until 11:00, and then I was up for an hour. I sat in the cockpit and read on my Kindle for a while with the bright lights of downtown St. Petersburg in the background. My neighbor on the sailboat next to me returned from a night on the town and offered me a drink, which I turned down.

~~~

The following morning began like all the rest here. I made coffee before sunrise and walked along the bayfront. The faint light of dawn illuminated the still water upon which floated various sailboats. A high-speed ferry boarded passengers bound for Tampa, across the bay. I walked past the marina of a fancy hotel, said "buenos dias" to a group of Hispanic workers waiting for their workday to start, then out to a park where I stretched and tried to meditate as the sun rose. People rode by on expensive bicycles, walked their dogs, jogged by. St. Petersburg is a clean city with a beautiful waterfront. Parks abound and the buildings are all across the street from the water. A long sidewalk runs along the waterfront, connecting various parks and marinas. I've never stayed anywhere urban with a nicer place to walk in the mornings.

At first light, I was back aboard *Sobrius* removing tape from the brightwork (varnished wood, "bright" from the high-gloss varnish which reflects the sun's damaging rays). Some of the tape was very hard to remove because the varnish and epoxy had hardened over it, and I vowed to remove tape daily while the varnish is still wet in the future. To this day there are still pesky bits of blue or green tape hiding around the shining varnished teak on the toerails of my little ship.

Next I reinstalled the varnished handrails and admired their beauty in their new coats of varnish and epoxy. I set them in 3M 4000 caulk but struggled with the screws that fastened them to the coachroof. I should have drilled these holes out first, as varnish had gotten in them and made them smaller in diameter. This caused the wood around them to crack when I drove the screws back in, and as I write these words, this still need to be repaired. A sailboat is a never-ending maintenance job - a labor of love to the sailor, or a dread to the landlubber who owns a sailboat and neglects maintenance.

I also pulled out all of the many screws around the sliding hatch in the companionway (this is the entrance into the cabin) and reset them in fresh caulk, thus sealing up another source of leaks.

Today Al, the broker who sold me the boat, was kind enough to take me to Sam's club and let me use his membership to purchase new batteries for *Sobrius*. I selected AGM (absorbed glass mat) batteries because they seemed modern and cool, and because they don't require adding water – they are permanently sealed. This makes them a bit safer because in the event of a capsize, if the batteries were thrown about the cabin the AGM batteries would not spill battery acid all over the inside of the boat. Really, who wants to be burned by flying battery acid when their sailboat is upside down and rolling under a huge wave? Not me.

Unfortunately, I neglected to read the amp-hour rating on the batteries before I bought them, and they were only rated at 55, which meant that I needed to go back to Sam's to get a third battery; my electrical budget required at least 150 amp-hours of battery power. Luckily Al was kind enough to take me there again (Thanks Al!). In the future, I need to overcome the urge to just get a purchase over with and instead take the time necessary to read everything pertinent on the product, like the amp hours on a battery.

After installing the three batteries, I began putting cleats and screws, which I had removed in order to varnish the wood, back on the rails. I bedded them all in 3M 4000 caulk, which is messy stuff. One must have paint thinner and a roll of paper towels on hand when using 3M 4000! I also reinstalled the tiller, which shined in the sun, revealing the gorgeous grains of the golden teak.

I also added two cleats by the mast to accommodate the headsail downhaul (which I would need the next day) and the spinnaker halyard.

~~~

Dec 4, ship's log:

"*Sobrius* is really starting to look good. I have her all ready to sail tomorrow and I look forward to a good sea-trial. I also added two blocks for sheet-to-tiller steering today and I can't wait to test the system tomorrow."

"This is my new life, and it is getting off to a good start. I am a sailor now. The big adventures are coming, the ones I've been craving and chasing all my life."

~~~

On December 5th, I set out early in the morning in an attempt to sail from my slip at the St Petersburg Municipal Marina out to the Gulf of Mexico, around Egmont key and back - a trip of about 60 miles. I had planned on going out to the Gulf through Egmont Channel and coming back in through the south channel.

The sail started easy and was smooth on the way out, going mostly upwind or on a beam reach. I experimented with rigging a sheet-to-tiller system, running the main-sheet through a block on the windward side of the cockpit to the tiller, where I tied it off. I also tied a shock-cord (like a bungee) to the tiller and ran it through a block on the leeward side of the cockpit to a winch so I could adjust the tension. With the tension of the shock cord and the main-sheet balanced, *Sobrius* tracked straight. The system worked well, but proved to be one that would need a bit of experience to perfect.

It was a fine day as I sailed through Tampa Bay to Egmont Key and out Egmont Chanel. I waved to some fishermen in a small boat as I passed under the Sunshine Skyway Bridge. I passed a large container ship soon after. Sunlight reflected off the water, shielded by my sunglasses under a straw hat blocking the sun from above. Dolphin visited briefly, swimming alongside *Sobrius*. I think I made eye contact with one. One of the things I loved about Tampa Bay was the abundance of dolphin; they were a common sight, and always wonderful and surprising to see.

The wind increased as we approached the Gulf, as did the seas. This channel is used by all the large commercial ships entering and exiting Tampa Bay, and I encountered one on the way out. It was a huge vessel coming in as I tacked upwind. We were pointed right at each other, and the big ship had right-of-way, as it was much more restricted by draft than *Sobrius*. I wasn't sure which way I should go to avoid it; the channel curved between us, and I was nervous and unsure of my ability to avoid a collision. But I told myself to just hang in there, this was the first of many big-ship encounters to come in my new life. I ended up sailing across its path, in front of it as it bared down on us, a bit later than was comfortable, not being able to judge its speed, but we passed without incident, due to good luck rather than good seamanship.

The water on both sides of the channel was shallow, and I had to sail out into the Gulf for nearly an hour before I got to the marker at which I had chosen to turn south. The wind was stronger out in the gulf and the seas were choppy with a small swell rolling. The whole scene had a completely different feel to it than that of being inside Tampa Bay. Being out in the Gulf was like being outside a house for the first time, seeing the big world as something new and daunting. The horizon was empty and endless. The whole world was water, moving erratically, blown by the wind, grey.

I tacked back and forth, sailing upwind towards a buoy at which I had previously determined I would turn south and cross deep water on the way to Egmont Channel. When I finally got to the buoy, I tensioned the windward jib-sheet, took the leeward jib-sheet in hand, moved to the leeward side of the cockpit and pushed the tiller all the way over to tack south. The boom gently swung across the cockpit as we passed through the wind, and the big genoa fluttered and moved across the bow as I released one jib-sheet and pulled in on the other. But then I heard the unmistakable sound of cloth ripping.

I looked up in horror to see the big genoa caught on a cleat on the mast. As I watched, the sail ripped along the entire length of its foot and began flogging madly. We were "in irons" – pointed into the wind with the wind holding us in this position - drifting towards shallow water, with a wild scene at the mast, lines and sail all flapping in the wind, attempting to beat and whip anything and everything, while the waves bounced us up and down, left and right. I sat in the cockpit and watched as calmly as I could, waiting for the solution to come to mind.

This was precisely the type of situation that a novice sailor fears – chaos and loss of control, with no obvious solution. But finally, the solution did materialize in my brain. "Heave-to" said my subconscious, recalling the maneuver from all the reading I had been doing. I needed to heave-to and fix the problem.

I stood up and pushed the boom into the wind to get us out of irons, allowing us to tack the rest of the way across the wind. I then lashed the tiller to windward. But instead of coming to a controlled stop and remaining there as I expected, *Sobrius* continued turning and the boom swung across the boat in an uncontrolled gybe. Instead of heaving-to we were spinning in a circle and the chaos-level was increasing.

My mind raced. What had I done wrong? Tiller to *leeward*, I remembered, not to windward. So I tacked us again and put the tiller to leeward. Throughout all this the torn sail and its sheets flogged, whipping wildly in the air, tying themselves into knots while the sail continued to tear out its foot. The wind was increasing and the grey water of the Gulf of Mexico bounced us around. Finally we successfully hove-to (tiller to leeward, mainsheet all the way out, headsail back-winded) and *Sobrius* came to a position of relative control. I clipped in to the jackline and carefully crept forward to the mast, where I released the jib-halyard and pulled on the downhaul. The torn sail fell to the deck, bringing the knotted sheets with it. We were drifting out of the channel and into shallower water populated with fishing buoys, which probably marked crab traps, as I worked to get the sail rolled up and into its bag. *Sobrius* was rolling with the waves and I was having to focus on my work on the deck, which brought about some seasickness. I tried to look up to the horizon all I could, but I had to work quickly to avoid drifting into the sandbars west of Egmont Key.

Eventually I got the sail into its bag and stowed below,

but I still had to put up another jib, which I retrieved from below and brought to the bow. I had to take this sail out of its bag and hank it on to the headstay. This involves attaching the tack to a hook at the base of the stay, and then clipping about a dozen bronze spring-loaded clips (hanks), which are sewn into the sail, to the stay. Then the halyard and downhaul are clipped to the top of the sail. Lastly the two jib-sheets are tied to the clew, at the aft end of the foot of the sail. This took another twenty minutes or so and made me more seasick. All the while we were drifting towards fishing buoys and shallow water. I did not feel well at all when the work was done and I was back in the cockpit, but I did feel the satisfaction of having faced and fixed my first major problem at sea. I was glad for all the studying I had done, as the answers came to me when I needed them, and I felt as if I had remained calm and confident throughout the ordeal.

I decided to abandon the idea of sailing around Egmont Key and instead turned and headed downwind back towards Tampa Bay through Egmont Chanel. The wind continued to increase and *Sobrius* continued to heel (lean away from the wind), as we sped back to Tampa Bay at maximum speed (about 6.5 knots). The maximum speed of a cruising sailboat is a function of its waterline length, and has to do with the wavelength of the bow wave, which is the wave created by the boat as it pushes through the water. Physics and math can further explain this concept, but alas, I cannot.

As we sped into the bay heeling and leaving a wake, the weather helm (the tendency of a sailboat to turn itself to windward, which increases as the mainsail overpowers the headsail) was very strong, and I really had to hold on to the tiller, pulling it to me with both arms and pushing my feet into the seat opposite me. I should have reefed the main when I had the chance while we were hove-to, but now I had shallow water on both sides, ships to deal with, and no means of self-steering. I had to hold the course. We were heeling a lot at this point, sailing fast on a broad reach, but I had to hold on at least until we were out of the channel and in safe water. My inexperience was showing, but perseverance held the day. My stomach was still not happy.

I gybed after we cleared out of the channel and created a new problem for myself. Instead of passing across the deck, the headsail wrapped around the headstay. I had released the sheet too early (like one does when tacking) and, since we were pointed downwind, the headsail blew forward of the boat, then twisted itself around its stay as we turned. I pulled on the sheet, turned the boat back and forth trying to free the sail, but it remained twisted and flogging. I didn't want to destroy another sail today!

Then I remembered something from my readings. I needed to blanket the headsail with the mainsail, that is, I needed to use the mainsail to block the wind from the headsail. I turned *Sobrius* directly downwind and let the main-sheet out until the headsail was downwind of the mainsail and thus out of the wind. Quickly I crept forward to the bow, and unwrapped the sail by hand. I ran back to the cockpit as quickly as I deemed safe, and put us back on track. Again I was glad to have studied all I had, but I was ready for the problems to end. They did not.

As we sailed downwind back towards the Sunshine Skyway Bridge, *Sobrius* wobbled and wandered back and forth, and was very hard to steer. Something seemed to be wrong, but I couldn't figure out what it was. *Sobrius* was hard to control, and the headsail seemed to be acting funny. In fact everything seemed off.

While I was looking around, not paying attention to the helm, *Sobrius* gybed unintentionally. The boom swung across the cockpit, over my head, caught the wind on the other side and slammed against the shrouds. The mainsheet, which is a 7/16" line going around a double pulley assembly so that four lines are parallel between the traveler and the boom, oriented vertically right in front of the tiller, slammed across the cockpit with a vengeance and smacked me right in the face hard enough to break the skin and give me a bit of a black eye. Luckily nothing was broken; an unintentional gybe can cause a variety of things to break or be damaged.

Again I had to gybe, and I did so intentionally this time, but my troubles were not over. As we changed course, something completely unexpected happened: the entire headsail detached from the bow and shot up the headstay; the entire sail went to the top of the mast in a great bunch. This was unbelievable. Somehow the tack of the headsail had come off the hook that holds it to the bow. This should not be possible, but the sail was up in the air, flapping like a great panicking bird caught in a trap, 40 feet above the deck. I went forward again, released the jib-halyard and pulled on the downhaul, which I was very thankful to have rigged. Without the aid of the downhaul, the wind would have kept the sail up, way out of reach, indefinitely.

At this point I was done with the headsails, and decided to stow the jib and sail the remainder of the way home under mainsail alone, and luckily there was enough wind to carry us. I carefully rolled up the sail, bagged it, and stowed it below. Back at the helm, I noticed something else was amiss; the backstays were very loose. The backstays are two steel cables that run from the extreme rear of the boat (the transom) to the top of the mast. They support the mast and essentially prevent it from falling forward. They should not be able to come loose. Something was terribly wrong, but I could not determine what it was. And as much as I was ready to be finished with problems, yet another was awaiting my discovery.

As I was inspecting the backstays I noticed that the anchor that I kept hanging on the stern railing was dragging in the water, trailing behind us below the surface. Luckily, the chain was caught on the locker lid, which prevented the rode (the rope and chain tied to the anchor) from completely paying out. If this had happened, the anchor would have settled on the bottom of the bay and when the rode fully paid out and became taut, and it would have either brought us to a violent halt, or tore part of the boat off trying to do so.

I pulled the anchor in without incident and continued sailing for home. Fortunately the rest of the journey was pleasant and we arrived at the marina just in time for a magnificent sunset. The sun goes down behind the marina when viewed from the bay, and the oranges and reds and yellows backlight the skyline of downtown St Petersburg. I pulled *Sobrius* slowly into her slip, and she snuggled into the X-lines that waited for her arrival. I had survived a rather difficult sea-trial. I had made many mistakes, suffered various troubles, endured tests of determination and ingenuity, and I had passed. I felt like a king as I took a hot shower in the bathhouse on the dock, which seemed to be gently rocking back and forth.

Singlehand miles: 65

~~~

When I inspected *Sobrius* the next morning, I discovered that one of the two bolts in the stemhead fitting, which attaches the headstay to the bow, had broken, and the other had bent to 90 degrees but still held. This allowed the headstay to slacken considerably, and in turn slackened the backstays. This is what allowed the headsail to release its tack and fly up the mast. If the other bolt had sheared as well, the headstay would have become completely detached from the deck and I might have lost the mast completely, which would have been a disaster.

Dec 6, ship's log:

"Yesterday was exhausting yet exhilarating. When I got back and had everything stowed, I felt invincible, as if I could do anything. I had faced adversity, the unknown, and raw nature. I did not conquer, but I coexisted; I made it out and back singlehanded."

Things I learned yesterday:

1. Stowe items properly before sailing so they don't roll around below-deck
2. When gybing, don't let the headsail wrap around the headstay
   Wait until the headsail is back-winded to release the sheet
3. Use a preventer (a line to prevent an unintentional gybe)
4. Look into getting a tillerpilot
5. Cut excess off all lines
6. Wear shoes
7. Reef early and change headsails early (as the wind increases)
8. When heaving-to, tiller goes to *leeward*
9. Practice sailing downwind
10. Replace as many bolts in the rigging as possible
11. Secure the stern anchor
12. Don't keep reading glasses around neck while sailing
13. Leave engine in gear (in reverse) while sailing
14. Secure dorade vents

~~~

When the bolts that held the stemhead fitting to the bow broke, which probably happened when the genoa was tearing and flogging madly, the bow was damaged considerably. The fiberglass under the stemhead fitting had been wallowed by the bolt that broke and the other one that almost broke probably when the headstay thrashed about as the genoa was being torn. This desperately needed to be repaired.

The stemhead fitting is a small rectangular block of stainless steel about three inches long and one inch wide that bolts through the bow to a metal plate on the outside of the bow. It serves as the main attachment point for the headstay, which is the steel cable that runs from the top of the mast to the bow. It holds up the mast, preventing it from falling backwards, and also supports the headsail, which attaches to the headstay via hanks and to the stemhead fitting via a hook through the headsail's tack. Both the mast and the headsail put an enormous amount of strain on the stemhead fitting and thus its bolts and the bow underneath it needed to be fixed properly. I'd never attempted a repair like this but I could visualize what needed to be done and was willing to give it a try.

In order to remove the bolts in the stemhead fitting to fix the fiberglass, I had to detach the headstay. A clevis pin held it in place, and the tension on the stay had to be released before it was possible to remove the pin. I tied the spinnaker halyard and the jib-halyard to the bow railing to support the mast, and I slackened the backstays first so the mast would bend forward a bit, allowing me to remove the headstay from the stemhead fitting. With the tension off the fitting, I then removed the fitting and cut the bent bolt with my Makita 4" grinder. I punched out the cut-off bolt with a hammer and a nailset.

I cut some small pieces of fiberglass cloth and mixed up a batch of epoxy. I first poured some into the two bolt holes, then pushed the new bolts through, and filled in around them with slightly thickened epoxy. I then applied small pieces of fiberglass cloth to the area around the bolts and beneath the stemhead fitting, which I bolted back on before the epoxy set.

I let the epoxy cure for 24 hours, after which I had to reattach the headstay. This proved to be very difficult. I needed to put a lot of tension on the headstay to pull it down to the stemhead fitting, which required pulling it downward with much more force than my arms could generate. I asked myself "what would Moitessier have done?"

Channeling the famous mariner and author, I first

slackened the backstays as far as I dared, then tied the downhaul line to the headstay with a rolling hitch. This line ran through its block and then back to a winch in the cockpit, where I could put a lot of tension on it. After increasing the tension and further slackening the backstays multiple times, I was able to wrestle the headstay back onto its mount on the stemhead fitting, insert the clevis pin and finish the job. Moitessier would have approved.

When I bought the bolts for the stemhead fitting, I went ahead and bought replacement bolts for the rest of the rigging. This totaled about 30 bolts. I assumed all the existing bolts were original, and thus 44 years old. Stainless steel tends to fail catastrophically when it gets too old, that is, it gives no warning and simply breaks. I was very lucky that the second stemhead-fitting bolt bent without breaking, otherwise the mast might have fallen backwards and onto my head.

While I had the epoxy out, I also reinforced the transom around the backstay chainplates and swapped out the bolts with shiny new stainless-steel replacements.

I accomplished the headstay attachment in the morning, and then spent the rest of the day working on mounting my new solar panels. While working, I listened to tales of mullet fishermen who had pulled up and rafted their boat to my neighbor's boat. The mullet were running and schooling in and around the marina, so lots of mullet fishermen were in the area, chasing the schools and throwing cast-nets. After a day and a half of cutting and drilling aluminum mounting plates, bolting these to the railing, and much wiring, I had the panels mounted and charging my batteries. No longer would I need to run the engine to charge the batteries, and I could dispense with the cheap battery charger I had bought for the purpose. This was certainly one of the best improvements I made to *Sobrius*.

~~~

On December 9th, I put on my wetsuit and snorkeling gear and got in the water to try to repair a hole in the hull with epoxy. The origin of the hole is quite a bit embarrassing.

I was trying to install battery straps to secure the three batteries to the hull so they wouldn't bounce around while sailing. I was using very short screws to screw cleats for the straps to the bottom of the battery compartment. I was pre-drilling the holes with a short drill bit, however I was only guessing at the thickness of the hull. Since *Sobrius* was built in 1972 and was a well-respected offshore cruiser, I assumed that the hull was probably about .75-inch-thick or more, and I was trying to drill holes only about .25-inch-thick.

However, my concentration slipped and when pulling the drill-bit out of the hole I had just drilled, I was absolutely shocked to see a stream of water follow the bit out of the hole, squirting up at me. Immediately I put my finger over the hole, which temporarily stopped the flow of water. As I sat there dumbfounded with my finger over a hole that might otherwise sink my boat, I was reminded of a time at work when I was nailing up tongue-and-groove boards building an interior bathroom wall in a new house and I nailed one of my boards to a vent pipe that was pressurized with compressed air (the pipes were pressurized to test for leaks). There too I pressed my finger to the hole while thinking of what to do. In that instance, I decided to put the nail (which I had pulled out) back in the hole, after which I got out some epoxy, mixed it up, pulled the nail, put epoxy in the hole, and put the nail back in with some more epoxy around it. This stopped the flow and I went on nailing up the boards, building the bathroom walls.

Back on *Sobrius*, I was sitting over the battery compartment with my finger over a hole in my boat, surrounded by tools and materials and wondering what to do. I didn't have epoxy out, but I did have some below-the-waterline caulk (3M 4000) ready to go, as well as the screw for which I had drilled the hole. With my one free hand, I got the caulk (which luckily was in reach and ready in a caulking gun), and squeezed some out. I took the screw and dipped it in the caulk, put some on my finger and squished some into the hole, then I drove the screw into the hole and some more caulk on top of it. I sat and stared at the hole for quite some time while chastising myself for such a foolish mistake. But the screw and caulk held the water out and all was well.

The very next day I got in the water with my snorkeling gear. As I swam under *Sobrius* looking for the hole so I could put epoxy in it from below, I was surprised by a bunch of fish which swam around me expecting a free meal, supposing that I was going to clean the hull. Instead I disappointed them by searching for the tiny hole, which I never found. I had a small syringe ready that I was going to fill with epoxy and use to squirt into the hole, but this repair had to wait until I hauled *Sobrius* out of the water weeks later.

I worried about this hole quite a bit, but *Sobrius* never sank. I was reminded of the first house I owned. I used to worry that it would burn to the ground whenever I went out of town. I expected to see a pile of smoldering embers every time I returned from a vacation. I now worried that my boat would sink whenever I was away from her and expected to see, upon returning to the marina, *Sobrius'* mast sticking up out of the water, marking her position like a gravestone.

Since I was already in the water (looking for the hole to fill), I went ahead and fed the hungry fish by cleaning the hull. As the myriad encrusting sea-creatures fell off the hull, the excited fish gobbled them up. Sheepshead, spadefish, small unknown fish, and even a grouper swam around gobbling up the buffet that I scraped from the hull. It was kind of fun.

~~~

Dec 9, ship's log:

"Today it was back to the basics: tacking, gybing, and

sailing downwind. Every maneuver needs to be thought out in advance and done in the correct order, and all of that needs to be practiced. A simple tack, singlehanded, requires precise timing and skilled movements. Otherwise things go wrong."

"But today things went well. Docking especially went well. "

"Tomorrow I will sail again."

Singlehand miles: 85

"Work today included mounting the tiller-tamer and two cam cleats for it. I caulked the solar panel wire-holes in the deck and taped the wires to the rail. I also re-mounted the water intake deck fitting with 3M 4000."

~~~

Dec 10, ship's log:

"Sailed out into the bay, practiced tacking, gybing and downwind sailing.
6 gybes, 8 tacks – all good!"

Singlehand miles: 98

~~~

On December 12th, I drove to St. Petersburg, back from St Augustine. I worried about the hole I put in the boat with the drill. In fact, I worried about this hole continuously since leaving *Sobrius* in such a state. Part of me fully expected to see the top of her mast poking up through the water in my slip as I walked down the dock. But she was still floating, and once inside I pulled up the floorboards and found the bilge dry. *Sobrius* was not taking on water.

That evening, I took one of the headsails that I hadn't

used yet to the dockhouse to inspect them. The sail, referred to as a "storm jib" by the seller, turned out to be a little bigger than what I thought a storm jib should be. I would say it is a #3 jib, or a "working jib".

The following morning I was determined to sail.

As I backed out of the slip on the morning of December 12, 2016, *Sobrius* would not go into forward gear, and instead I began to drift toward my neighbors' boat behind me. "She's not going into forward" I yelled as we approached their boat. A woman in the cockpit looked at me in silence with big eyes, apparently at a loss for words and unsure what to do about the boat drifting onto her. I left the cockpit, pulled out the fenders and got them between *Sobrius* and the other boat and pilings, to which I tied off while the couple on Sin Bad Sea looked on. Max, the man of the ship, came up with a GoPro camera to film the action. Apparently his camera was a new acquisition, because only a man who had just bought a camera would think "I should film this" instead of "I should put out a fender so this boat doesn't crash into mine." However he quickly came to his senses and put the camera down to help me tie *Sobrius* off to the pilings.

As I was trying to figure out how to handle this situation, I noticed their engine was running, and thus they were also planning on going out for a sail. After quietly pondering the situation for a moment I decided I needed to get *Sobrius* back into our slip to diagnose the problem. I figured I should break out the "dinghy" and row a line over to my slip, which I did (on my 12-foot surfboard) and tied it to the dock. I then rowed another line over and tied it to the leeward piling in my slip, rowed back and pulled the line tight and tied it off to the piling at my stern so it stretched across the marina about 4 feet above the water. Max, the camera-man from Sin Bad Sea, got onboard with me and held the taut line while I pulled us over on the other line.

Back in my slip I donned my mask and jumped overboard, thinking I might have lost my propeller, however it was still there attached to *Sobrius* as it should be.

Looking in the engine compartment revealed that the prop shaft had pulled out of the transmission coupling. Ironically the surveyor had warned me that this might happen as the prop-shaft set-screw needed a locking set-screw – a second one holding the first one fast. It seems odd to me that the only thing holding the propeller shaft to the engine is the friction of a set-screw pushing against the shaft, but then again, I'm no diesel mechanic [as I write this, a year later, I am about to replace the transmission coupling with a split coupling, because this happened again, after running aground…].

Oddly enough, I found a small plastic bag in the navigation table with three set-screws of the size I needed and an Allen wrench. Apparently this had been a recurring problem. I put the shaft back into the transmission and fastened it tight with two set-screws and fired the engine back up. We were going sailing after all.

This time *Sobrius* went smoothly into forward after backing out of the slip. I was glad to have encountered and fixed this problem here at the dock instead of while sailing home to St Augustine. This was yet another experience that reinforced the fact that many sea-trials are necessary between purchasing a sailboat and sailing it on a long journey.

~~~

Out on the bay, the air was light, the sun was bright, and I enjoyed my first easy and relaxing sail on *Sobrius*. I practiced tacking and gybing, as well as downwind sailing. I tried out an old headsail, one that I was told was original to the boat. It still worked, although it was a bit blown out.

I rigged a preventer by running a line to the starboard bow-cleat from the cockpit and around to the end of the boom. I then positioned the sails "wing on wing" – with the mainsail starboard and the jib to port, supported by the whisker pole, on opposite sides of *Sobrius*, like a bird with its wings spread out catching the wind. This worked well, but took a lot of concentration to keep both sails filled and not gybe accidentally. It was a tranquil time on the water; *Sobrius* and I sailed as the sun set and a dolphin visited.

Singlehand miles: 108

~~~

In the days that followed, I continued working on *Sobrius* and running errands. I took two of the sails, the torn genoa and another "racing" genoa to Advanced Sails for repair. The sail loft was a big open room, big enough to unroll very large sails on the plywood floor. Two sewing machines occupied spaces cut into the floor, so the operator could sit comfortably at a sewing machine that was at floor level. I met Keith, a friendly man with glasses, who inspected my sails and came up with a very reasonable price to fix them. I expected Keith to say that the genoa was torn beyond repair, but it didn't seem like a big deal to him. I then went in search of someone who could copy the key to start the Yanmar diesel engine.

First I went to Home Depot, but they could not copy the key. Then I tracked down a locksmith, who told me the same thing. A second locksmith told me that he would have to come out to the boat in order to make a key, and that sounded prohibitively expensive. I was beginning to worry about this key, and I wondered how other sailors dealt with this problem, which must be common. I finally went to a Yanmar dealer who sold me two keys right off the shelf. Apparently Yanmar keys are all the same and mine didn't need to be copied, just replaced.

Back aboard *Sobrius* I did some repair to the fiberglass gelcoat on the deck and I tried, unsuccessfully, to remove the traveler. I was thwarted by frozen bolts and gave up. I wanted to replace the traveler-car, because it looked like the point where the shackle attached to it was almost worn through and about to break. This is where the mainsheet attaches and is very necessary for a sailboat, but the car had two other attachment points, for blocks, and I just moved the shackle to another point and moved on to the next project.

I also realigned the bow pulpit, which was off-center, perhaps from a collision in the past. This required drilling new holes, new bolts, and using block and tackle to pull it into position. I removed a large piece of ugly wood from the bow deck and filled the holes beneath it. I still don't know why it was there. I usually don't remove things until I know what they are, but for this I made an exception, and as I removed it I hoped that its purpose wouldn't become painfully obvious in the future.

For my evening mini-project, I wanted to go ahead and pull the trigger on an autopilot. I was torn between getting one of the major brands (Simrad or Raymarine) or a more-expensive handmade Pelagic. The Pelagic was made by a sailor/engineer who lived in San Francisco and looked pretty cool. After much hand-wringing and consternation, I ordered the Pelagic, which was recommended by some folks on the St Augustine Cruiser's Net Facebook group. This had been a very difficult decision requiring more than a few e-mails and phone calls to Brian, the sailor/engineer who made each unit by hand in his shop in California. But in the end, I decided that I should order the best one.

One of the recurring themes I read about singlehanding was that tillerpilots break all the time. The Pelagic was a bit more expensive than the major brands, but I hoped the extra expense would yield more longevity. The last thing I wanted was to be without autopilot during my journey back to St. Augustine. I knew the journey was going to be difficult, and I wanted the things I bought to work properly. I wasn't disappointed.

~~~

December 15

    This was my scheduled day to haul *Sobrius* out of the water for a bottom job at the nearby Salt Creek Marina. I was nervous as I sailed the 3 miles to the haul-out slip. Docking, pulling into slips, avoiding collisions, maneuvering in tight areas worried me more than any other aspect of sailing, and Salt Creek, where the haulout facility was located, was shallow and narrow. I had the fenders out and lines coiled, ready to throw, as I pulled into the slip where *Sobrius* was to be hauled out.

    Two relaxed-looking men were there waiting for me, their demeanors contrasting my apprehensive state, as I threw big coils of line right into the chest of the first, then the second man. When all was well and I was confident that my work was done, I closed up *Sobrius,* shut off the engine, and climbed ashore. *Sobrius* was lifted out of the water and the bottom was pressure-washed while I walked three miles back to the St Petersburg Municipal Marina to get my truck, and then drove right back to the Salt Creek Marina.

Singlehand miles: 111

~~~

    I worked long and hard for the rest of the day on *Sobrius.* I replaced the head-discharge seacock because the old one was frozen shut. I completely removed the head-sink-discharge seacock and glassed over the hole in the hull where it used to be. *Sobrius* didn't have running water, and so I didn't think I would need a sink in the head, and thus the through-hull fitting was superfluous. The fewer the better – another recurring theme in the books I had read.

    For the next two days, I worked on the keel. The

Dufour Arpege has a cast-iron fin keel, about seven feet long and four feet tall, which is bolted to the hull with twelve large stainless-steel bolts. While this is a common arrangement, the bolt-on keel did not leave me with a feeling of confidence. Also reducing my confidence was a visible gap between the keel and the hull. Most of this gap was thin, but I could put my finger inside the gap in one place. I assumed this was allowing water intrusion and thus corroding the keel-bolts and rusting the keel from the inside.

I devised a plan to fill the gap with epoxy and then cover the joint with layers of fiberglass cloth and epoxy. I ran the idea by a few people and got mixed reviews. Al, the broker who sold me the boat, thought it was a good idea. John, the guy working on the Pacific Seacraft next to me, thought it was a bad idea. He thought I should instead unbolt the keel, lift the boat off the keel and fill the gap with epoxy, and lower the hull back on the keel before the epoxy set. He showed me an article in Practical Sailor that backed his idea. Flummoxed, I decided to investigate the keel bolts. I tried to loosen one of the nuts inside the bilge, and the bolt spun with the nut. This was the deciding factor, I would go with my plan to partially encapsulate the keel in epoxy.

Right away I went to a fiberglass store where I purchased a big roll of fiberglass cloth, a gallon of epoxy resin, a gallon of hardener, a tub of thickened epoxy, brushes, and gloves. They also gave me two big pieces of cardboard to spread on the ground on which to lay out the materials and cut the cloth into strips of various sizes. The fiberglass people were very helpful and, of course, they liked my idea.

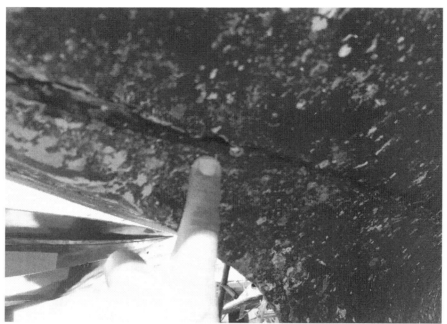
the keel/hull joint before repairs

The iron keel was also quite rusted and pitted, full of indentations ranging in size from BB's to golf balls. I had arranged to have the yard sandblast the keel, and a worker diligently attempted this, but the yard's sandblaster was grossly undersized for the job. When he was finished, I went over it again with my Makita 4-inch grinder, which was much more effective. Next I filled the gap between the keel and the hull with thickened epoxy. I also used thickened epoxy to fill some of the larger pits in the keel. I then laid out the two large pieces of cardboard that the fiberglass store had given me and began to cut fiberglass cloth into strips of 4-inches, 8-inches, 12-inches, and 16 inches which I laid out on the cardboard. I put on a one-piece paper suit, respirator and gloves, and was ready for action.

When everything was organized and laid out on the big pieces of cardboard on the ground, I began my all-day project, which I couldn't stop until finished. I needed to keep putting layers of epoxy and cloth on the keel before each previous layer set. The working time of a mixed batch of epoxy was about 20 minutes, after which it started turning into an unworkable goo, and then became rock-hard. The entire day was a race to apply the epoxy before it hardened.

I mixed epoxy resin and hardener in a plastic tub and first brushed it onto a strip of cloth, then I brushed more epoxy onto the keel, and finally I applied the wet cloth to the wet keel, covering the hull-to-keel joint, thus covering the offending gap. I then brushed on more epoxy and used my gloved hands to squeegee out any air trapped behind the cloth. I started with the 4-inch strips and overlapped these with increasingly larger strips. I worked as fast as I could to avoid wasting epoxy and ending up with a tub of rock. It was an all-day race, but at the end of the day, the keel was nearly encapsulated in four layers of fresh cloth. As you can imagine, this was an extremely messy affair. I left the marina when they closed at 7:00 pm, after dark, and drove downtown. I spent the night in a hotel, which was quite a luxury after living on the boat, and was back at the marina the following morning to do it again.

the keel after day-one of repairs

On day-two of the keel project, I still had a layer of large pieces of cloth to apply. These were much more difficult to apply than the smaller pieces. They were very messy and hard to deal with as I picked up the dripping sheets of cloth and tried to coax them onto the keel with some semblance of control. But by lunch time, I had the final pieces on and the project was looking good. While the epoxy set, I took a long lunch break at a nice café where everyone else was clean and well-dressed.

My next task was to find all the air pockets that I had missed during the application and open them up with the grinder. After this was done, I sanded the whole keel as best I could with my 6-inch random-orbital sander. The final job of the day was to fair the keel with thickened epoxy. I used a 10-inch drywall knife for most of this, and worked until I felt like I couldn't get the keel any smoother. It was dusk as I left the boatyard and went back to the hotel.

On the morning of keel-project day-3, I donned my paper suit, respirator, goggles and gloves, and sanded the keel to the extent of my endurance. I used my Rigid 6-inch random-orbital sander, which is a fine tool indeed. When I felt like sanding could do no more good (or maybe it was when I ran out of sanding discs), I painted on one final coat of 2-part epoxy paint and called it done.

I left the marina and went home to St Augustine for a few days while the yard painted the bottom. Upon returning on December 23rd I drilled and screwed the stanchions in place. The stanchions are the vertical steel rods around the edge of the deck that support the lifelines – the horizontal lines that prevent people from falling overboard. Up until then the stanchions could be pulled out of their seats, which was not safe at all. This day I also replaced the sacrificial zinc anode on the propeller, which prevents galvanic corrosion, which would otherwise destroy the propeller.

the finished keel

Sobrius was put back in the water and I had another nice sail on the way home in Tampa Bay, practicing tacking, gybing and sailing wing-on-wing. I think she sailed a little bit faster on account of the smooth and fair keel, but this could have been my imagination.

Singlehand miles: 127

~~~

On Christmas Eve, I installed the new AIS (automatic identification system), which included the main unit inside the boat, a GPS antenna, and a VHF antenna. This required some decisions to be made, as the VHF antenna had to be at least eight feet away from any person's head (because it transmits a powerful "very high frequency" signal) and at least three feet away from the other VHF antenna. This meant it couldn't go at the top of the mast, where the other VHF antenna was, nor could it go anywhere near the deck, where my head would be.

I ended up mounting it on the port spreader (the horizontal mast support about fifteen feet above the deck). This was quite a job, requiring me to climb the mast and sit in a bosun's chair (a canvas seat that hangs from a halyard and is hoisted up the mast). In order to do this alone, I first hoist a mast ladder that attaches to the mast via the mainsail track. The ladder is made of nylon strap and has large loops for steps. I hoist it with the main halyard. Then I hoist the bosun's chair with the jib-halyard and cleat it off at the height where I will want to use it. I then climb the mast ladder and step down into the bosun's chair.

The GPS antenna was much easier to mount, on the stern rail.

~~~

Christmas Day, 2016

As I have neither wife nor children, each Christmas I like to go on some sort of adventure. Christmas of 2015 was spent in the Okefenokee. Two earlier Christmases I spent surfing at Pavones, Costa Rica. Surfing on Christmas morning is great, because nobody else is out, even if the waves are really good. Pavones is a world-class wave, and getting it by yourself during a good swell is a rare treat. On this Christmas, I wanted to try again to sail out into the Gulf of Mexico and around Egmont Key, as I was trying to do earlier when my genoa tore out and I turned back. I determined this time to sail out through the Southeast Channel and anchor for the night in the lee of Egmont Key, on the gulf side.

a Christmas sail

I left early in the morning and sailed across Tampa Bay, under the Sunshine Skyway Bridge, and out of the bay via the Southeast Channel and into the Gulf of Mexico, where I turned north and headed toward Egmont Channel. The wind was fine until this point, when it suddenly died and I was assaulted by a swarm of flying insects. They covered *Sobrius* like a plague, and the majority of them seemed to die right away, as if flying to my little sailboat was their last wish. I washed off the legions of dead with buckets of water and wondered why they all died.

After about an hour, the wind came back and we proceeded north at a leisurely pace in the warm sunshine. I anchored off Egmont Key, just south of the channel, and dove on the anchor to set it. The CQR anchor was just lying on the bottom on its side, not dug in at all. I picked it up, and facing the boat, kicked with my fins and pushed the point of its plow into the bottom. The water was not cold at all, like I would expect it to be on Christmas, but I didn't spend more time in it than was necessary to set the anchor.

When I told this story to one of the sailors at the marina the next day, he was incredulous that I swam in the gulf off Egmont Key, and went on to tell me how the area is known as a haven for large tiger sharks. The big ships, he told me, would often dump their food scraps overboard in that area before entering Tampa Bay. This attracted tiger sharks, who are known to be voracious eaters of anything resembling food. I rolled my eyes at this story and told him that there are sharks everywhere, and that they've already had most of my life to get me if they wanted me. The truth is that I *am* scared of sharks, but I choose to swim in the ocean anyway. I don't want my fear of them to limit my world to land only.

Back onboard, I set the anchor-drag alarm on the chartplotter, which I had just then discovered while fiddling with the buttons. I also turned on the all-around white light on the mast and I left the AIS on. I was a bit worried about drifting downwind off the anchor and into the shipping channel just behind me.

The sunset was beautiful and I took some video to share with my family before sleeping soundly in the silence and gently rocking water. This was my first night on *Sobrius* outside of the marina, and it was serene.

~~~

On the morning of December 26th, I awoke to a gorgeous and bright sunrise shining over Egmont Key. The wind was blowing at about 10 knots out of the northeast carrying on it the cries of seagulls. I put on my gloves and sat down on the deck at the bow. I took the anchor rode in hand and slowly pulled *Sobrius* forward and coiled the rode in the anchor locker beneath me.

When we were directly over the anchor, it released its grip from the hard sand bottom and we began drifting away from the island. I stowed the anchor in its locker and then moved to the mast. As we drifted away from Egmont Key and towards deeper water, I hoisted the main, then the jib, and moved to the cockpit, taking the tiller in hand. I put us on a course toward the channel that weeks before had been the scene of a badly-tearing genoa. To drift off of an anchor, catch the wind in the sails, and start moving forward is an amazing thing indeed. No engine sullied our peace this morning. It was just me and *Sobrius*, the sun and the sky, the seagulls and the dolphin, and we sailed as the sun rose over land.

I had to tack into the wind to progress up the channel, careful not to stray into the shallow water on the north side. By the time we got to the bay, the wind had increased and we were heeling nicely and making 6.5 knots. I heard the forlorn call of a loon while we sped along. The sound of the loon reminded me of a week I spent in Canada with my father, fishing on a remote lake and staying in a log cabin. As we sailed further into Tampa Bay dolphin visited, and a sea turtle made a brief appearance.

We were on a close reach sailing fast, but I was annoyed at the constant luffing of the leach of the jib. As far as I could tell, the sail was trimmed properly, yet the trailing edge of the sail constantly fluttered. But then I noticed something I hadn't seen before. I tied off the tiller and went forward; a phrase came into my head: "leach line". The sail had a leach line, and I leaned out over the windward rail, grabbed a hold of the white cord near the clew, pulled it, and secured it to the little plastic cleat on the sail. Like magic, the luffing stopped.

As we approached the Sunshine Skyway Bridge across the bay, the AIS alarm sounded. There were no ships in the area, and I couldn't imagine with whom I might be on a collision course. I couldn't tie the tiller off to go below and shut off the alarm (I can only do this on a close reach), and I assumed the annoying alarm would eventually stop. We were about to cross under the bridge, and we did this to the incessant beeping. It never quit.

On the other side, I put us on a close reach, tied off the tiller with a bungee cord, and went below to investigate the cause of the alarm. The AIS showed two ATON's (aids to navigation) as the culprits, one on either side of the bridge opening. I vaguely remembered reading somewhere that ATON's could be equipped with AIS-transmitting hardware. I took a mental note to turn off the alarm when sailing in inland waters in the future.

Singlehand miles: 190

~~~

December 27

Yesterday evening I prepped the deck for the application of Kiwigrip non-skid paint by first washing the deck with soap and water, then cleaning it with paint thinner, sanding it with 80-grit sandpaper, and finally taping off sections of the deck to paint. This morning the tape was set but it was losing its grip due to the morning dew. Fortunately, most of it held. I dried it off, but the condensation just kept coming. I was anxious to paint the deck and have *Sobrius* looking sharp because my father was going to visit on the 30th. I waited until the sun rose up over the surrounding boats and evaporated the rest of the condensation, then I began painting the deck.

First I scooped out globs of the thick grey paint and spread it with a notched trowel, one that I used for setting tile, and then I rolled it out with the special roller that came with the paint. I did one section at a time, and backrolled the previous section after rolling out each new section. The Kiwigrip stands up and forms spikes when it is backrolled, which is what gives it its grip. I rolled each section a third time after the job was finished, and finally I removed the tape before the paint was dry. I waited 7 hours, as the instructions on the paint-can dictated, before returning to *Sobrius* and carefully walking on the surface. I was very pleased with the results, both visually and practically. I haven't slipped on deck yet.

While out, I visited West Marine and purchased charts for Florida's east Coast and the Keys. I bought another chart book for The Bahamas. I also went to the airport for a meeting with Customs and Border Patrol, where I registered with the Small Vessel Registration Service.
This way I will not have to go through customs when I return from a foreign country on *Sobrius*. I need only to make a phone call to check back in.

~~~

December 29

I couldn't sleep past 4:00 am this morning, so I got up

and went to work replacing the lifelines in the dark with a light strapped to my forehead. The lifelines, which run around the boat like a fence, are the last line of defense for a sailor who has lost his balance. The old lines were thin, frayed, and ugly. I replaced them with new, thicker line, grey in color and very strong. *Sobrius* looks surprisingly better and stronger with the new lifelines.

Next I wanted to take a look at the propeller shaft and its connection to the transmission. I removed the cushion and plywood support under it in the starboard quarterberth and opened the access panel to the engine and transmission, and crawled in with a flashlight to see if I could determine how to permanently fix the problem of the propeller shaft sliding out of the transmission. Upon inspection, I noticed two things that could be improved. First I determined that I needed to replace the "key" between the shaft and the transmission coupling. This is just a small block of steel that fits in a groove shared by the shaft and the coupling. After a bit of research, and at the suggestion of the employee I spoke to at the propeller store, I ordered the keystock from McMaster-Carr.

Secondly, I determined that the set-screw that holds the prop shaft in place would be prevented from slipping if it had a small indentation in the propeller shaft in which to sit. So I got out a drill and a drill bit and bored a small divot in the prop shaft where the set-screw came into contact with the shaft.

Back on deck I cleaned the bird-droppings off the new paint. Then I went back inside and cleaned and emptied the bilge, removed the old water tank under the port settee and its hoses and cleaned underneath them. This opened up a lot of storage space, so I rearranged things and put two 5-gallon jerry-cans filled with water under the settee where the old water tank had been. I was happy to have bought the jerrycans that clearly said "leakproof, able to be stored on its side." I filled and put another one on its side under the settee where I sleep. Things were coming together inside *Sobrius*. I was feeling like we were nearly ready to sail for home.

Later I checked the bilge, which I had cleaned and dried, to see if any water was coming in, and to my great dismay, the bilge was full again. My heart sank as I pondered the full meaning of having a leak of unknown origin in the hull somewhere, especially since I had recently done so much work to the keel and expected it to be completely water-tight. But then I remembered reading in one of the many books I had read over the last year about tasting the water when a leak was noticed. I dipped a finger in the water and put in on my tongue, which sensed no salt. It was fresh-water, not salt-water. The offending water in the bilge was coming from my new water tanks which were laying on their sides and apparently were not "leakproof" and one could not "be stored on its side".

~~~

December 30, ship's log:

"My parents came to visit me today. While my mother toured the Salvador Dali museum, which is right down the street, my father and I and I went for a sail in the light but adequate wind. The weather was fine – sunny and about 80 degrees. He loved *Sobrius* and was impressed with all the work I had done, and with my sailing ability, which made me feel like a success. No matter how old I get, I still want to impress my father. Sailing has brought us together, giving us something to share and providing subject matter for long conversations."

The older we all get, the more precious spending time with my parents becomes.

sailing with my father

December 31

When I awoke on the last day of 2016, the wind was strong and the air was cold. I could hear whistling coming from the rigging of other boats in the marina, and the trees on the shore were swaying in the wind. I had been wanting to try out my "storm/working jib" in strong winds and as I drank my coffee I decided to give it a go. I got the small sail out and hanked it to the headstay, led the jib-sheets through the jib-cars and tied them to its clew, attached the halyards, secured the jacklines, put a reef in the mainsail, and started the engine. While the engine warmed up, I put on my lifejacket/harness, gloves, and a warm hat. I was also wearing my very warm red sailing jacket and a black hat. Before pulling away, I attached my GoPro video camera to the stern pulpit with two hose-clamps so I could video the action.

As we pulled out of the relative calmness of the marina and into the choppy water of the bay, I heard the VHF radio say "this is the United States Coast Guard." But then the radio abruptly died. The battery in the handheld VHF that I kept in the cockpit when I sailed had not been charged. Earlier I heard on the weather-radio channel that there was a small craft advisory today. I wondered if the Coast Guard was calling to warn me not to go out. The wind was cold and strong, the sky was grey, and there were no other boats out on the water. I hoped I was not making a bad mistake.

I hoisted the sails and steered us onto a close reach. We accelerated, *Sobrius* heeled over, and spray flew off the bow with each little wave we crossed. I was taking video as I tied off the tiller, climbed up onto the coachroof and carefully walked to the mast. The jib-halyard needed tightening, and *Sobrius* charged ahead at full speed while I rode her like a surfboard and used the winch to trim the sail.

These were the heaviest conditions in which I had yet sailed. The wind was blowing 20-25 knots with gusts at "near gale" according to the report from National Weather Service which I heard on the VHF radio earlier that morning.

With one reef in the mainsail and the small headsail that the previous owner referred to as a storm jib, we heeled considerably on a close reach, with the leeward rail at the waterline. This sail has a luff of only 25' 6" and a foot of 11' 5", but I felt like I probably had too much sail up while we beat into the wind at 6 knots. However, sailing downwind was fine and we slid across the water at 7-8 knots, faster than the theoretical hull speed, which is about 6.5 knots. It was dramatic how the perceived conditions changed when I turned us downwind: no more spray, surfing the waves instead of charging into them, not heeling, sailing faster but feeling less motion.

The sail was absolutely thrilling and I took some good video, which I edited into one short video and posted on YouTube (Pauly Dangerous and *Sobrius*, a 1972 Dufour

Arpege, Sailing in Near-Gale Conditions on Tampa Bay
https://youtu.be/dhoT6kY0KAw). *Sobrius* performed well, my foul-weather gear performed well, and the camera performed well. I suppose I did too. However, the cacophony coming from below-deck made me realize that I need to better secure things down there when I sail.

Singlehand miles: 202

~~~

Jan 1, 2017

The weather on the first day of 2017 was much warmer and calmer than that of the last day of 2016. As soon as I emerged from the cabin of *Sobrius*, coffee in hand, and looked at the beautiful day, I wanted to sail again.

I tested out the stiff genoa that the sailmaker had repaired earlier, the one he referred to as a "racing genoa". "As a singlehander" he told me "I don't see you having much use for this sail". He went on to explain that it was too stiff to be easily handled by one person, rolling it out and rolling it up on deck. He was right about its stiffness, but it worked very well in spite of the difficulty I had managing it on deck. I did my best to roll it up on deck, but afterwards I had to take it to the park across the street and lay it out in the grass to roll it up properly.

I learned today that I need to make the turnbuckles less apt to snag the jib-sheets. I also learned that it is about impossible to climb back onboard from the water without the ladder. I went swimming while becalmed and experimented with this. I made a rudimentary rope ladder by tying loops in a dock line, but the rope bit into my feet too much. I decided that I need make a secondary rope ladder that works. I feel like it is absolutely necessary to have an emergency method of getting back onboard should I ever be so unlucky as to fall overboard, or to lose the swim-ladder. I see now the truth in all I have read about the difficulty of climbing back onboard. Many sailors have perished while trying to do so after falling overboard, even when tied to the boat via a harness – dragged beside the boat until they drowned, unable to reach the safety of the deck so tantalizingly within reach.

My anxiety and fear of the journey home to St Augustine diminished with each project completed and with each sea-trial. One of the last projects I needed to do was to rebed the chainplates, which are the steel plates that serve as anchoring points for the shrouds (the six steel cables in the center of the boat that support the mast). I removed them, one at a time, cleaned and inspected them, cleaned and caulked underneath them, and reinstalled them with the new bolts I had bought weeks before. Rebedding the chainplates was a huge accomplishment, as their condition was largely unknown. A couple of them showed signs of leaking too, which suggested saltwater-intrusion and possibly corrosion. There was corrosion, but there will be no more. This project made me feel much more confident about the integrity of *Sobrius* and her ability to sail on the open ocean.

I could feel the time to sail for home was approaching.

Today I put the name *Sobrius* on the transom. I used the somewhat unattractive and utilitarian reflective stickers from the hardware store. I like the reflectivity, and the stickers will increase the visibility of the vessel. In order to prevent being run down by a big ship while I sleep, it is very important to be seen at night, so the ugly stickers increase my safety factor. In the future, I will properly paint the name "*Sobrius*" on the transom, but at this time I was ready to use safety as a justification for taking the easy way out.

Another addition today was a shiny and stout little cleat in the center of the teak toerail on the transom. There is something I love about bolting stainless steel parts to *Sobrius*. The cleat is intended to be an anchoring point for a backstay adjuster. I was reminded of my days as a mountain-biker while installing the glistening steel piece. Simple mechanical things intrigue and bewitch me, especially when they are shiny and well-made.

I had a bit of a mishap today on the way out of the harbor. As we entered the bay the wind and the waves increased and *Sobrius* heeled. I had not properly stowed the sliding hatch-boards (that close off the companionway) but instead left them on deck. I watched in dismay as they slid off the coachroof and one of them disappeared into the water. This is something I will need to replace immediately, as I can't close up *Sobrius* without it.

Singlehand miles 230

~~~

Jan 4

I completed the install of the tiller-pilot on this day, which I started the day before. This was a complicated bit of work which required a lot of reading of the instructions, studying diagrams, and making a couple of phone calls to Brian, he who made the device. The job included cutting a hole in the companionway bulkhead where I installed the control module. I mounted the power unit to the inside of the opposite companionway bulkhead, then wired it to the breaker panel and the female connector in the cockpit. I had to make an aluminum extension to the teak cockpit rail to accommodate the actuator.

While I was crawling under the cockpit wiring the female connector for the autopilot, I noticed that the plywood bulkhead that supported the fuel tank was not secure, and thus not doing its job. So later in the day I added a plywood support piece to the bulkhead under the diesel tank. It looked like very little had been supporting the tank – possible disaster averted!

~~~

Jan 5

I woke up this morning after a fabulous sleep (I only woke up once in the night) and decided to sail. I needed to test the autopilot, and it seemed like an opportune morning to do so. But first I had to devise a system to prevent it from falling overboard. So, as the sun rose, I installed 4 stainless-steel D-rings. I don't know what my attraction to these little pieces of hardware is, but somehow I came to look forward to every opportunity to install D-rings, or padeyes, like jewelry on *Sobrius*.

The system I devised used blue shock cord to hold the business-end of the tiller-pilot to the rail when not in use. The other end of the unit has a pin that fits into a hole in an aluminum bracket that I made and installed. The tiller-pilot pivots on this bracket when in use. I tied a loop of shock cord to this end of the tiller-pilot and fastened two carabiners to the cord. The carabiners clip into the d-rings and hold the tiller-pilot firmly to the rail the whole time it is on deck, in use or not.

Confident that I wouldn't lose my new piece of equipment overboard, I was ready for another sea-trial.

The Pelagic tillerpilot functioned perfectly, and sailing with it will be a whole new ballgame. Now I can go forward safely on all points of sail and even alter course from outside the cockpit using the remote control. More importantly, while sailing offshore, I can let it steer while I sleep.

Singlehand miles 242

~~~

Since I had lost one of my sliding hatch-boards, I needed to find or make a replacement as soon as possible. After unsuccessfully trying to find used replacements at a sailboat-salvage warehouse, I eventually decided to make new ones out of "Starboard", a plastic sheet-material. The new sliding hatch-boards are better than the original set. I made them stronger and they fit better. I also like their bright white color as it brightens the interior when they are in place.

My propeller finally came in on this day, and I went to pick it up. This is something I had been waiting for since I bought the boat. However, on the way to the store to get it, they called to tell me that there was a problem with the propeller, so I had to turn around emptyhanded. After I got back to the marina and *Sobrius*, they called again and asked if I could bring them the old propeller, but they were closing in an hour, and they were a half-hour drive away. So, with a half hour to do so, I quickly put on my wetsuit, mask, snorkel and fins. I got out a hammer, two wrenches, and a screwdriver, then jumped overboard to remove my old propeller. I had to take off the locknut and the main nut. The propeller shaft is tapered, so getting the propeller off after the nuts have been removed is most easily performed with a propeller-puller. But since I didn't have one, I used a large hammer and beater-block, and after a bit of underwater work, I had the propeller in my hands and got it to the store in time.

~~~

Jan 8

The new propeller arrived, but the difficulties continued. I installed the propeller, underwater, holding my breath, but it didn't go up the prop shaft quite as far as the old propeller, and thus fewer threads for the locknuts were exposed. Worse, I stripped the locknut in the process. I wanted it to work so bad, I was in cold water, and my quickly-approaching departure-date was on my mind. I tried to take the propeller back off, banging on it with a hammer and a wood block until I was exhausted and cold, but the prop would not budge. In the end, I put the locknut on without the primary nut, forcing it on while stripping its threads.

propeller install, take 1

The next day I decided that this was not right, and I

borrowed a neighbor's propeller-puller and pulled the propeller off in short order. All I needed was the right tool (and the courage to ask to borrow it).

Another neighbor asked if I had been in the water today. "Yes" I said "I had to pull the propeller."

"You always pick the coldest days to go in the water" he replied. The air was 37° that morning, but the water was not so cold. In fact, the weather was much nicer underwater.

The problem was solved with the elimination of one of the nuts and the addition of a locking washer made specifically for the purpose.

~~~

Another job that needed done was rebuilding the winches. I had never done this, so I consulted YouTube for a demonstration, which I quickly found. After unbolting the port winch from the deck (there were only two winches on *Sobrius*) I removed the snap ring at the top and the winch body slid off the gear assembly inside. I laid all the pieces out, in the order in which I removed them, on paper towels on the small table in the galley. Everything got cleaned with WD40, then sprayed with Corrosion X, dried, and lubricated with marine grease. This process reminded me of my time working on bicycles, from another life.

The winch project took up the first half of January 9th, and the second half of the day I spent rebuilding the head with a rebuild kit. This was a fairly easy process, and in the end the head worked perfectly. After this I went shopping and provisioned *Sobrius* for the journey home with canned soup and chili, canned fruit, nuts, crackers, energy bars, apples, bananas, olives, peperoni, V8, and fruit juice.

~~~

On the January 10th, I screwed the aft bulkheads into

place, covered the ventilator holes in the hull at the bow, added forward blocks to the toerail for using a preventer, mounted the binoculars to the cockpit bulkhead on a little shelf I built, and filled the water tanks. I had 27 gallons of water divided among five tanks, about three more gallons in small bottles, about three gallons of juice, and a 12-pack of coconut water. The fuel tank was topped off and I had another five gallons of diesel in a yellow jerrycan.

When *Sobrius* was ready, I drove back to St Augustine. The morning of the 11th, I rented a car and drove back to St. Petersburg and returned the car to a small airport near the marina. At this point I was ready to go, but I relaxed for the rest of the day and planned to leave in the morning.

Departure
January, 2017

The things we fear are the things we should embrace. Our fears enslave us and keep us anchored to the past and ignorant of the future that could be. Bad karma prevents us from facing our fears, and thus makes conquering them impossible. A negative view of the world makes us fear what is good and keeps us stuck on a meaningless treadmill of our own construction. Overcoming fear is escape, and escape leads to enlightenment. Enlightenment is the ultimate goal and leads to something bigger than life as a human on Earth. Earth is a school for gods-to-be. It doesn't matter where we have been, because we've already been there. All that matters now is where we are going next, and we can't go somewhere new if we are afraid of leaving.

~~~

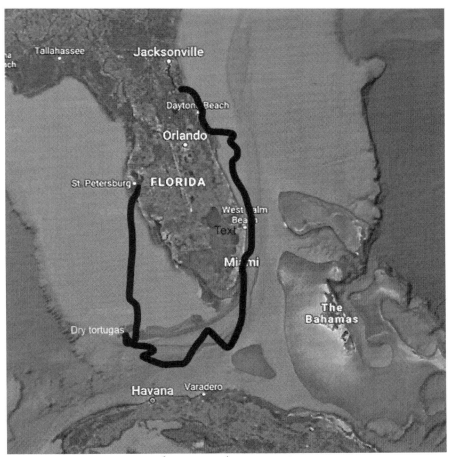

the approximate route

Jan 12, 2017

    I slept well last night, especially considering that today is the day I depart to sail by myself 1000 miles to St Augustine, stopping only at the Dry Tortugas and Miami, should I choose to do so. Today is my day of reckoning, the day I put everything I have learned and all my preparations to the test. There is no more time to prepare *Sobrius* for the journey, no more time to study, nothing else I can learn and no more questions to ask before leaving. Tonight, and for the rest of the journey, I will only sleep 20 minutes at a time. I will sail 24 hours a day in what will probably be three legs of three or four days each. Whatever weather comes, I must deal with it accordingly. Whatever breaks or fails on *Sobrius* I must fix or do without. Whatever obstacles get in my way, I must sail around. The time has come for me to assume the role of singlehand sailor. This is what I have wanted for a nearly a year now, and the day is here!

This morning I made coffee and ate an apple, then began final preparations for the journey. I installed plastic anti-chafe covers on the lifelines at the bow, to protect them from the headsail, and the headsail from them. I washed the deck, as I didn't want to start the journey with bird-droppings on *Sobrius*. I stopped service on my electrical account at the marina; I removed fenders and docklines from the dock and put them aboard. I hanked on the genoa, and called the marina office to let them know I was coming to drop off my key. *Sobrius* and I departed at 9:00 am under clear skies and very light wind.

~~~

As we motor past the office dock I hold out the marina key that I need to return, looped on the end of my boat hook, trying to give it to the secretary as we drift by. But we are going a little too fast and she looks surprised as she jogs down the dock to keep up with us. Before she gets to the end of the dock she reaches out and grabs the key at the last second, before we drift out of reach. I wave goodbye and she waves too, with one eyebrow slightly raised. I am leaving as a novice sailor. Hopefully I'll be an intermediate sailor by the end of this journey, or at least an advanced novice.

We motor out of the marina and into the bay, like I have done a dozen times before. But this time it is different; I will not be returning to my slip at the St. Petersburg Municipal Marina. The slip is no longer mine, and there is nowhere to go but home to St. Augustine, 1000 miles away.

In the bay, I shut off the engine and hoist the sails, catching the light wind. Silently we glide across the flat water, and I watch the St Petersburg skyline fade away one last time.

The breeze decreases as we approach the Sunshine Skyway Bridge and I watch the speed display drop. For the next hour we only sail at 0.5 knot, about the pace of a slow old man walking somewhere he doesn't want to go. Movement across the water is barely perceptible and a red buoy we are approaching appears stationary. I don't want to run the engine on the first day of the journey, not knowing when I will have an opportunity to fill up or how much fuel I might need. I also don't want to start the journey giving in to the desire to move above a certain minimum speed. This is to be a sailing journey, and I am determined to use the engine minimally. I'm in no hurry.

With patience to spare, *Sobrius* and I sail across Tampa Bay, past Egmont Key, through the south channel, and into the Gulf of Mexico. The wind has increased a bit and we make all of 2 knots. We are now out farther than I have yet sailed and I experience the unique feeling of being on my first big sailing journey: freedom, adventure, anticipation, the unknown. I am on the edge of my comfort zone, but so far, I love it.

~~~

day 1 in the Gulf of Mexico

It's now 5:20 pm and we are about to cross the dotted line on the chartplotter that marks three nautical miles from shore. The sun is low on the horizon, straight ahead and reflecting off the very light chop on the water. A flock of terns squawk and dive excitedly as they pursue some mobile food source invisible to me. The wind is coming out of the east at 12 knots and soon I will turn south toward the Dry Tortugas, 180 nm (nautical miles) away. I'm sitting in the cockpit hand-steering while looking at the skyline of Sarasota in the distance. Very soon I won't be able to see land anymore, and then it won't be until the day after tomorrow before I see it again, at the tiny island of Garden Key.

We are now making what seems like very good headway at 4.2 knots, after an incredibly slow morning. The wind has increased and is propelling *Sobrius* forward; we leave a wake in the water behind us and the journey is well-underway. I feel an incredible sense of accomplishment to have gotten to this moment, the beginning of the biggest adventure of my life. It is happening now, and this is what the journey is all about. I am sailing, alone, and on my own boat. I am deep in nature, and nature is deep in me. Very little in this world matters besides what is happening right here, right now. Tranquility reigns supreme, and I want for nothing.

~~~

But as quickly as I realize that I want for nothing, a want arises. I want to share the moment with my father, and I call him one last time before sailing out of telephone-range. We talk about the weather forecast, which seems acceptable – the wind is supposed to increase to the mid-teens and blow from the northeast. I describe the scene to him – the distant skyline of land to the east, the calm seas, the autopilot and the sails. We go over my plans one last time. I try to share with him what I can of my adventure, one I know he would have liked to do himself.

The sun sets, I watch for the green flash, but see only warm colors. The stars come out, *Sobrius* continues south. I steer in the cockpit for a few hours, the lights of Sarasota fade away. I am alone on the water, leaving land for a few days. I am relaxed and falling into my element. The seas are calm and the wind is just right for my first day out.

sunset on the first day of the journey home

Throughout this journey, I will need to sleep in 20-minute increments and do so whenever the opportunity arises, sometimes regardless of whether or not I am tired. Opportunity to sleep comes when there are no ships visible and nothing around to run into. Right now, land is six miles away and we are sailing nearly parallel to it and slightly away. No ships are visible, and the chartplotter shows no obstacles in our path. I haven't seen any fishing buoys for over an hour, and no ships are indicated on the AIS. I unstrap the tillerpilot from its holder, pivot it to the tiller and attach it to the little post that I installed there. I turn on the tillerpilot by pushing a button on the control module mounted on the cockpit bulkhead and a red light starts flashing. With another button, I adjust it a few degrees to starboard to get it steering us in the right direction, then go below and lay down in my bunk, which moves with the sea. I turn on the 22-minute countdown timer on my watch and close my eyes as the autopilot steers us south.

This is the first time I have tried to sleep while sailing by myself. Months ago, while reading about singlehanding, the author mentioned that trying to sleep when nobody is on deck can bring about a very nervous and uncomfortable feeling, and I smile as I realize that I am indeed quite comfortable with the idea.

Soon I feel a vibration on my wrist and then hear my watch beeping. Quickly I sit up, realizing that I did indeed sleep, and feeling a small sense of victory in this. *Sobrius* has been sailing on her own for 22 minutes now with nobody on watch, and I am eager to take a look around. I poke my head out of the hatch and look out at the dark horizon for any lights that would indicate ships in the area. I see none. I look at the sails, and they are both still trimmed correctly. The chartplotter shows that we are travelling in the proper direction, and it shows nothing hard that we might run into. The AIS confirms that there are no ships around. I go back to my bunk, lay down and close my eyes. The countdown timer on my watch reset itself as soon as I turned off the alarm and has already been counting for a couple of minutes, which is why I set it for 22 minutes. I have two minutes to look around, and then twenty to sleep. I clear my mind and try not to think about the fact that I only have such a short time to sleep.

I go through this routine three times, after which I feel awake and want to sit in the cockpit and hand-steer for a while. The night is dark and beautiful. The only sounds are made by the wind and the water and the interactions of them and my ship. The air has no scent, and my sinuses are wide open, taking in large breaths of the pure and oxygen-rich air. I have no bimini to block the view of the stars above, which are much more bright and numerous than when viewed from land. Tranquility reigns.

Our first day of sailing covered 105 nautical miles; the nearest weather buoy reported east winds at 10-15 knots.

~~~

I sleep a few more times; I can't say for sure how many; memory doesn't record such details when sleeping this way. I am wide awake and hand-steering before the sun rises. The sky is dark and the water is nearly invisible. The first morning of the journey has brought increased wind and seas, both coming from the northeast, and we sail along on a broad reach. We are making 6.5 knots, which is the maximum speed – "hull speed" – of *Sobrius*. The darkness gives way to light on the eastern horizon, to our left and slightly ahead. The cloudy sky becomes backlit in warm colors, then the sun itself makes its appearance on our side of the world. There is no land in sight, it's just me and *Sobrius* out here on the Gulf of Mexico, sailing by myself, my dream realized. I smile at the thought.

~~~

Before leaving one of the things I wondered about was whether or not I would be scared out on the ocean by myself. I thought I might worry that the boat would simply sink. After all, it's just a half-inch fiberglass hull with a 3000-pound iron keel bolted to the bottom. I take a mental inventory and find no great fear. I experienced real fear during the Okefenokee canoe trip, but out here I feel fine. I don't think *Sobrius* will sink, and if so I have my 12-0 surfboard, the SPOT, my camelback, and two handheld VHF radios. My water is stored in 5-gallon containers and I could bring at least one with me if I had to abandon ship. It would float since fresh water is less dense than salt water. I have soft-wood plugs to plug broken through-hull fittings, should one break. I have lots of tools for fixing things. I have a wetsuit that will prevent hypothermia if I have to spend time in the water (assuming I can put it on in time). And I wear my self-inflating life-vest/harness and stay clipped to the boat nearly all the time. I feel well-prepared, even though I don't have a proper life-raft or an EPIRB (emergency position-indicating radio beacon). There's always going to be safety gear that I could have but don't, and I hope I have enough.

As the day wears on, the wind and the seas slowly increase. We are making 6-6.5 knots, which is maximum speed, and the seas are coming from behind and port, so the motion is not uncomfortable. But Sobrius slowly heels more and more, leaning to starboard with the force of the wind.

I'm thinking about reducing sail by removing the genoa and replacing it with a smaller headsail, and so I feel I must do it, as the saying goes: "If you're thinking about reefing then it's time to reef." But I don't really want to reef, it's more like I feel like I have to. The sky has lost its warm colors and is now grey, the seas are rolling at about five feet, coming from aft and port, and it feels like we are moving fast. But the wind is slowly increasing, as are the seas, and Sobrius heels a bit more than I think is proper.

I turn Sobrius into and across the wind and the mainsail swings to the other side of the cockpit; I let its sheet out all the way. I leave the headsail tied to what is now the windward side of the boat, and so it becomes back-winded. I lash the tiller to leeward and Sobrius heaves-to, coming almost to a stop and pointing just off the wind. In this configuration, the headsail tries to push the boat downwind while the tiller tries to steer upwind. The mainsail is out all the way so it does little. The overall effect is that the boat moves very slowly, a little bit upwind, and requires no helmsman. I clip the stainless-steel carabiner on my harness to the white and flat nylon jackline and carefully move forward. Sobrius pitches and rolls in the five-foot seas. The sky and water are the same shade of grey; land is about 50 miles away and well out of sight.

On deck, I free the headsail downhaul from the cleat I installed, weeks ago, on deck at the base of the mast, release the halyard from a mast-cleat, and pull down the genoa with the downhaul. I am careful not to let it fall into the water, but since it is back-winded it is mainly over the center of the boat; I reach out with my free hand and pull on the sail so it falls on deck. I am watching the boom and hoping it stays in place. I don't want it to swing across the boat and brain me, but *Sobrius* remains hove-to and the boom is happily staying put.

While working on deck, my eyes and attention are focused on the deck and rigging and sails, but not the seas. Waves come unexpected, unanticipated. The body must keep balance without the aid of the eyes. *Sobrius* seems to move in random lurches; seasickness threatens, safety is paramount.

On the bobbing bow, I wrestle with the genoa, untie the sheets from its clew, and roll it into a disheveled bundle; I coax it into its black sail bag. My legs straddle the bow, my feet are hanging in the air above the water, then they plunge into the water, back out again. The bow points to the grey sky, the water recedes, the bow points back to the sea, the water rises to my feet. I unhank the sail from the headstay, pulling the spring-loaded bronze clips loose one-at-a-time until the sail is free. I release the halyard from the ring at the top of the sail and clip it to the bow pulpit. I carefully drag the large black bag of sail back to the cockpit, staying clipped to the jackline all the way, and drop the sail into the cabin below.

Now I must repeat the process again, reversed, but with a smaller sail. I drag it to the bow, clip the hanks to the headstay, attach the halyard, and unroll the sail. I try to tie on the sheets but the lines need to be lengthened, so I go back to the cockpit, pulling my tether along behind me. To cross a sheet laying across the jackline, I first clip my second tether to the other side of the sheet, then release the first tether; this way I am always attached to *Sobrius*, holding on all the time, careful not to slip. I release the sheet from its cleat and carefully return to the deck and tie the jib-sheets to the clew of the jib.

Finally, the jib is changed and ready to hoist and I

move to the mast, free the downhaul, and pull on the jib-halyard, crank it tight on the winch, and fasten it to its cleat. The jib is up and flogging in the wind, flaying its sheets all over the place, since I left them uncleated.

I return to the cockpit as quickly as I safely can, clipping and unclipping my tethers as I do, so that I am never unattached to the jackline. Back in the cockpit I tension the windward jib-sheet and the job is finally done. I take a deep breath, and then another, sitting in the safety and comfort of the cockpit.

Still hove-to, I need to get us moving again. First I release the windward jib-sheet and pull in on the leeward jib-sheet as the headsail comes across the deck. I unlash the tiller and haul in on the mainsheet and we get moving on a beam-reach, but heading north instead of south. I head us upwind and tack, releasing one jib-sheet and hauling in on the other. I then turn us the rest of the way downwind, let the main out a bit, and proceed south.

My first headsail change of the journey was slow and laborious, and it made me a bit seasick. But it is now done and I sit in the cockpit and feel relaxed and safe. On to the Dry Tortugas!

~~~

We are now making 6 to 6.5 knots, the same speed we were making before I changed headsails. But with less sail area aloft, we are heeling much less and the motion of *Sobrius* is considerably more pleasant. This is a lesson I need to remember. Reefing doesn't necessarily mean reducing boat-speed, and it certainly does make the ride more comfortable.

My stomach, however, is not comfortable. All the work on deck has made me slightly ill. My mood is worsened by the grey sky and relatively rough seas, also grey. My mood is grey. I set the tillerpilot and go below for a nap.

I set the countdown timer on my grey watch and I lay

down in my bunk. Next to me is my 12-foot surfboard, which is also my life-raft and dinghy. It also prevents me from falling out of my bunk when *Sobrius* rolls, so I guess that makes it a lee-board as well. The surfboard dominates the aisle in the center of the salon and is tied to the stainless-steel mast-compression post. On the other side of the aisle are four 5-gallon jerrycans of water lashed to the opposite bunk. Another 7 gallons of water is in a blue container bungeed to the floor further forward. I also have various containers of juice in a locker next to my head, which is resting on a pillow, and my Camelbak contains 100oz of water and emergency food and flares. This is the bag I will take with me should I need to abandon ship.

The tillerpilot tries to keep me awake with its incessant mechanical whirring and whistling, but I am drifting off to sleep while *Sobrius* presses on across the Gulf of Mexico. Laying down in my bunk is so relaxing. Anything in a moving sailboat besides laying down requires effort. One Is always keeping balance, holding on to something, countering the constant motion of the ship, and thus one is always at work while sailing. But laying down, all the work ceases, and sleep comes quickly, like a missed lover.

I sleep for three 20-minute increments, getting up each time to check the horizon for ships, the chartplotter for course, speed, and any obstacles. I also consult the AIS for any boats that I can't yet see. In the cockpit, I check the trim of the sails and I scan the horizon for lights. If all is clear I need only to lay back down – the timer on my watch resets itself. Polyphasic sleep is all the singlehand sailor can afford.

~~~

I feel better after my rest, seasick no more and no longer depressed by the color of the sky and the demeanor of the sea. My mood is further improved by a visit from a pod of dolphin. They approach from windward, leaping and rolling, swimming under *Sobrius*, riding in my wake. The dolphin ride in the swell just beneath the surface, *Sobrius* rides the wave of wind just above. Occasionally I hear a thump on the hull, as if they sometimes bump into us. I wonder what they are up to underwater – if they are playing some sort of dolphin game. Perhaps the game consists of trying to outmaneuver each other until one collides with my hull, which the other counts as a score and laughs at his or her friend.

The sailing today is thrilling. We reach along at 6 – 7 knots in about 15 knots of wind, also pushed from aft and port by the five-foot waves. The tiller requires much movement in order to keep us going in a straight line. Each time a wave rolls underneath and lifts us, *Sobrius* turns to windward, and I pull on the tiller to counteract the turn. This is repeated about every 15 seconds, all day, all night, *Sobrius* and I moving together.

Sobrius moves like a butterfly - up, down, left, right, an erratic thing of beauty, traversing the dancing waves of unknown origin formed by the same wind that propels us wherever I point the tiller. Boat and sea and wind and sailor all interact in a series of seemingly chaotic movements that somehow result in the boat moving in the direction desired by the sailor. I don't know if mathematicians can describe all this motion and intention with numbers, I certainly can't, but somehow my body knows what to do, and we keep moving south, towards the Dry Tortugas. My eyes stare forward, my feet and legs brace my body safely in the cockpit, my left hand holds tight to a cleat, my right hand grasps the tiller, and my right arm works like a piston, pulling and pushing however necessary to satisfy my eyes, which stare off at the horizon, monitoring the relative angle of the waves and periodically consulting the chartplotter for course.

After the orange sun sets and the full yellow moon rises, I sleep some more, letting the tiller pilot steer. The noise from the wind, waves, lines banging into the mast, and the tillerpilot would keep me awake were it not for the red plastic construction-site ear muffs that I wear when I lay down. The tillerpilot is a diligent helmsman, constantly making fine adjustments to the tiller, whirring and clicking all the while. In the space of 20 minutes, I fall asleep, I dream, I wake to the alarm on my wrist, and I rise – a bit disoriented. For the next two minutes I check the horizon, the sails, and the instruments. All is well, and there are no ships or obstacles in my little world, so I lay back down, close my eyes, and quickly fall back asleep.

~~~

I get up in the middle of the night wondering how much battery power the lights, instruments, and tiller pilot have consumed and if the two 55-watt solar panels had been able to charge the batteries enough during the day to keep everything running all night. When I designed the system, I calculated the energy consumption of everything, and concluded that 100 watts of solar power and 150 amp-hours of battery power would be adequate. I have 110 watts of solar power and 165 amp-hours of battery power. But at midnight I check the battery voltmeter, and the news is bad – 12.5 volts. This means the batteries are already getting low and that there might not be enough power to run the tiller pilot, *Sobrius'* lights, and instruments through the night. Perhaps the cloudy skies of yesterday prevented the solar panels from fully charging the batteries. The navigation lights, chartplotter, and AIS need to stay on, however, the tillerpilot is expendable. It also consumes the most power, so I resign myself to hand-steering for the rest of the night, and I partly welcome the opportunity to experience the sea at night and gaze at the stars. [In retrospect, I believe I misread the analog voltmeter. It probably read 13 volts, with the needle halfway between 12 and 14, and since 13 is not on the meter, I probably interpreted this as 12.5 in my sleep-deprived state. When trying to function on less-than-normal amounts of sleep, one must move more slowly and think twice as long about each decision.]

I sit in the cockpit and remove the tillerpilot from the tiller and strap it to the rail, taking the tiller in my right hand. I eat a chocolate bar that contains caffeine. Its wrapper reads "AWAKE", and awake it keeps me. I feel quite alert as we sail across a black sea and under a black sky on my second night as a singlehand offshore sailor.

The scene is magical and beautiful. The moon illuminates the sea; myriad wave crests reflect its yellow light, which the moon is reflecting from the sun, beyond the horizon. The sea is a shifting and shimmering black mass beneath the flickering light on its surface. As bright as the moon is, it can't hide the light from all the stars, which appear like glitter across the sky. Light above, light below, on Earth as it is in Heaven.

~~~

Before I left St Petersburg I was told by another sailor to watch out for the light towers between Tampa Bay and the Dry Tortugas, as they were the only hard things I might run into. I found them on the chart, and in my head I pictured small lighthouses perched on rocky outcroppings surrounded by the sea. I stare off at the horizon watching for them. The chartplotter shows one somewhere in the distance, and eventually I see the faint flashing light of a tower on the horizon.

Hours later, or so it seems, I pass a lonely steel tower emerging from the sea topped with two flashing white lights and a fog-horn, standing firm in over 100 feet of water, no land or rocks in sight. "Why is this here?", I wonder. There is nothing to mark, no rock to avoid or channel to locate. Perhaps the light tower is simply a reassurance for sailors sailing from Tampa Bay to the Dry Tortugas that they are indeed on the right course. I keep looking back to see if it's still there, and it is hours later before the light disappears over the horizon aft. For the rest of the night I watch the horizon ahead for the lights of the buoys surrounding the Dry Tortugas, not sure at what distance I will be able to see them.

For hours I simply sail. There is nothing to see but the night sky and its reflection on the black water. There is nothing to hear except the wind and the waves passing by my little ship. The air has no smell, and my mind is calm. I focus my attention on the position of a particular star relative to the shrouds of *Sobrius*, keeping the star in the same place – within a triangle formed by the shroud, the mast and the lifeline. This keeps me steering in the same direction. Occasionally I check the compass heading on the chartplotter, keeping it as close to 180 (directly south) as I can. I am part of the ship, pulling and pushing on the tiller, responding to every motion with a counter-motion, navigating, steering, nothing more.

Steering a sailboat at night while staring at the stars is one of my favorite things. While an autopilot is extremely useful, I am glad not to have one that can work all the time. I value this time I spend steering, otherwise I would not be so in tune with the boat and the sea and the stars. The act of steering a sailboat is one of the great pleasures of sailing, and I think one should be cautious when outfitting their boat so as not to give up the necessity to at least occasionally steer the ship, for if the skipper never steers, he then becomes a passenger.

~~~

The wind has continued to increase and the unwelcome compulsion to do another headsail change and to also reef the mainsail dominates my mind. I've been avoiding this chore, but I can no longer deny that it must be done. I haven't reduced sail at night yet, but there's a first time for everything, and on this trip almost everything is a first. This time, however, I decide not to heave-to but instead do the headsail change and reef while underway. I go over the steps in my head, trying to remember the order of tasks presented by Andrew Evans in his book *Singlehand Sailing, Thoughts, Tips, Techniques & Tactics*:

- Lower foresail to relieve pressure on tack
- Unroll new sail on windward side
- Disconnect lazy sheet, attach to new sail
- Hank on new sail below existing sail
- Remove tack of existing foresail and shackle on new sail
- Return to cockpit and tension lazy sheet
- Initiate auto-tack (with remote control of autopilot)
- Release jib-halyard
- Pull foresail down
- Unhank existing sail
- Clip halyard to new sail
- Leave old sail on windward deck
- Raise new sail
- Return to cockpit and trim new sail
- Retrieve old sail
- Connect lazy sheet to new sail

The work is dark and ominous, but I remain clipped in to the jacklines 100% of the time. The most dramatic part of the sail-change is untying the lazy sheet from the jib while underway. I have to lean out over the water to access the clew of the jib, which is full of air and pulling *Sobrius* forward. The black water rushes by underneath and I must use both hands to untie the line. Falling overboard would result in watching *Sobrius* sail away under full sail and autopilot, eventually disappearing over the horizon as I bobbed in the sea, kept afloat by my lifejacket. While untying this sheet I am doubly clipped in, with one tether clipped to the jackline and the second clipped to a shroud. I feel like a rock-climber dangling over a cliff.

I have to tack into the wind in order to drop the headsail, which takes us off-course while I work, but the motion of the boat is much more comfortable compared to when we were hove-to during the last headsail change. While underway, *Sobrius* remains consistently heeled and only moves up and down as we cross waves. While hove-to she rocks side-to-side as well as up and down. I find that I definitely prefer changing headsails while underway, although I also prefer doing it in the daytime. The night adds an element of fear to the operation.

When the old sail is down and the new smaller sail is up, I gybe *Sobrius* and get us back on-course, and once again we are heeling less than before and sailing more comfortably. I move to the mast and start the process of reefing the mainsail. I loosen the downhaul and boom vang, release the halyard and pull the sail down about 24 inches and try to attach the first reef cringle to the hook on the boom, but it won't reach. I have to return to the cockpit and loosen the mainsheet so the boom can rise. Back at the mast I push the boom up and there it is, I secure the reef cringle to the hook on the boom. I find the reefing line and pull hard and make it fast to a cleat on the boom. I finally tighten the downhaul and the vang. The reef is done, the sail is made smaller.

This should be a very quick process for an experienced sailor, but for me it is not quick at all yet. When the process is over and I return to the safety of the cockpit, where I can sit still and relax for as long as I like, I think about how I can improve my technique.

The night is dark and the only lights visible are the stars that peek out from behind the clouds. I'm thankful that I am not afraid of the dark, or being alone at sea. Before departing I wasn't sure if this would be the case. The level of fear that I might experience at sea was one of the many unknowns of this journey.

~~~

Late in the night, I detect a faint glow on the horizon. The glow becomes many lights. But I'm too far away to be able to see the lights for which I look, the beacons surrounding the Dry Tortugas. These are not beacons or light houses, my AIS confirms that what I see is a fleet of shrimp boats. My father warned me about this exact scenario. He encountered the same thing on his way to the Dry Tortugas many years earlier, also at night. I heard his warning but was unimpressed and wondered how, on such a massive body of water, could a fleet of shrimp boats get in the way of a sailboat. However now, looking ahead at this moving obstacle course, I am certainly impressed with the difficulty I face in getting around them. Fishing boats towing gear have right-of-way over sailboats, and they are dragging huge nets some unknown distance behind them while lumbering about in the dark and frequently changing course. They will indeed expect me to avoid them. I alter course intending to pass them to the west.

It's not long before my AIS alarm goes off, warning me that we are on a collision-course with one of the fleet. The alarm on the AIS is adjustable for both closest point of approach (CPA) and time to closest point of approach (TCPA). I have it set for one mile and 15 minutes. If it calculates that I will pass within one mile of another ship, the alarm goes off 15 minutes before our closest point of approach. The alarm is beeping and it is loud, however I mounted the AIS on the navigation table, way out of reach from the cockpit. I think I'll just let it go off until it stops. It's got to stop eventually, I think. But it doesn't stop; it just keeps on beeping relentlessly, annoying me beyond my endurance. Defeated, I set the tillerpilot and go below to turn it off.

The AIS is an amazing piece of equipment with a display screen that shows me what ships are around me on a little map. If I select a ship on the map, the AIS tells me its name, direction of travel, speed, closest point of approach, time to closest point of approach, what type of ship it is (fishing, in this case), length and weight of the ship, etc. The ship setting off my alarm is called *Odin*, the Norse god of war and death. I need to stay away from *Odin*. I check the next closest boat, and its name is even worse: *Fuck It* (no, I didn't make this up). I really need to stay away from all of these boats.

I grab the binoculars and go back above. I want to see what direction the boats are going in order to plan my route around them. They should all have a red light on the port side of the bow and a green light on the starboard. A white light should be on the stern. This is maritime law, and allows skippers like myself to determine the relative direction of travel. But all I see are yellowish lights everywhere – no green, no red. I can't tell anything from their lights, and about ten shrimp boats crowd the horizon.

Again the alarm goes off, and I have to again set the tiller pilot, turn it on, and go below to stop the infernal beeping. I come back up and decide that I should change course and instead pass the fleet to the east, as they look like they are travelling west now. I prepare to gybe, which is a difficult and sometimes dangerous maneuver but it's time to change course now. It's nearly impossible to tell just how far away the shrimp boats are, and I know they tow huge nets behind them, so I really don't want to be anywhere near them.

I pull in the mainsheet, bringing the boom closer to the center of *Sobrius*, ready the windward jib-sheet by wrapping it around its winch and taking up its slack, move to the leeward side of the cockpit and uncleat the leeward jib-sheet, holding it tight. I pull the tiller to my chest, turning us to port. The wind switches from one side of the mainsail to the other and the boom swings across the cockpit over my head, bringing the mainsheet and its block with it. I release the jib-sheet and quickly pull the other sheet with both hands, holding the tiller with my knees. I take up the slack as fast as I can, making the winch scream its metallic cry and pull hard on the jib-sheet, cleating it off after I've pulled in all I can, and I take the tiller back in my gloved hands.

We are now sailing northeast, but I have to look around to find the shrimp boats in the black night to get my bearings. I steer us to starboard, tighten the sheets, and put us on a southeast course. We are sailing fast in the dark and windy night, rolling with the waves, approaching the east flank of the shrimp boats, some of which are changing course. I suppose that they are chasing schools of shrimp, and the skippers of the vessels somehow know where the shrimp are going, and they follow the shrimp, caring not about the sailboat interloper.

The alarm goes off again. *Fuck It* is on a collision course with me. This is not good. I alter course to port, on a beam reach directly east. I stare at the boat and try to determine its course. The night seems particularly dark as I sail east. We are moving fast, at 6 knots, into five-foot seas. The action is thrilling, but it all seems risky, the maneuvering and dodging of shrimp boats. I can't really tell, in the dark, how far away they are or how fast they are moving. I am trying to be conservative and stay as far away as possible, but I am a novice sailor. This is the first time I've been in a situation like this and the penalty for error is destruction and death.

After sailing east for about a half hour, I feel that I am well out of their way, and I pull the tiller to me and turn *Sobrius* to the south. But again the alarm goes off and I must set the tillerpilot, go below, turn the alarm off, try to determine with whom I will pass within one mile and to what direction I must alter course. I make a decision and return to the cockpit.

I want more speed to get around the fleet. I think I can pass to the east of them, but I need all the speed I can get. I start the diesel engine and wait for it to warm up. When the pitch of the engine's one cylinder rises and smooths out, I put the throttle all the way forward and turn us more south. We are making a run for it, around *Fuck It* and *Odin* and the rest of the fleet.

But what I see baffles me. As we begin to pass, the light of *Fuck It* turns to face me. Is this psychotic nocturnal shrimper trying to run me down? I'm at a loss. I've altered course to stay away from them four or five times now, I'm clearly trying to avoid them, but *Fuck It* has it in for me. I hold my course and stare into the light, trying to determine if we are on a collision course. If the bearing between us changes, then we will not collide, but if it stays the same, we will. But the alarm is silent. Though the bearing between us does not change, the light on *Fuck It* is bright and not getting bigger. It must be the stern I'm looking at, not the bow. Yes, *Fuck It* is moving directly away from us, not directly toward us. We are safe, and I begin to relax.

This was our last obstacle in the shrimp fleet. We pass to the east of the shrimpers and leave them behind. I turn off the engine. The night becomes a quiet and peaceful place again. The water sloshes against *Sobrius'* hull; the wind sings softly in the sails. There are no other sounds. Ahead in the blackness I see only water, moon and stars, and the faint smell of diesel exhaust from the shrimp boats fades away.

Finally I can relax and enjoy the evening as I sit in the cockpit, steering us south and looking at the stars above and their reflections on the water below. I watch for the yellow flashing buoys that surround the outer edge of the Dry Tortugas. We are sailing at 6-7 knots in about 20 knots of wind and 5-foot seas. I've been steering all night and am ready for sunrise and anchoring. I'm tired, but the scene is mesmerizing. It's a setting that few humans get the opportunity to experience; the open sea at night, alone, is tranquil beyond measure.

~~~

Eventually I see a yellow flashing light on the horizon, poking its head up above the waves, then hiding below. I want to count the seconds between flashes as this number identifies the buoy and thus its location. Time passes and the buoy continues to play hide-and-seek, but eventually I determine that it's flashing in four-second intervals. From consulting the chart, I know that the one closest to the inlet has a six-second interval. The one I see is a few miles further to the east of the inlet.

Hours pass and the sun begins to rise; the sea changes from black to grey as the sky goes through a series of color changes – purple, red, orange, yellow, blue. The morning is beautiful, but I am weary. We are now passing to the south of the Dry Tortugas, and I can turn us to the west. The channel I seek is on the south side of the National Park, which is surrounded by shallow reef. I need to gybe, so I pull on the mainsheet and center the boom over the cockpit, then I ready the leeward jib-sheet, move myself to the leeward side of the cockpit, push the tiller away from me, and *Sobrius* turns west. The mainsail shifts to the other side with an audible low-pitched snap, then the headsail does the same. I slowly ease and then release the windward jib-sheet and at the same time pull in on the leeward sheet and cleat it off.

I spot another flashing light, but it only stays above the horizon for a second or two in the waves. Eventually I can see it long enough to count six seconds between flashes. I'm getting closer.

In my peripheral vision, I see a bright light pointing right at us. What is this? Is there a ship approaching? I check the AIS and see no ships in the area. The light disappears, but it comes back and points at me again. It is so bright, but there is no ship in view beneath the light. My mind is tired. I consult the wisdom of the chartplotter, and the chartplotter knows the answer. The source of the bright light is the lighthouse on Loggerhead Key. I laugh at myself. My mind is running slowly.

~~~

A low island in the distance, a lighthouse, a brick fort, these occupy a small space in my vision, perched on the grey horizon, behind a light mist between water and sky. In the foreground bobs a vertical white cylinder, a buoy marking the outer edge of the Dry Tortugas National Park. Atop the buoy flashes the yellow light that I'd been watching in the predawn hours, watching and slowly approaching. I am tired and mentally exhausted from the two previous days and nights of singlehand sailing, sleeping in 20-minute sessions, dodging shrimp boats, and hand-steering all last night. But now I must perform; I must think through every action twice as long as I normally would, to ensure I don't make any mistakes. The inlet I seek is surrounded by rock and reef hidden beneath the water. All the water looks like ocean, but the all-knowing chartplotter knows of the dangers beneath. Red-right-return, red-right return, keep the red buoys on the right, green on the left. But I can't currently see red or green buoys.

The gentle roaring of the increasing wind fills my ears as the constant waves lift and drop *Sobrius*. The island beckons; my patience sharpens. The approach seems incredibly slow, like watching the minute hand of a clock; the island grows as fast as a shadow moves across a sidewalk. Hours pass and little changes. The dark blue water lightens. The brown of the island takes on a richer hue, less grey. The red brick of Fort Jefferson becomes more red as the haze of the distance fades.

What restful pleasures await me? I hope for a peaceful and protected anchorage; the wind seems to be blowing twenty knots as we broad reach toward the inlet. My tired eyes and sleep-deprived brain use palpable energy to identify the red buoy and the green buoy beyond marking the entrance to the inlet. The penalty for a mistake here is destruction and a long swim, possibly a slow death. Red – right – return, keep the red buoy to starboard and the green to port, but the early-morning light yields minimal color-perception.

Rest is near. The fort in all its 19th century majesty grows and looms to port. A small island, brown with rock yet topped with a bit of green, sits above the water straight ahead. The chartplotter warns me of shallow reef to starboard, submerged and deadly, ready to eat my keel, like an alligator waits in the reeds for its next victim.

I turn to starboard, just slightly, trying to find the proper alignment with the inlet so I can safely approach.

There is a woosh, and before I know what is happening the boom swings over my head and the quadrupled mainsheet under enormous tension slams into my left arm hard enough to hurt. The boom bangs into the shrouds sending shudders through *Sobrius*. My arm goes numb. What happened? I think. We gybed unintentionally; when I turned, I allowed the wind to catch the opposite side of the mainsail and push it across the boat. I had a preventer rigged – a line tied to the boom led to the bow and through a block and back to the cockpit where it was cleated. This should prevent the boom from moving, but apparently the cleating failed. The boom slammed into the rigging and I look to see if anything is broken. *Sobrius* seems to be OK.

I take stock of my arm and shoulder. Feeling returns and I too am OK. My mind is weak from lack of sleep. I must not make any more mistakes. The inlet is potentially dangerous, and I must approach the channel properly and stay in it, failure to do so would be catastrophic. I decide to take down the jib to simplify my sail into the channel.

I study the chartplotter and the buoys that I can see. The low angle of the sun makes the colors hard to make out, so I approach with extreme caution. We are now sailing upwind so I have to tack on approach, careful not to get too close to shallow water; the chartplotter shows a large submerged rock just east of the channel, but it all just looks like water from where I am. I pass the red buoy and we are in the channel; the waves start to decrease; I relax a little. Far to the east, reefs sap the energy of the waves and give us some protection. I study the chartplotter some more. We have to continue north for a while before turning west towards the anchorage by Fort Jefferson.

I point us into the wind, start the engine, and set the tillerpilot. At the mast I drop the mainsail, but I leave it ready to hoist in the case of engine failure. With a careful eye on the chartplotter, we motor around Fort Jefferson, a huge red-brick structure surrounded by blue water. The water has become very calm and the lack of motion is appreciated. A pelican sits on top of one of the channel markers and I think it is looking at me. The water around the fort is very shallow and we have to navigate a wide arc around it in order to stay in the deep water of the channel. The chart shows a clearly-labeled area for anchoring, but it is not very close to the fort, where I need to check in. Although the water is calm, a strong wind still blows out of the east, and the anchorage area denoted on the chart is completely exposed to the wind. But there is a harbor right next to the fort in which two sailboats lie at anchor. This area is protected from the full strength of the wind by the small strip of land on Garden Key. There is also a large dock at the fort. My mind is tired.

I hail the park service on my handheld VHF. I am advised to use the dock to come ashore and check in. But the wind is blowing hard and the dock is very high off the water, designed for much bigger ships. I don't like that idea. I foresee disaster in the docking attempt. Too much wind, too much fatigue, lots of broken pilings and shallow reef downwind of the dock. I call them back and request permission to anchor and paddle in. "Of course" he says.

The two other sailboats anchored in the small bay outside the fort look like peaceful resting soldiers after a long march. The water is clear, reflecting the color of the bright-blue sky, and 15 feet deep. I can see the light brownish-yellow sand and sparse green grass on the bottom. The narrow spit of sand and shrubs that extends from the fort blocks much of the wind, and the water here is calm and lovely.

I select a spot and put *Sobrius* in neutral, and we glide into the wind, idling. I am more awake now and I move to the bow and pull the CQR anchor out of its locker. I'm fatigued, sleep-deprived and a little delirious, so I move slowly and deliberately, always holding on to something as I creep to the anchor locker at the bow. The anchor is heavy and clumsy, but I get it out and maneuver it under the bow pulpit and dangle it above the water, holding onto its chain rode. When *Sobrius'* forward motion is arrested by the wind, I carefully lower the anchor into the water, holding the chain as we drift backwards, letting the anchor catch the sandy bottom and bite into it before I let go. I let the chain out along with another 50 feet of rode and make it fast to the large aluminum bow-cleat. I hold the rode in my hand to check for vibration that would indicate that the anchor is dragging. The rode is taut and still.

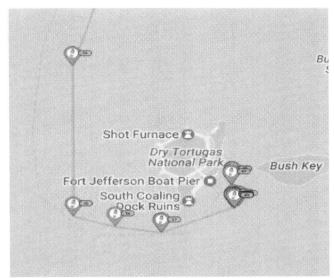

entrance to the harbor, from my SPOT tracking device

Confident that we are not dragging anchor, I let go of the rode and stand all the way up, one hand on the headstay, and survey my surroundings: a small strip of sandy beach, short green bushes, birds, a dock leading to a fort with a drawbridge and a mote, two other sailboats, a vast blue sky. I am here and the time is now, and here and now are good. I have successfully completed my first singlehand passage aboard my own sailboat, which I have meticulously and lovingly restored over the past two months. This I have studied for, dreamed about, longed for. I've read at least 20 books in the last year about sailing, singlehanding, bluewater cruising. I've taken a one-week class, a singlehand lesson, crewed on two offshore voyages and many local races, and sailed *Sobrius* on a dozen sea-trials, all to prepare myself for this voyage.

This leg of my journey has been a success, but is only about one fourth of the total distance home. The realization washes through me like a warm wave across the sand; I am doing it, living out my dream!

Our second day of sailing covered 122 nautical miles; the nearest weather buoy reported 18-20 knot winds.

~~~

Fort Jefferson from the harbor

I spent four days at Fort Jefferson, anchored about 200 yards from shore. I would paddle my board to shore twice daily and walk around the fort, check the weather forecast on the computer in the gift shop, and talk to whoever I ran into.

The fort covers almost the entire island, which is within a National Park. Park rangers stay on the island, but nobody lives here full-time, and there are no services available. The gift shop is the only store. Anyone visiting the island must bring all of their own supplies, including food, fuel, and water.

One of the highlights of my stay here was being served dinner aboard a Coast Guard ship which was tied off to the same dock that I didn't want to use earlier.

On the bridge that led over the moat surrounding the fort I struck up a conversation with Chris, captain of the Coast Gard cutter *Diamondback*, and he invited me to join him for dinner on the Coast Guard ship. The hot meal was a fantastic and unexpected treat: shrimp, pasta with white sauce, greens, garlic toast, tomato and mozzarella, a Pepsi, and even an ice-cream bar for desert – all while seated at a proper table. *Diamondback* is an 87ft coastal patrol boat with a 12-person crew whose missions include search and rescue, maritime law enforcement, marine environmental protection, defense readiness, and port, waterway and coastal security.

Chris told me all about his duties as a Coast Guard Captain, most of which included looking for and picking up Cuban refugees in the Florida Straits. Apparently "wet-foot-dry-foot" is over, and he thinks now there will be less refugees trying to get to the USA from Cuba. However, Chris warned me to be on the lookout for refugees and to contact the Coast guard if I saw any. He said sometimes they were desperate and could be hostile. This is something that had never crossed my mind. Chris also confirmed what I had assumed from the weather forecasts – that the conditions in the Florida Straits were not favorable to small craft at the moment. He said the seas were 10-feet and that he had come here to give his crew a break, as some of them were seasick. The winds were blowing 20-25 knots from the east, counter to the Gulf-Stream current, and wind blowing counter to a current creates steep and menacing waves. I was happy to be safely at anchor. Every day I was there the wind blew hard across the small island and howled in *Sobrius'* rigging, reminding me that I shouldn't be out there sailing until the weather calmed down.

~~~

a *window with a view of the moat*

    Fort Jefferson is a grand old place indeed; a brick behemoth rising out of the sand, topped with cannons that never fired on the enemy, a remote outpost surrounded by the Gulf of Mexico and the Florida Straits. The place reminds me of a medieval castle, and is entered by crossing a drawbridge over a saltwater moat. Skinny windows in the brick stare at one crossing the drawbridge, behind which guards armed with muskets must have once stood.

The long halls of Fort Jefferson run the length of each side of the brick building. The floors are dusty grey slate, large squares and rectangles of differing sizes fit together like some simple puzzle. Brick columns, square edged, protrude from brick walls and support brick arches. The bricks are red, brown, black, white, or some combination of these colors. Large openings where windows would have been installed had the fort ever been finished look out across a shallow moat to the bright blue waters of the Florida Straits, a meeting place of the Gulf of Mexico, the Caribbean Sea, and the mighty Atlantic Ocean. There are no walls on the side of the halls facing into the large grassy courtyard. With these openings, on both sides, the halls of Fort Jefferson are well-lit and ventilated.

Atop the roof above the second story grass grows on the sand and shell that cover the roof, which catches water and directs it to pipes which fill underground cisterns. Rainwater is the only source of water on the island. A path leads around the perimeter of the roof; like the platforms in the Okefenokee, there is no safety railing separating pedestrians from a long fall into the shallow moat.

Rising out of the green grass are trapezoidal mounds of earth that once supported cannons guarding this remote outpost from enemies that never came. I suppose the most effective weapons are the ones that are so overwhelming in their threat that the enemy never ventures within range. A lighthouse rises high above the fort, a pointed cylindrical appendage that once led mariners to this tiny island.

the harbor at Garden Key, Sobrius is on the left

Sailboats are anchored in the harbor beyond the walls and lighthouse. *Sobrius* sits among them in the clear blue-green water that reflects the bright sun. Their four masts rise up towards the sky. Cumulus clouds move across the scene. A thin strip of sand and scrubby trees separates the water from the sky and provides some shelter from the waves and the relentless wind for the anchored sailboats who patiently wait for their next adventure. The air is clean and has passed over many miles of sea before reaching me. I take in deep lungfulls while standing atop the fort, staring out over the water.

I walk along the narrow trail on the earthen roof of the fort and come to a shiny black cannon that has been restored. The barrel is long and thick, open at the business end and capped with a fatter cylinder at the other end. The barrel rests on a triangle of steel that holds it via two fat pegs protruding from the rear of the barrel, where the two cylinders meet. The supporting structure rests on two steel rails that appear to be connected to something beneath a low brick wall in front of the cannon. The other end of the rails rest on wheels upon a semi-circular track, allowing the cannon to be aimed left or right. A historical plaque mentions that the cannons here were modern weaponry at the time they were installed, in the late 19th century.

Fort Jefferson cannon

I walk on, a solo tourist with time to kill, slowly ambling along the roof, enjoying the view and the fresh air. My only plan is to depart when the weather dictates, until then I do what I please from moment to moment. I don't need to entertain, consider, or look out for anyone else, and so I decide what to do spontaneously. I step down off the path to a low wall where a cannon once stood and look in a hole in the wall. I look at the crushed shells on the ground that is a roof. I walk to the lighthouse and peek inside.

~~~

The Dry Tortugas were discovered by Ponce De Leon in 1513. Many sea turtles lived here at the time, and they, along with the islands' lack of fresh water, provided the inspiration for the islands' modern name (tortuga is Spanish for turtle). The shallow reefs of the area have sunk many ships, and thus the lighthouse at Fort Jefferson, on Garden Key, was built in 1825. The fort was part of an effort to protect shipping commerce to and from the Mississippi River. It was one of many forts built after the war of 1812. The fort was to be an advance outpost for ships patrolling the Gulf of Mexico and could be used to resupply ships, or to allow them a safe place sit out bad weather, as *Sobrius* and *Diamondback* were doing now. Heavy cannons, 420 in all, protected the fort so effectively that it was never attacked. The fort eventually became a prison, housing mostly Civil-War deserters. After the war, it became too expensive to maintain and was used as a quarantine facility.

The construction of the fort must have been daunting, with no fresh water and the nearest source of supplies at least a day's sail away. On top of that, the workers were also exposed to hurricanes, intense summer heat, and yellow fever, which killed many. In fact, the fort's doctor – and his son – were killed by the mosquito-borne disease, and he was replaced by a prisoner – Dr. Mudd, who was serving time for conspiracy to assassinate President Lincoln. Dr. Mudd housed John Wilkes Booth and treated his broken leg in the days following the assassination of the president. Dr. Mudd was tried and convicted for harboring Booth. His sentence was life and he was sent to Fort Jefferson to serve out his sentence. However, he was pardoned by president Andrew Johnson for his efforts to help during a yellow fever epidemic at the fort, the one that took the life of the fort doctor.

~~~

As I look out over *Sobrius'* deck I am awed by the scene. Bright blue water, windswept and lighter on the edges, blue sky decorated with gliding birds above, and a small spit of land dividing the two, yellow sand, brown rocks and low green trees. We face the east wind with the skinny beach directly ahead, thankfully breaking up the relentless wind. To starboard is an expanse of shallow water, empty and serene. To port is the brick fort, its dock to the left and a small beach to the right. Two seaplanes are tied up to the beach, and their passengers stroll the beach; a couple of them can be seen on the top of the fort, carefully exploring the rooftop environment and marveling at the cannons.

Beneath *Sobrius* two large and dark shapes can be seen slowly moving about. When I first saw them I thought they were sharks, but closer inspection revealed them to be goliath grouper (formerly called jewfish). They seemed to be taking refuge in the shade below my little ship. I swim around *Sobrius* a few times daily, and the grouper are as big as me, and not scared of me at all. I've captured them on my video camera, and even heard and recorded a vocalization, like a grunt, when one tried to communicate with me. It was probably saying "back off, fool!"

Four days here have been very relaxing, and I have needed it after singlehanding for three days. I feel much apprehension about sailing to Miami, which looks to be about 340 nautical miles away, including tacks. The shallow reefs of the Florida Keys lie to the north and the unapproachable country of Cuba to the south. There is nowhere to run if the weather gets bad in the straits. I've been studying the charts of the Keys and there seem to be very few options for a sailboat to find shelter in the keys during a storm. But like all the books I've read say, it's safer to stay out in the deep water and away from land during bad weather.

The wind on my last day here is 15-20 knots out of the east and should weaken and turn more south in the coming days, just right for sailing to Miami if I leave tomorrow. Hopefully the seas will have calmed down by then. I desire a peaceful sail.

It is decided, tomorrow morning I will leave the Dry Tortugas, perhaps never to return. The fort is grand and fun to explore, and the scenery is tranquil. But the coral, like in many other places I've dove, is almost all dead, and the tranquility is crushed throughout the day by the constant arrival and departure of seaplanes. The planes are quiet when they land, but they take off right between the sailboats in the harbor, and they are LOUD! Further crushing the tranquility is the twice-daily arrival of the ferry, bringing about 100 sightseers from Key West.

Regardless, it has been peaceful and restful staying here in the harbor. The water is clear and I swim every day, which I love to do. The goliath grouper are magnificent, as are the sunsets and sunrises. I've read all the historic plaques in the fort, imagining life here in the late 1800's. It's like a sprawling castle, topped with earth and cannon, a little-known piece of American history looking out over the Gulf of Mexico and the Straits of Florida.

~~~

While taking my final swim this afternoon, I discovered that my propeller zinc is gone, along with the bolt that held it in place, and no longer protecting my new propeller from galvanic corrosion. It breaks my heart to think that the propeller that was so difficult to obtain and install is suffering this ailment. I asked around at the fort if they had any zincs that I might be able to use, but the only ones they had were not at all the right size or shape. I resigned myself to the fact that I would have to wait and try to find one in Miami.

On the other hand, I accomplished something today that will greatly improve the efficiency and comfort of my sailing. I moved the AIS to the ceiling right next to the companionway so that I will be able to read and operate it from the cockpit. There will be no more having to set the autopilot and going below when the alarm goes off, or sitting and listening to the infernal alarm while steering clear of a ship, unable to turn it off. I wish it would just stop on its own when we are no longer in danger, but once the alarm starts it seems to just go on beeping forever.

There was a serious mishap while moving the AIS, which could have ruined my day. When I thought the job was all finished, after moving the unit, the VHF antenna cable, the power supply wires, and the GPS antenna cable, I switched it on and nothing happened. I got out my DC voltmeter and determined that power was not being supplied through the wires. Earlier I had noted a fuse in the wires, so I checked for power before and after the fuse. The voltmeter told me there was power before the fuse, but not after, hence the fuse had blown. Indeed I had left the power on while moving, and disconnecting, the unit. I must have crossed the lines and created a short, blowing the fuse. The fuse probably saved the AIS from serious damage, which would have been a real problem for me and the rest of my journey. I rely on the AIS to alert me of other ships on a collision-course, and to alert them of my presence. I was very lucky to find a replacement fuse in the navigation table, left by a previous owner, and all ended well.

I also moved one of the preventer-blocks to a D-ring I installed amidships near the bow, behind the anchor locker. The issue I am trying to solve is chafing between the preventer line and the jib-sheets. I hope this works. Additionally, it puts the block in a much safer location, as opposed to it being on the rail. The less I need to work near the rail while sailing the better. I simply must have a good and trustworthy preventer; I must never again suffer an unintentional gybe. Furthermore, I think I should avoid gybing altogether in winds over 20 knots.

~~~

I look forward to seeing my old friend Cristina again in Miami. She was my first love, back in high-school. We reconnected and fell back in love a few years ago when she lived in New York City, but it was not to be. I think I will always love her, although I know we can never live together or even be a couple. She wants me to visit in Miami and to introduce me to some of her sailing friends. Two are offshore racers, and one is an Olympic gold-medalist. I am astounded that she has become a sailor since moving to Miami from New York, where we, at another time, were planning on building a life together. Then after being out of communication with each other for about two years, I discover that we have both become sailors. We must have some deep universal connection.

It seems that a powerful storm will roll off the Florida coast early next week, so perhaps I will stay in Miami until the weather clears. I hope there is not too much traffic between here and there so I can get some sleep. I'll try to stay well offshore in deep water to avoid the reefs around they Florida Keys and shrimp boats like *Odin* and *Fuck It*.

I feel some apprehension about tomorrow's sail. Maybe because I have been facing 20+ knots of wind in the anchorage for the past three days. It howls and it rocks my little sailboat. It is relentless; however, it should start easing tomorrow. Logic tells me that we will do fine, but the emotion I feel is counter to the logic. Sobrius will start out with the same sail plan as she had up when we arrived: one reef in the main and the #3 jib. I'll have to keep an eye out for thunderstorms and be prepared to drop the headsail when one approaches. They can produce violent winds.

I upgraded the tethers on my lifevest today. The bowlines (knots) at both ends of the tethers had been coming loose, which could have sent me overboard with a false sense of protection. I removed the two 5/8" lines and replaced them with one 1/4" Amsteel line, tied in its center with an alpine-harness loop to the lifejacket and terminating at carabiners at both ends. I also taped the bitter ends of the lines with rigging tape to prevent the perfection knots on the carabiners from working themselves loose. I hope they perform well, my life depends on it!

~~~

I told my friend Jon, before I bought *Sobrius*, that I

needed a new life. I hope this is it. I do not miss society; I am happy living on its fringe, visiting it from time to time, but on my schedule, on my terms. I do not wish to be influenced by pop-culture, television advertisements, politicians, hucksters and con-men. There are many – countless – ways for a man to live his life. Our culture is but one way – the way that the salesmen, the advertisers, the hucksters and con-men want us to live: go to work, go home, see advertisements, buy the products that they put in our heads, reproduce, be sports-fans, spend money, buy a new expensive car every three years, buy a new expensive wardrobe every season... Don't worry about the environment, the pollution, the unsustainability of our culture – that's all a lie – they tell us. Spend, reproduce, go to work, go to church, obey.

While capitalism promotes ingenuity, creativity and entrepreneurship, it also promotes the love of money, which has fostered many cancers on our society. We need to learn to create and nurture a culture that does not allow industries that profit from harming mankind. Love of our neighbor and our planet must reign; love of money and power must be removed from our culture. Ending the ability to wield political influence with money is one step we must take. We separated church and state when our forefathers created this nation, and now we must separate business and state.

We are not free when corporations that sell us products are able to influence politicians and write laws that promote their products. We need checks and balances in this system, so that we don't end up with private prisons lobbying for longer sentences, the makers of addictive pharmaceuticals lobbying for distribution of their drugs, arms manufacturers lobbying for war, and the polluting fossil-fuels industries lobbying for less environmental protection or to keep clean energy technology oppressed.

Out on the ocean by myself, I feel detached from all this, and it is glorious.

The real world is all around us. It is outside our houses,

outside our cities. There is still some left; we haven't destroyed everything yet. The oceans are still wild and free. The men, women and children of pop-culture fear wilderness and stay home. I fear the ocean too, but I love the ocean, I study the ocean, I ask her to allow me to be present. We all experience fear, but some of us choose to confront and attempt to overcome our fear. I prefer the wilderness to society, be it forest, desert, or water. Give me adventure in raw nature, now that is life!

~~~

January 16

I almost left today, but the winds continue from the east at 20 knots and I assume the seas must still be 10 feet. I really don't want to beat into that for two or more days, especially with the wind and swell going against the current. Besides, I'm in no rush, and I really like it here.

I want to stop in Miami to see Cristina, to meet her sailing friends, and to try to get a zinc for my propeller. There is a bad storm forecast for Monday moving west to east off central Florida with 30-40 knot winds (today is Wednesday). So I really can't stay past tomorrow, but why not wait another day and let the wind and waves between here and Miami die down a bit?

~~~

Once again it is my final evening in the little harbor in the Dry Tortugas. The orange sun is setting in a clear blue sky; two black frigate birds with their long and angled wings hover over Fort Jefferson. The wind has finally begun to ease, but still blows at about 15 knots out of the east. Just this slight easing of a few knots increases the tranquility of the twilight compared to the previous evenings. Seagulls circle over the ruins of the coal docks next to the main dock. Palm trees lean with the breeze on the west edge of the little island. The sun passes behind the horizon, backlighting a line of blue-grey cumulus clouds. Two fishing boats approach from the southwest. They come every night. Someone blows a conch-shell horn to mark the sunset. I hear it but can't tell where the sound comes from. More birds fly in from a day of searching for food, much like the fishing boats. Gulls, a pelican, and terns fly in a cluster; an odd turkey vulture, completely out of place, joins the scene, passing through without flapping its wings. The horizon in the east, opposite the sunset, turns pink while the western sky greys.

I'll miss this place. It gave me much-needed rest after the first singehand crossing of my life. I was so fatigued when I entered the harbor – it took all my focus to not make a terrible mistake. In fact the only injury I sustained in the three-day crossing was in the harbor. I lost footing while carrying the stern anchor to the bow, so I could lie to two anchors, like my father taught me to do 30 years ago right here in this very same anchorage. I slipped and my fingers got caught and pinched between the flukes of the Fortress anchor. One was cut, two others were bruised – a very small price to pay for such a prodigious journey.

St Lucia to Puerto Rico
February/March, 2016

Great things are achieved by first taking baby steps. Goals are never accomplished immediately; rather great goals are accomplished through a series of steps. Sometimes these steps are methodically planned and methodically taken, and sometimes they are more haphazard. Regardless, the beginning of achievement requires the smallest of steps.

During my first year of sobriety, I saved some of the cash that I would have spent on beer and instead put it in a wooden cigar box. I intended to spend this on some sort of great adventure to celebrate my first year of sobriety. This was part of my strategy to quit drinking, a reward that I could look forward to and thus steel my resolve to stay sober. This is but one of the many strategies I used, and the entire method can be found in my book *Alcoholics Not Anonymous, a Modern Way to Quit Drinking*.

When I got home after the Okefenokee canoe trip, I began reading books about sailing. The first of many was *Get Real Get Gone, how to become a modern gypsy and sail away forever* by Rick Page and Jasna Tuta. I was immediately taken by the idea espoused by the title. Sail away forever, never to return to my old life – which is exactly what I wanted to do, having already abandoned my old life by giving up drinking and not yet having found my new life; I was ready for a big change and another big adventure.

Soon after the canoe trip I used most of the money that I saved to enroll in a one-week sailing class with American Sailing Association. This was my reward to myself for one year of sobriety. I was looking for a new life as a sober person, and sailing seemed to fit the bill. I would never have been able to afford to be a sailor nor would I have had the resolve to do so when I was a drunk.

To one who loves to sail but does not have a sailboat,

any time spent sailing is a wonderful experience, and the sailing class delivered. Three students (including me) and an instructor sailed for about 7 hours a day for five days. The first day we sailed a small open-decked Hunter, about 20 feet long. The next four days we sailed on either a Hunter or Jeanneau 36. I loved the sailing and discovered that the most anxious part about it was maneuvering through the marina (hence my reluctance to take *Sobrius* out until I devised the X-lines).

During this time learning to sail, I was obsessed with the grand idea of selling my house, buying a sailboat large enough to live on full-time, and sailing away forever, somehow making a living on the sea. I kicked around many ideas, like being a travelling carpenter, learning to repair sails, starting a non-profit organization, embarking on great adventures and writing books about them, cleaning hulls, treasure-hunting… I reasoned that with the money from the sale of my house that I could buy an adequate sailboat and have enough money left over to live for two years. Within these two years I figured that I could devise a way to make a permanent living while sailing.

My father was a sailor in his younger days, and he was happy to hear that I enrolled in the sailing class. I also told him about my idea to sell my house (which he had helped me buy) and buy a sailboat, on which I would sail away forever. He didn't like that idea so much. Instead he suggested that first I should find a sailboat that needed crew and get a bit of experience. I rolled my eyes at this idea (over the phone so he didn't see the eye-roll). But I got on the computer and discovered crewbay.com.

Using this website, I soon found a British man named Robin in St. Lucia who wanted crew to help him sail his Catalina 42 across the Caribbean Sea to Puerto Rico. After convincing him to allow me to crew, he convinced me to buy, for the trip, a handheld VHF, which I could use to call him and ask for rescue should I fall overboard at night during my watch, and a Spinlock self-inflating life-vest equipped with three flashing lights and a sprayhood. This amounted to a total investment of over $600, which made me feel that I was investing in my future as a sailor.

These items were expensive, but I was all-in at this point. In addition to them, I also bought a GoPro underwater video camera and a flashlight to go with it. With the video camera, I intended to make an educational video featuring coral reefs to be used to start a non-profit organization that would allow me to have a career while living on a sailboat exploring the world. The sailing obsession was growing.

I graduated from sailing school, and within a week I was driving to the Fort Lauderdale airport and flying to Trinidad, where I had to spend the night in a cheap hotel. Here I was told by the proprietor not to drink the tap-water, as it made him sick the last time he drank it. It is such a sad state of affairs when a nation's tap-water is undrinkable, and generally points to a lack of infrastructure preventing contamination, usually sewage, from getting into the water supply. I bought a bottle of water for a dollar and got some sleep, which required the use of my construction-site ear-muffs due to the prevalence of barking dogs and crowing roosters making themselves heard throughout the night.

The next morning, I enjoyed a beautiful flight to St. Lucia, with views of St. Vincent and the Grenadines along the way. Viewed from above, the water was dark blue with whitecaps from the trade-winds. Small islands, the peaks of submerged mountains, dotted the surface and sailboats filled the protected bays. The occasional vessel moved between the islands, some alone, some in pairs.

We landed at a small airport on the Island of St Lucia, exiting the plane down the stairs to the tarmac, and cleared customs in a small waiting room. Robin picked me up at the airport in a beat-up pickup truck with the steering wheel on the right side, where the passenger sits in an American car. It turns out they drive on the left side of the road in St. Lucia, which was a British colony until 1979, when they gained their independence. He was tall, about 6' 6" and large but in-shape, with short blond hair and a British accent. He had been a rugby player in the past, and he looked the part.

~~~

The first known humans to live on the island of St Lucia were the Ciboneys, hunter/gatherers from South America, and lived here from about 1000-500 BC. Their culture disappeared and they were replaced by the peaceful Arawak Indians, who left behind pottery, weavings, evidence of farming, and evidence of boatbuilding. The Arawaks called the place "Island of the Iguanas." Around 800 AD they were killed off by the more aggressive Carib Indians.

The first European known to live here was a one-legged French pirate named Francois le Clerc, aka Jambe de Bois (Wooden Leg). In the 1550's he set up an outpost on Pigeon Island, on the northwest corner of St Lucia, and from here launched attacks on Spanish Galleons.

The first English to arrive were blown off course while heading to Guyana and attempted a settlement on St Lucia. But the Caribs killed nearly all of them. The 19 survivors eventually fled in canoes and somehow made it all the way to Venezuela. The English attempted another settlement in 1639, but once again the Caribs would have nothing of it, and this time all of the English were killed.

The French arrived from Martinique in 1651 led by De Rousellan, of the French West India Company. Following the noble customs of Europe, he married a local Carib woman and thus managed to coexist with the Indians. In 1660, he had a treaty with the Caribs, and he then bought land from them and grew his settlement at Soufriere establishing a sugar cane plantation. However, it was apparently his presence alone that kept the peace, and after he died in 1654 the Caribs became hostile to the French.

The British again tried to gain a foothold on St Lucia in

1664 by sending 1000 soldiers to the island. However all but 89 died from diseases. Meanwhile the French were still able to live and work in their settlement at Soufriere, occasionally battling with the Caribs, while the Dutch built a fort on the south of the island at Vieux Fort.

During the French Revolution, French Royalists were executed with the guillotine in Soufriere. In 1794 the French governor abolished slavery, much to the chagrin of the wealthy plantation owners. Like today, industry influenced politics, and soon after emancipation, the British invaded the island and restored slavery.

The British, Dutch, and the French fought many battles for control of the island and over the next century-and-a-half St Lucia changed hands 14 times. Eventually the British gained full control via the Treaty of Paris in 1814. The British ran sugar-cane plantations worked by Africans who were slaves until a gradual emancipation in 1834.

St Lucia gained their independence from Britain in 1979, and the culture today is a mix of French, British, Caribbean, and African. The official language is English, and the education, legal, and political structures are heavily influenced by Britain. The French culture is retained in the creole language spoken by most residents, the town and family names, the music and the arts.

~~~

I arrived in St Lucia on a Tuesday, which happened to be the 35th anniversary of the island's independence, and I stayed on the boat, *Sophie Ems*, a Catalina 42, in the marina in Rodney Bay until we sailed away Saturday evening. Meanwhile Robin stayed at a friend's house on the island, getting some time on land. While there, I did some carpentry on the boat, including a repair to the cabin sole (the floor inside the boat), which had been damaged by termites, and I built a fishing-rod and oar rack which I attached to the ceiling of the cabin. Robin was very happy with this, as it gave him much-needed storage and added a nautical look to the boat. I was very grateful to be included on this trip and to have been given the opportunity to sail across the Carribbean Sea, so it felt good to be able to contribute to his boat.

Near our marina was a modern SCUBA-diving outfit, with whom I dove twice. They had a nice and professional operation and a clean and new dive-boat, which about 20 of us boarded Wednesday morning and motored out to the sea.

We stopped in Marigot Bay to pick up some more customers. Marigot Bay was one of the most beautiful places I have ever seen, a picturesque cove with an island-themed resort complete with wooden bridges, waterfalls and fountains, and clean "huts" climbing up the mountainside. In the harbor were sleek-looking yachts, and one mega-yacht with mirror-finished stainless-steel accents glistening in the bright tropical sun.

An old Rasta-man with long dreadlocks rowed to the mega-yacht in a tiny square dinghy with "Jah Live" painted on the side and took hold of the anchor chain in self-juxtaposition. Since this enormous five-story power-boat was the topic of conversation at the moment, I remarked that the Rasta-man was probably happier than the owner of the mega-yacht, and the captain of our boat chimed in "I know them both, and he is!"

Marigot Bay

~~~

We dove on coral reefs near the shore, which dropped off steeply as the island is of volcanic origin and rises out of deep water. It was wonderful to be diving again. I hadn't dove with SCUBA gear in many years. The sensation of breathing underwater is fantastic! Not only is breathing underwater absolutely amazing, but the experience is like flying; the diver is essentially weightless, slowly gliding over large structures, moving up and down in order to better see the reef and the fish. Since I had a video camera with a flashlight attached to a short pole, I could illuminate dark sections of the reef. Black caves suddenly filled with light and revealed oranges, reds, purples, fish both large and small, the occasional eel or lobster. I filmed everything that seemed interesting and later edited my video and posted it on YouTube ("SCUBA Diving in St Lucia" https://youtu.be/E4I33DuYte8).

~~~

A pair of bright blue-tang dart in and out of reef crevices, swimming away from me as I follow with my camera. Brown surgeonfish watch me warily, perhaps diagnosing my ailments. A trumpetfish imitates vegetation, suspended vertically in the water just above the reef. Bizarre boxfish spit mouthfuls of water at the sand on the bottom, trying to scare up little invertebrates for a meal. Schools of yellow wrasse mill about in clusters just above the reef. Damselfish dart out of large hollow box-shaped sponges trying to scare me off, fearlessly defending their property. Various colorful fish that I can't identify swim around the reef. A sharpnose eel slowly swims like a snake across the bottom while SCUBA divers congregate and watch. A black-and-white spotted moray eel hides in a cave and does not move when I shine my light on it and stare. It seems there is so much action and so many different animals moving about reef that the inhabitants take little notice of the humans as we swim by, staring and pointing at the reef-dwellers.

St Lucia coral

A significant portion of the world's coral reefs are in a state of declining health. Two species of coral, elkhorn and staghorn, are nearly extinct. Here large areas of the sea-floor were covered in dead staghorn coral. There was a good bit of live blue club-coral, but there was also a lot of it that was dead and covered in algae. However, even in this state, the reef was beautiful and awe-inspiring. There were not as many fish as I remembered from the diving experiences of my youth, but many fish still animated the reef.

One of the main reasons for the decline in health of the world's coral reefs is the rising temperatures of the oceans due to climate change and global warming. Coral are very sensitive to temperature changes, and increasing water temperature causes coral to expel the symbiotic algae that live inside the coral's tissue. The coral then turns white, which is referred to as bleaching, and then the coral slowly starves to death.

Another cause of coral-reef decline is acidification of ocean water caused by the absorption of carbon dioxide from the atmosphere. Carbon dioxide concentrations in the atmosphere have been increasing since the beginning of the industrial age, and the ocean absorbs this gas, which causes the pH of the water to drop (become more acidic). This increase in acidity reduces the availability of calcium carbonate, which coral needs in order to build its structure. Additionally, all sea creatures that build shells need calcium carbonate and thus the entire food web of the ocean is negatively affected by ocean acidification.

Overfishing is another killer of coral reefs. Hungry people must eat and feed their families, and families tend to grow as people seem to enjoy reproduction. Taking too many fish from the reefs has cascading effects. Some herbivorous fish, like parrotfish, control algae growth, and the taking of these species directly upsets the fragile balance of coral and algae. Given an advantage, algae overgrows the slow-growing coral and smothers is. Algal growth is also fueled by nitrogen, which comes into the sea with sewage and fertilizer runoff.

Coral is also physically delicate, and simply touching coral can kill portions of it, leaving the surviving portions susceptible to infection and invasion by competitors, like algae and sponges, which are now dominating areas once rich with coral.

Reef health is also impacted by exotic fish and diseases introduced by the Panama canal, the hulls and bilges of ships travelling between oceans, and the exotic pet trade. Elkhorn coral and sea urchins have been decimated by diseases which originated near the Panama Canal and were probably introduced by ships coming from the Pacific. Sea urchins are herbivores and help maintain the coral/algae balance. Elkhorn coral is a tall and branching coral upon which many species of fish and other reef-creatures depend. It is a "keystone species", and entire ecosystems are supported by its presence.

Lionfish, native to the tropical South Pacific reefs, are now omnipresent throughout the Caribbean and Florida's coastal waters. These efficient predators are thought to have been introduced by the exotic pet trade, that is, released by aquarium owners. Just as Florida is infested with giant Burmese pythons, exotic fish, exotic poisonous snakes, huge monitor lizards, Brazilian pepper trees, and countless other species of plants and animals from the exotic pet and plant trade, so the reefs of the Caribbean are infested with the beautiful yet destructive lionfish. Lionfish methodically rid coral reefs of their normal resident-fish, once again upsetting the balance upon which coral-reef health and stability rely.

As coral dies, algae and sponges begin growing on top of dead coral. The dead coral erodes, and the once-heterogeneous reef becomes flat and turns to sand, then completely disappears.

Coral reefs are dying world-wide and this should be seen as a harbinger of much worse things to come. Coral reefs are like the forests of the ocean, providing habitat for countless species and nurseries for many more. We humans cannot afford to lose coral reefs. Once they are gone the oceans will forever produce much less food and will change in ways that will seriously degrade our quality of life and threaten the ability of humans to inhabit the earth, our only home.

Fortunately there are things that can be done to help reverse reef-decline.

Clean-energy sources, like solar and wind, can replace the dirty fossil-fuel industry and lessen climate change and global warming.

Sewage treatment is known technology that can be spread to areas where it is not in use. Education about sewage and various ways of properly treating and disposing of it, can help people make better decisions.

Coral-reef restoration is actively being studied by scientists and put into practice by non-profit organizations. Coral can be farmed in aquaculture operations and planted in the sea, where it can take hold and grow.

Fishing-exclusion zones, like national parks in the water, allow reef fish to grow to maturity and spawn. Many ocean fish produce large numbers of very small planktonic offspring which can drift about and colonize new areas.

Education can help people fish more responsibly, and fisheries management can and does prevent the collapse of fisheries.

Fertilizer runoff from land can be controlled, and the use of fertilizers can be limited. Organic farming is one solution. Vegetarianism is another. Growing meat is way less efficient than vegetables and ends up causing a lot more pollution. Purchasing organic vegetables and limiting our meat consumption are things we can all do.

The invasive and ever-present lionfish is edible and tasty, and also easy to shoot with a spear. This is guilt-free seafood!

The exotic pet trade need not exist at all. It's not good

for the animals, and it's not good for ecosystems. For example, nearly all saltwater aquarium fish are taken from coral reefs, as they will not breed in captivity. For every one fish that survives to a consumer's aquarium, about 100 die before getting there. We can go see exotic animals in their natural habitats instead of buying them as pets; it's more fun too.

All of these problems have solutions, even the growing number of humans who must eat and excrete can be reduced via education and birth-control, or "family planning". This is a subject that is rarely talked about and even seems taboo. But we need to start talking about limiting the human population. If we don't limit it ourselves, disease, famine, and war will. But again, education can help. Education, especially of females, can also help control our population size, which is the root of all environmental problems. Studies have shown that more-educated women start reproducing later and have less children overall. We should all view reproduction as a choice, and not as a foregone conclusion.

~~~

Even considering the abundance of dead coral, the diving in St Lucia was so nice that I could not help but think about it for the rest of the day, and it so occupied my mind that I felt compelled to dive again the following day. I walked in to the dive-shop the next morning accompanied by the other crew-member from the boat, a retired lawyer from the Midwest named Linc. There was no more room to join the SCUBA-divers, but we were told we could join the snorkelers on the same boat, and we did.

The diving was again fantastic. We got in the water just off a tall pointy mountain, one of the famous Pitons, where the water-depth dropped off steeply. I was able to freedive in fairly deep water while still close to the group of snorkelers that I needed to stay with. Again I recorded the experience with my video camera ("Freediving St Lucia"

https://youtu.be/I6OVJHZMOwI)

The Pitons

I enjoy freediving just about as much as SCUBA-diving. For those of you that are unfamiliar with this, freediving involves using only mask, snorkel and fins while holding your breath, while SCUBA diving uses the same plus a tank of compressed air, a regulator through which you breath normally, an inflatable (and deflatable) vest which is used, in conjunction with a weight belt, to control buoyancy, and a dive computer.

Freediving is well-named, because you feel much more "free" while doing it. Obviously you can't stay down as long, but it is quite possible to dive to the same depths (or even deeper) as SCUBA-divers, and each dive feels like a separate adventure and accomplishment. It also makes one feel very close to nature, much like a fish. The ability to hold one's breath and dive to depth is within us all and merely takes a bit of training and conscious effort; the subconscious takes care of the real work.

Our ancestors evolved in the ocean, and oddly enough, our bodies are adapted to freediving. Internally, our bodies undergo rapid changes in response to breath-holding and being underwater. This is known as the mammalian diving reflex. The body responds to being underwater by first slowing down the heart-rate by about 25%. Next peripheral vasoconstriction occurs, that is, blood flow to the fingers and toes slows, followed by the hands and feet, and ultimately the arms and legs stop allowing blood circulation, leaving more blood for the brain and other organs. This is achieved by the narrowing of blood vessels. As depth and thus water-pressure increase, blood shift and the spleen-effect occur. With each 33 feet of water-depth, air is compressed to one-half its volume, and thus a diver's lungs become compressed as the diver descends. The body prevents the diver's chest from being crushed from increased water pressure by moving the blood conserved by peripheral vasoconstriction to the chest area and the alveoli of the lungs, thus replacing the area that the air, which is becoming compressed, used to occupy. The spleen, once thought to be a redundant organ, comes into play while diving by releasing stored blood for use in blood-shift. Water is also removed from the blood to make more room for oxygen. All of these symptoms are increased with colder water, and either do not occur, or barely occur, if the face is not submerged in water, especially cold water.

Freediving is a fascinating experience, and while it may seem impossible to the non-diver, it is something most anyone can achieve with practice. There really is nothing quite like it. Freediving also has the side-benefit of making one feel more comfortable in various situations in the water, like surfing big waves, which I had the opportunity to do later in Puerto Rico.

Some of the best opportunities for freediving in Florida, where I live, are in its many freshwater springs. Clean, clear water, always 72 degrees, rises up out of the Floridan Aquifer in many springs across the state. Sometimes these springs feed into rivers, like the Suwanee, the Ocklawaha, and the Santa Fe, and sometimes they are simply landlocked sinkholes that plunge straight down into the aquifer.

These are all fantastic places connecting two worlds: the terrestrial world in which we live, and the subterranean water-world below, places where few humans have seen. It always excites me to be in a place like this, where I am one of a very small number of witnesses to its majesty and beauty. While many may frolic on the edge or the surface, the masses are kept away from the depths by their fears and lack of training and effort. One must overcome obstacles in order to experience the depths of the springs. One must train.

~~~

The first obstacle to my enjoyment of Florida's springs was a deep fear I had of alligators. For reasons unknown I have experienced recurring dreams about these dark creatures for most if not all of my life. Because of this I was always too afraid to schedule a trip to any of the springs, even though I had heard many people talk of the fun they had floating in an inner-tube down the river at Ichetucknee or Ginnie Springs. It just sounded terrifying to me. However I eventually gave in to a girlfriend's coaxing and agreed to go to Ginnie Springs, where I was overwhelmed by the natural beauty of the place and had a wonderful time snorkeling in the clear water.

In order to overcome a fear, one must confront the fear. This is a simple rule that can be nearly impossible to follow. It is always easier to go through life following the path of least resistance, but this leads to patterns that become entrenched. In order to escape the traps of entrenchment, one must first recognize that they are entrenched, doggedly following the same less-than-ideal path over and over again, day after day. A leap of faith is required to escape. A plan must be crafted and executed.

We can either go through life letting fear direct our paths, or we can attempt to face the fear and get over it, thus escaping the traps of entrenchment and opening up the future to vast possibilities.

I first began confronting my fear of alligators at Ginnie Springs, a place where hundreds of people float down a section of the Santa Fe River in inner-tubes and rafts of all sorts. Since this section of the river is spring-fed from about eight springs in a one-mile stretch, the water is colder than the rest of the river and this decreased temperature and the abundance of people make this section of the river a less-than-ideal habitat for alligators. However there are alligators there, although I've only seen small ones.

Ginnie Springs was an ideal location for me to take my first step towards overcoming my fear of alligators. The next step I took was the canoe trip through the Okefenokee Swamp. Through exposure to alligators, I came to terms with them, learned about them, and began to overcome my fear of them.

~~~

Another way to combat fears is through lucid dreaming. One must be able to first realize they are dreaming, and then to take control of the dream and confront their fear. This is really a long-term project and one should not expect immediate success, but the rewards are magnificent and endless. In order to have a lucid dream, one must first recognize that they are dreaming. This can be achieved by recognizing things that are out of place or that don't make sense, and this requires practice while awake, by simply being observant of one's surroundings.

I have had recurring dreams of alligators for most of my life, but through one lucid dream, and much effort through actions while awake, I have all but eliminated these nightmares. Usually my alligator dreams involved me being in water, often at night, and I see alligators. They never attack me, but I am always very afraid of them. In the one lucid alligator-dream that I had, I was on the bank of a swamp in a moonless night. Tall reeds surrounded smooth black water in front of me. A lone alligator looked at me from the water, about one hundred yards out. I swam out to the alligator, knowing I was dreaming and deciding to take action confronting my fear. The alligator seemed to acknowledge what I was doing and I think perhaps the gator was relieved to be freed from having to scare me in my dreams. I have not had an alligator dream since, and this has been a great relief.

Another recurring dream that plagued me was an elevator nightmare. I would step into an elevator, turn and face the doors. The doors would close and the elevator would start descending, faster and faster. I would usually try to grab onto a handrail as the elevator accelerated down, but soon the elevator would be going faster than gravity and I would be pulled up to the ceiling, where I would be plastered flat, spread-eagle. The elevator never hit bottom, but the dreams were always terrifying. In my waking life, I used to always avoid elevators, taking the stairs instead. But the last time I had an elevator dream, somehow I realized that it was a dream, and as the doors shut, I sat down, cross-legged in the elevator and said out loud "shit, I'm having another elevator dream" upon which the dream ended, without the elevator dropping, and I have not had one since.

Another lucid dream I had involved a technique that I read about in a book, which said that if you look at the palms of your hands while dreaming, you will become lucid and gain control of the dream. I was able to do this once, and it was like having an in-road to my subconscious. First I looked at the palms of my hands, and noticed that they had white spirals painted on them, at which point I became lucid. I looked up and people were arguing in front of me. I quickly solved the problem, which I believe was symbolic to something in my mind, then immediately flew away, straight up into the air with incredible speed. I landed somewhere else, facing another issue, and quickly solved it, and again flew away. This happened a few times, and when I awoke, I felt as if I was a bit closer to enlightenment, having gone into my own mind and straightened a few things out.

After getting over my fear of alligators, a new world opened up to me in Florida's freshwater springs. The natural beauty of these places is unsurpassed; the water is clear and deep, and the depths are challenging. While they are an adventure in themselves, the springs also provide a good training ground for freediving in the ocean. It really is a fascinating sport and makes me feel like a fish. Even though it is temporary, the ability to swim underwater without breathing is wonderful, and the more one trains and practices, the longer one can stay underwater and thus the deeper and further one can dive. It's like travelling to another world down there, seeing things few others have or will ever see, doing something that most people would not consider doing.

~~~

All of the springs connect to caves and an aquifer, and some of these caves are big enough to enter. The first time entering a cave, I just put my head in and look around, and go back to the surface. With more dives, I gradually penetrate deeper into the cave. Clearly safety is the first concern when doing this. Baby steps…

Ginnie Springs, in north-central Florida, has some great caves for diving. The most popular cave is in the namesake spring, a beautiful round depression filled with crystal-clear water which empties into the Santa Fe River through a shallow creek. The swimming hole is about fifty feet across, fifteen feet deep in the middle, and is surrounded by tall trees. There is a boardwalk along the edge of one side, and two sets of wooden steps leading down into the water. The bottom around the edge is rock and about four feet deep, dropping off steeply where the cave entrance is located. The bottom in front of the cave entrance is sandy, and the entrance is divided into two openings by a large rock. Inside the cave is a wide flat ceiling, and as you swim deeper into it, the bottom slopes downward and large rocks give way to a big round cavern with a safety rope showing the way out. Sometimes the cavern will have a group of cave divers inside training, but since there is nowhere else to go they just sit in one place and shine their lights about the cavern. At the bottom of the cavern is another cave entrance, but it is blocked by an iron grate and a sign on which the Grim Reaper warns divers to go no further saying "nothing beyond here is worth your life." Over 30 million gallons of water a day flow through this grate. Looking back from the cavern, the cave entrance is a small blue light, becoming two blue lights on approach.

Swimming into this cave is very exciting, as the freediver's life is totally dependent on a successful exit. It is of extreme importance to take "baby steps" when venturing into something like this: just a little taste the first time, a bit deeper the second time, and deeper still with succeeding dives. It's also important not to push it on dives like this, inside a cave. The diver needs to be very aware and conscious of his or her body and limitations. A feeling of lightheadedness after surfacing is a sure sign that the diver should go no deeper on the next dive. Another safety technique is to swim with one hand right in front of the forehead, so that if you bump a rock, it won't be your head making contact. I also like to pull myself along with my other hand in order to minimize kicking with the fins, which might stir up silt on the bottom and thus reduce visibility and possibly hide the exit route.

Please note: the best way to freedive safely is to take a course and become a certified freediver. It is definitely a life-threatening sport and should not be taken lightly.

About a quarter mile further upstream on the Santa Fe

River is a set of three holes in another spring feeding into the river. The hole farthest from the river, Little Devil, is a crack in the bedrock about twenty feet across and six feet wide in the middle. The opening is about six feet below the surface, and the crack goes straight down about forty feet. The rock walls have an odd texture consisting of many concave depressions, as if thousands of grapefruit and lemons were thrown against a clay wall, leaving behind impressions of their round shapes. The crack narrows with depth and is only about four feet across at the flat, sandy bottom. Solitary catfish hide in the dark. Looking up, the view is a skinny bright green light overhung with trees, shimmering and dancing with the movement of the water's surface. I like to climb in and out of holes like this, using my hands instead of my fins, to avoid kicking the rock.

Closer to the river is Devil's Eye, a round hole in a large swimming area near the edge of the river. Mullet, largemouth bass and sunfish swim about, as do small snapping turtles, all largely ignoring the swimmers. The hole is about twenty feet across and descends from the flat sandy bottom of the swimming hole from eight feet deep at the top to about twenty at the bottom. The bottom is flat and the round wall is rocky and full of crevices in which hide the occasional catfish, turtle or crawfish.

At the bottom is a cave entrance, opening into the main cave network. The cave entrance is small, but big enough for the cave-divers to enter wearing all their gear. The first room is very strange, with stalagmites, flowstone, smooth round walls and shelves. Deeper still is a low passage connecting to the cave system, and another route blocked again by the Grim Reaper and his macabre warning.

These caves were formed when they were not underwater, during Ice Ages deep in the past, as water flowed down through the limestone bedrock dissolving it as it went, just as terrestrial caves are today. Water dripping down through limestone bedrock deposits dissolved substances as it comes into contact with air, and over millennia odd rock formations are created. Stalactites descend from the ceiling in smooth bumpy spikes. Stalagmites are the same but rise up from the floor. Eventually the two might connect to form a column. Flowstone is formed by sheets of moving water and create flat and curved structures, sometimes resembling drapes or sliced bacon. The caves here continue deeper and go way beyond the ability of a freediver, although rumor has it that one has made the connection from Devil's Eye to Devil's Ear. Not me!

Back on the surface, a red buoy floats over the entrance to Devil's Ear, just past where the clear water of the springs meets the brown water of the river. On the upstream side of Devil's Ear, it's possible to stand on the rocky bottom of the river and relax before diving. While the water on the upstream side is warm and brown, the downstream side is cold and clear from the spring water emerging from Devil's Ear. The water in Florida's rivers is not brown from dirt or mud or anything ugly, the color comes from tannic acids released by oak leaves and other decaying plant material in the wetlands which form the headwaters of the rivers.

Descending straight down into Devil's Ear, the water quickly becomes clear. Like Little Devil, this is another vertical crack in the bedrock, only lager and deeper. The opening at the bottom of the river is about twenty feet in the orientation parallel to the river, and about ten feet perpendicular. The walls are rock and full of small holes in which various creatures might be hiding. Halfway down a large tree trunk wedged in the crack bisects the vertical passage. A thick chain is wrapped around the trunk and keeps the red buoy in place. The bottom, at about sixty feet deep, is composed of large-grain sand and many small shells. A strong current of water flows out of a cave entrance on the upstream side of the bottom. The entrance is about six feet tall and three wide. Jagged rocks lead in and down, curving to the left into a large dark room. The current is strong here and penetrating requires holding onto the rocks. Exiting is easy, simply letting go of the rocks causes the freediver to be spit out of the hole and gently back up towards the surface. Again, the diver should ascend with one hand over the head so as not to hit the tree trunk or rocks. This is a good safety measure to use on every ascent, as there may be something unexpected, like a boat, a log, or an alligator, above the ascending diver.

The cave system here is massive, and cave divers come from all over the world to explore it. They use extensive and specialized gear and resemble astronauts preparing for a space-walk. They often have four air-tanks on their backs, and leave other emergency tanks in various places in the water, like at an exit point. They use dry-suits, and have lights and line-reels attached about their suits. Some even use devices that look like torpedoes that pull the divers through the water while they hang on. They take their sport very seriously, going over their gear and having long discussions planning the dive before getting in the water. This creates quite a juxtaposition to the throngs of college students at Ginnie Springs who come here to float down the river on inner tubes and rafts while drinking copious amounts of beer. You can watch a video I made while diving in Ginnie Springs on YouTube (Freediving Ginnie Springs https://youtu.be/f02wCgLqEXY).

Another exciting freediving location requiring one to get over fear is called the Catfish Hotel. This is a sinkhole near the bank of the Suwanee River, connecting to a cave that leads to Manatee Spring. The cave entrance at Manatee Spring is large and easy to access, but the water current exiting the cave entrance is so great that entering is impossible. It will literally blow the mask off a diver's face.

The Catfish Hotel looks like a pond covered in duckweed, with only the central portion of the water clear. A stairway leads down to the water. The "pond" is surrounded by a park, so there is little fear of alligators, although they could theoretically be in the water, as they can absolutely do as they please and go wherever they want. But this is certainly not their ideal habitat. A sign at the top of the stairs states that the bottom is ninety feet deep and a cave entrance can be found there.

Duckweed is a small floating plant with flat round green leaves each about the size of an M&M. Their root structures hang down about five inches and the plants cluster together forming what looks like a solid structure (it isn't) on the surface. Bubbles from SCUBA divers keep the center of the pool free of duckweed, which otherwise extends all the way to the steps leading into the water, obscuring completely the depths below. When I dove here, the first thing I did was to put on my mask, clear away some of the duckweed by the stairs and peer underwater, and what a sight it was! The water was clear and deep, starting at about only four feet at the steps and quickly dropping off into the oblivion. Although clear, the water was kept dark from the duckweed, but the clearing in the middle allowed the sun to shine in and creates a shaft of light descending diagonally down the center of the pool.

I put on my gear and swam under the duckweed, which from below looked like a solid rocky surface penetrated with roots, to the center of the pool. Here I floated and relaxed, looking down into the clear green water and the bright shaft of light, breathing through my snorkel and clearing my mind of thoughts, just letting the vision in front of me occupy my mind. I could not see the bottom, and the irrational and ancient part of the brain sends warnings of monsters lurking in the depths below. But the modern, rational part of the brain says "no, there are no monsters living in the depths of the freshwater pool, nothing but catfish, as the name implies."

~~~

I wear a wetsuit and a weight-belt, and the result is that at the surface I float, and this is useful for relaxing in the minutes before a dive. After meditating and breathing slowly and deeply for a few minutes, I roll forward, push my feet into the air, and begin a vertical descent. As I swim slowly down through the clear green water and the bright yellow shaft of light, I alternately blow little puffs of air into my mask and then hold my nose and blow again, this time putting air into my inner ears. I do this continuously as I descend, so that I never feel any pressure on my face or in my ears, otherwise the air space in my inner ears and mask would decrease in size as the air compressed, creating severe pain in the ears and trying to pull my eyeballs out of my head into the mask.

The water is featureless as I descend, and there is nothing to see at all until I get about thirty feet down, where I begin to see a dark blackness down and to my right. I alter my course slightly toward it. Slowly it begins to take shape and at about sixty feet down I can see that it is the cave entrance. At about sixty feet, I become negatively buoyant, and thus sink without having to swim downward. This is because the air in my lungs has compressed to only one quarter of its volume at the surface.

The weight of a column of water thirty-three feet deep is the same as the weight of the column of air above a person standing at sea-level. Thus we call the pressure of water at thirty-three feet "one atmosphere". The pressure at one atmosphere of depth (33 feet) is double that on the surface, and thus the volume of air is compressed to half its volume on the surface. At a depth of sixty-six feet, air is compressed to one quarter of its volume on the surface.

A flat rock wall above the cave comes into focus, and soon I am sitting on the sandy bottom, ninety feet deep. The cave entrance is in front of me. The initials of a few divers are carved into the rock. Although I could not see the bottom from the water's surface, I can clearly see the surface from here, a small bright green area with the legs of my dive-buddy Jenn poking into the water, the shaft of sunlight leading from there to me.

I only sit here for a moment, taking in the view and storing it in my long-term memory, before standing, pushing off the bottom, and slowly swimming up toward the light and Jenn's legs. As I ascend, the air in my lungs expands, and it feels like breathing in. Likewise the air that I pumped into my mask expands, and bubbles escape from its sides and join me for the trip to the surface, where it will rejoin the atmosphere and endlessly drift about the Earth, perhaps never returning to the Catfish Hotel. I might not return to the Catfish Hotel either, because after a few dives, I got out and eventually read the rest of the sign by the steps, which clearly said "no snorkeling, SCUBA diving only".

~~~

St Lucia, on land or in the water, was a fun place to visit. Multiple cultures and languages seemed to co-exist there. The marina was alive with foreign languages and foreign accents. There were many European sailors, and also many from South Africa. Apparently American cruisers rarely venture this far south in the Caribbean, but many Europeans sail here by way of the Azores in a regatta each year. Most of the locals are black, and speak English, French, or a mix of the two. Also, many are Rastafarians and speak the Rasta lingo. Fresh fruits and vegetables and coconut water are sold on the street daily, and I drank the delicious and healthy coconut water every day. The climate was warm and humid, with daily, but short, rains. The landscape was lush green and mountainous, and the water a dark blue, as it got deep quickly.

I had another motive besides adventure for taking this trip, and I didn't tell Robin, the captain of the sailboat, until we were in Puerto Rico. I used this trip to quit smoking marijuana. I had tried to quit the previous year, and didn't smoke for a full month, during which I experienced the unexpected withdrawal symptoms of waves of anger followed by depression, digestive problems, irritability, and insomnia. After I experienced four nights in a row of debilitating insomnia the days before my band had an important gig, I gave in and was soon back to my old habits. That was only four months after I had quit drinking, and perhaps I had tried to quit smoking too soon.

I reasoned that being out of the country and away from all my habits and haunts would be beneficial in my effort to quit smoking pot. I assumed that the other men on the boat would not be smokers (they weren't) and I assumed that I would not be exposed to marijuana in St Lucia. Here I was wrong. On my first day there I was offered weed for sale by a group of dreadlocked men that I jogged past. I just shook my head and kept running. The Rastafarian culture is prevalent in St Lucia, and I saw and smelled marijuana every day while there, and was offered it at least one more time in St Lucia and again later in Puerto Rico. But I had plenty to do in St Lucia and was constantly occupied and distracted to the point that I never suffered cravings or withdrawal.

~~~

We left St Lucia in the evening of my fifth day there, sailing to the northwest. At night on the sailboat, the three of us took turns at watch for three-hour shifts. This simply entailed occasionally scanning the horizon for the lights of other boats. Our boat was equipped with an auto-pilot that was nearly always on. We navigated with two iPads that communicated with the autopilot. I never saw a paper chart, and the steering wheel was only used during docking or anchoring. Most of my time on watch was spent reading my Kindle. However, the first night I had to stand and watch the horizon in order to not get seasick.

Seasickness is, at least partially, brought on by a disagreement between the inner ear and the eyes. The inner ear senses movement as the boat constantly rocks back and forth. The eyes, if they are focused on the boat, may not register any movement, because the body, and thus the inner ear, are not moving relative to the boat. This is greatly exacerbated when one is below-deck, inside the cabin. In order to relive or avoid the onset of seasickness one must look at the horizon, and as little at the boat as possible. Relief is not instant, but seasickness is reduced to mild nausea, which eventually goes away (after about a day in my case). However my appetite was also greatly reduced during the voyage, and Robin told me this was common.

The first morning at sea was glorious! I emerged from the cabin to bright sunshine and clear blue water as far as the eye could see in all directions. The endless undulating of the sea was occasionally interrupted by the bursting of flying fish as they jumped out of the water and glided impossible distances over the water and away from whatever predators were chasing them below.

Flying fish do actually fly, using their long pectoral fins like wings, not flapping but gliding like paper airplanes. They commonly turn in the air, which is always surprising to see, and sometimes increase their flight-time by kicking off the water with their tail-fins mid-flight. They are endlessly entertaining to watch, especially since there is little other action by which to be entertained.

Twice during the sail we were graced by mesmerizing visits of dolphin. They played in the bow-wake, the wave created by the front of the boat, rolling and dancing about, clearly having fun. I ran to the bow with my GoPro and recorded video of the first pod of dolphin that visited us. I was able to dip my camera below the surface of the water to get a few short underwater clips, which turned out to be fascinating, and is also posted on YouTube ("Caribbean Dolphins from the Sailboat Sophie-Ems" https://youtu.be/MCtOnK8iWK0).

dolphin visit the Sophie Ems

There is not a whole lot to be done while sailing on a long crossing with a crew and an autopilot that is always on, so I spent much time reading. My Kindle got a lot of use. It was especially helpful while on deck during my 12:00 am to 3:00 am watch. I think it would have been hard to stay awake otherwise.

~~~

On the second full day at sea, we came into sight of Isla Aves, a very small island owned by Venezuela. The island is a military outpost and manned by the Venezuelan Navy. It was our intention to stop here and pay them a visit. It is an island very rarely visited by cruising sailboats, or anyone for that matter, and we had gifts for the Navy personnel that stayed there.

At first all we could see was a white building, seeming to emerge from the water on the horizon. It really looked more like a cruise-ship in the distance than an island. As we got closer I wanted to take pictures, but since this was a military outpost of a foreign country, I was not sure if this was a good idea. I opted to put away my GoPro with its underwater video from diving on the reefs of St Lucia and the dolphin, just in case the Venezuelans were watching us with binoculars. None of us had been there before, and we did not know what to expect. I pictured stern, anti-American men in uniforms with guns formally greeting us, asking us why we were there, and ushering us away. I imagined them angrily confiscating my camera. Nothing could have been further from the truth.

Isla Aves

When we were within range, Robin attempted to hail Isla Aves on the VHF radio, but got no response. We tried over and over as we approached the island, and the radio silence heightened our anxieties.

A friend of Robin had visited the island many months

before and told us that he had spoken with them about us coming to visit, and that they would have a mooring ready for us. When we were in the small bay next to the island, we spotted a mooring ball, although at this time we had still not been able to hail them on the radio. We successfully picked up the mooring line and tied off. I put on my mask and snorkel and jumped into the very clear water to inspect the mooring and determine if it was secure. The mooring line was tied to a fisherman's anchor hooked to coral and did not look sufficient to keep our boat from drifting away, so we opted to drop our anchor as well.

We still had no response from the Venezuelans on the VHF as a dinghy approached from the island.

As the beat-up inflatable craft approached, I wondered what they would say first, and if my rudimentary Spanish would be sufficient to communicate with them. I'd never spoken Spanish with a Venezuelan. The boat, with half a dozen young dark-brown men in shorts and t-shirts, came alongside of us and I would never have guessed that their first words to us would be "pegamento de goma?" and "cigarettes?" It took me a while to figure it out but they were asking for glue to repair their dinghy, and of course, cigarettes. We had been told to bring them rum, fresh fruit and fishing lures as gifts, however Robin went below and quickly returned with a dinghy repair kit, which he handed over to the grateful Venezuelans.

They invited us to board their boat, and we were whisked to the "dock", which was a wall of horizontal 2x6 planks underneath and shaded by the main building. While holding the dinghy off the wall as the waves lifted and dropped the craft, careful not to allow the waves to push the inflatable craft underneath where it would clearly be crushed by the force of the waves, they looked at us and motioned towards the wall, clearly anxious for us to take action. It took a few moments for us to realize that they wanted us to climb the wall.

As the nimblest of our crew, I leapt onto the structure and climbed up the wet boards. I was astonished to find that there was no floor at the top, and instead I had to scurry across a fat and rusty pipe to reach the safety of a grate floor about ten feet away. This was quickly turning into a bizarre experience. Robin, a much bigger man than me, made it up the wall and across the pipe to safety, while carrying a backpack with our gifts, passports, and valuables inside. However the third member of our crew, Linc, slipped and fell, landing in the classic pose astride the pipe, luckily without injury.

Next, we were faced with what I believe was the most dangerous-looking stairway I had ever seen. It connected the dock to the upper level deck, hanging over the water and the fish below. It rose precariously without landings or obvious support about three stories to the first floor of the building. The stairs were made of yellow and blue plastic grating, the handrail was plastic and flimsy. It seemed to defy gravity as it hung there without obvious means of adequate support. Luckily there was the relative safety of the clear blue water below it. Robin went first and I let him get almost to the top before I followed, and the whole thing rocked side-to-side as we climbed. It was noted by the three of us that the Venezuelans who lived here were all considerably smaller than us, especially Robin, and we wondered later if he was the heaviest person yet to have climbed it.

The precarious stairs led to a concrete deck that supported the main building. Here we all felt safe for the first time since leaving the *Sophie Ems*. In view was a small crane from which dangled a large deflated red dinghy, which was in even worse shape than the one we had just climbed out of. A large water tank, and outdoor shower, and some unidentifiable machinery occupied the rest of the floor. A sign read "Bienvenidos a Bordo Isla De Aves" (Welcome Aboard Isla De Aves).

The building was a four-story structure vaguely

resembling stacked shipping containers. It had probably been shipped here in pre-constructed modules. After letting us roam around for a minute, we were ushered through a steel door. Inside the building reminded me of a high-school. We passed an industrial-looking kitchen, ascended interior stairs, and ended up in a carpeted room with plastic chairs and a large television.

An accordion-style partition wall separated this room from another which was apparently used for playing video games. On another wall a stern-looking Hugo Chavez greeted us from a military portrait. Our escort motioned for us to sit down, and then turned on the big television. I expected some sort of instructional or educational "welcome to Isla Aves" or Venezuelan propaganda program. But instead it was bad American TV with Spanish subtitles, assaulting us with a loud advertisement of a horror movie, and Robin immediately asked them to turn it off. They were probably just trying to be accommodating and assumed we would like to watch some television, as we had obviously been at sea for a while. But having grown accustomed to the tranquility of life on a sailboat, this was the last thing we wanted to see.

While we sat patiently, curious young men slowly appeared and spoke among themselves in Spanish. Lastly, a young man with a big smile on his face appeared and welcomed us in English. The Comandante introduced the other men one-by-one, and we all shook hands. These were all members of the Venezuelan Navy. One or two were in some sort of uniform, but most were casually dressed in shorts and t-shirts, flip-flops or bare-feet. All were young, and again the experience reminded me of high-school. By this point I had a big smile on my face as this bizarre experience was becoming quite entertaining.

The Comandante was very polite, and informed us that he was practicing his English, which made him quite happy; I believe he was the only one on the island who spoke any of our language. He explained to us that we were his guests and that they were very happy to have us on their little island.

I was very curious about the reef and the fish, and I particularly wanted to compare the health of the underwater ecosystem there to that of the areas I dove in St Lucia. After exchanging pleasantries, I asked the Comandante if we could snorkel, if it was OK to spearfish, and if I could take pictures while here. He told us the island was a nature preserve and that fishing was forbidden, but since we were his personal guests that it would be allowed. As for picture-taking, we were informed that it was fine but that we shouldn't tag him or the island on Facebook, or Instagram, for security reasons. We were then offered lunch and we graciously accepted.

Over a delicious meal of pork, salad and potatoes, the Comandante practiced his English and Robin and I practiced our Spanish. We presented him with the gifts we had brought, the first being two bottles of rum. The Comandante pulled them out of the brown bag, read the label, smiled and hugged the bottles, telling us that his birthday was soon and they would be greatly appreciated. The fruit we brought disappeared into the kitchen, and the fishing lures were a big hit. The resident fisherman, a muscular and dark-skinned fellow, scrutinized each package of hooks, lures and various tackle that Robin had picked out for them. Robin and I tried to explain in two languages what each piece of tackle was for and what kind of fish they might catch, however I doubt that much of this communication was either understood or necessary.

After lunch, the Comandante wanted to show us the helicopter pad on top of the building, and we followed him up more stairs. Sure enough, the top of the building was flat and painted with a big red bullseye. Around the edge, lacking any sort of railing, extended horizontal netting, which might catch someone if they fell. This was supported by rusty steel bars and the netting was torn in some places. It did not lend any sense of security, and Robin didn't get within twenty feet of the edge.

The view from up there was extraordinary. The island was shaped like a comma, one end skinny and one fat. The building was at the skinny end, which was tipped with rocky reef. The wider end was sandy and covered with birds, hence the name Isla Aves ("Bird Island"). Inside the comma was the small bay where the *Sophie Ems* was moored. From up on the roof, patches of coral were visible throughout the clear blue water. On the outside of the comma was the open sea with its dark blue water, waves and choppy surface, and in the distance we could see a passing catamaran, which surprised Robin.

"Is it common to see sailboats passing from up here?" asked Robin.

"It is very rare to see boats. Yours is the first sailboat we have seen since your friend was here six months ago" the Comandante replied.

~~~

The Venezuelans were keen to snorkel with us, and asked if we had extra gear, and we did; Robin kept extra snorkeling gear on board for his occasional charter guests. We descended the scary staircase and climbed down the 2x6 wall into the leaky rubber dinghy and motored back out to *Sophie Ems* with seven or eight of the Venezuelans, all smiling and clearly excited to be going snorkeling. The Comandante informed me that they never got to do fun things like this. Back at our boat, we doled out snorkeling gear, I got out my camera and a spear, and we jumped into the water and began swimming and diving.

A current was slowly pulling us away from the boat and the island. I had assumed that one of them would follow along in the dinghy, but that didn't happen, so I immediately decided not to spear anything, even though one of the Venezuelans pointed at a barracuda and communicated with sign that I should shoot it. I think this would have been a very bad choice, as the spear I had was made for shooting lobster or small fish, with a three-pronged tip. The barracuda would not have died instantly, and thus would have fought back, while bleeding and attracting sharks, and I would have had to swim against the current back to the boat with all this going on. The picture in my head was a dramatic and bloody scene, which included me getting bit by the large-toothed fish. No, I shook my head and did nothing of the sort.

While they may seem dangerous, barracuda are quite common and their company is to be expected when diving or snorkeling in the tropics. They swim or hover menacingly above reefs, looking for fish to eat, and are curious, often inspecting humans in their presence. It is possible that they identify humans as large predators (as we sometimes are) and hope to get free scraps of food from our actions. These ominous-looking fish swim with their mouth slightly open showing their many large and pointy teeth. However, they virtually never attack people. They usually eat small fish, and would have nothing to gain by biting a person.

The few people that have been bit by barracuda were usually wearing shiny jewelry, which may have been mistaken for small fish. They catch their prey by sighting an unsuspecting fish from afar and bolting at it from above. They are extremely fast, so fast that an observer might not even be able to see them, or just register the movement as a blur. They hit their prey with open mouth and often cut the fish in half, then turn and pick up the pieces. The half-dozen barracuda we saw here were two or three feet in length, but they can get up to seven feet long. Big ones like that are quite impressive, and scary! Once while diving on a wreck off of Palm Beach, Florida, I saw one as big as myself and looking like a gladiator with multiple fishing lures hanging out of its mouth.

The water around Isla Aves was clear and the snorkeling was fun. The resident fisherman was a strong swimmer and a good freediver, but the rest of the crew snorkeling with me seemed novice, and we soon were quite far from the boat and approaching the open sea, and I became worried for the safety of the group. I waved my spear in the air, trying to attract the attention of those on the boat, but got no response. Some of the swimmers appeared to be tiring. Not all of us had fins, and I began to fear the worst, that one would begin to struggle, and I would try to help, and the picture in my head was not a good one.

I waved some more, swinging my yellow spear in the air, but still got no response. I decided to swim for the boat. I knew I could make it back, but I also knew some of them could not. No one on the boat noticed me until I was all the way back at the boat, where I informed the driver of the dinghy that his men needed him. He quickly got into his craft, started the outboard motor and nearly ran me over as I swam out of his way.

~~~

The three of us had expected to sail away at this point, but the Comandante pleaded with us to come back to the island compound for a tour of the island itself and some guitar playing. He was very persuasive and in the end we gave in, and rode in the dinghy back to the 2x6 wall, and the sketchy stairway. We walked this time out a long walkway to the island and spent a little time walking around the beach, which was pristine and beautiful. Waves broke on coral reef on the north side of the island, while the south side was a sandy beach facing the bay and the *Sophie Ems*. Shells and old broken bits of coral were plentiful on both sides.

After the beach walk, we went back inside and the Comandante brought out a guitar, and he and I took turns playing. While I was jamming, he took some video, and when I was done he showed me his phone, already with a short video of me playing, posted on social media, and with responses from his friends. He took up the guitar and played and sang some tunes in Spanish.

Robin, me, and Linc, left to right

The friendly Venezuelans really didn't want us to leave and invited us to stay the night. The water was so clear that I was tempted to make a plea to stay so I could snorkel some more, on some of the surrounding reef instead of in the bay right near the boat. But the experience had already been as much as we could handle, and we were firm about having to continue on. After many group photos, exchanges of contact information and goodbyes, we descended the wobbly stairs to the floorless dock, climbed into the leaky dinghy, and were escorted back to our boat. It was time to make our way to Puerto Rico.

~~~

Fajardo, on the east coast of Puerto Rico, was our destination. I had previously made contact via crewbay.com with a woman who had a sailboat on the south coast. I had tentative plans to sail with her at some point, except that she had told me that her boat might only be ready for day-sailing. I had been in contact with yet another boat, also via crewbay.com, which might be a way to sail back to Florida. I didn't have a return ticket home and my plans were up in the air; I liked it that way. I was sailing and on an adventure, and that was all that mattered.

As we sailed away from Isla Aves and the friendly Venezuelans, the winds were strong, and we made good time on a broad reach at about 6-7 knots. We were three quiet men in a serene world sailing across the Caribbean Sea. The tranquility was momentarily suspended when we caught a fish, but soon returned. We were visited by dolphin, gazed at beautiful sunsets, and were surprised by countless flying fish, all of which eluded my camera.

Late at night, as I read my Kindle in the cockpit while on watch, I was startled by a loud noise and a thump on the boat near the rear of the cockpit. I saw movement by the rail. I slid over to inspect, turned on my headlamp, and saw a brown bird laying on its side under the spinning blades of the wind generator. I reached for it, but unfortunately I startled the bird, and it fell into the sea trying to get away from me. Blood stained the deck. I suppose it collided with the wind generator while flying too close to the boat, probably sizing us up for a landing area.

On the day before arriving at Fajardo, Robin informed us that we were making too good of time and that we were going to have to slow down, otherwise we would arrive at Fajardo in the night, which was not acceptable. In order to slow down and arrive in the daytime we reduced sail and for the last day we only sailed at 1-2 knots. There was a swell coming at us from behind and starboard, so the ship rocked a lot, for over 24hours. This made for rather uncomfortable sailing, difficult sleeping, and hazardous cooking in the galley. At one point while I was cleaning up after lunch, the entire tray of dishes I had just cleaned and dried went flying off the counter, scattering all over the floor, and one coffee cup broke.

This was no good since we all went barefoot onboard, by Robin's orders, so I made great effort to find every scrap of broken glass on the rocking boat. Luckily Robin kept a small cordless vacuum cleaner on board, and I put it to use.

I had a rash of bad luck on this particular day. It started while I was on watch in the morning and the other two were asleep. I was putting out a fishing line, as we were crossing a deep shoal, when the boat started turning dramatically, causing an accidental gybe, with the boom swinging violently across the boat and banging into the shrouds. Apparently my foot was pressing buttons on the autopilot, which was precariously mounted near the floor of the cockpit and which I had forgotten about. I instinctively jumped up and grabbed the wheel, which of course I could not turn, as the powerful autopilot was in control. I had to yell to wake up Robin, because I had no idea what was going on. Needless to say, this was very embarrassing. Later that day I stubbed my toe on a jib-car, which was still sore a month later. Next I spilled scalding hot tea on my bare leg. I had to laugh at this, even though it hurt, as I was clearly having an unlucky day.

But my bad luck continued. I woke in the middle of my sleep. The boat was rocking dramatically and I couldn't find my phone, which had the alarm set for midnight, which was the beginning of my watch. I looked everywhere in my cabin. The mast, which was keel-stepped, passed through my cabin, and was close to my head when I slept. Being hollow and aluminum, it transmitted a lot of sound, and with the boat rocking as it was, lines banged into it and all sorts of noise rang in my ears. This put my subconscious into a state of anxiety, as if I had been hearing constant alarms and sirens.

I was worried that my phone had fallen into the bilge next to the mast. I searched every square inch of the dramatically-rocking room. While I was standing looking through my gear and my bunk, which had a bookshelf above it, behind me, I was suddenly flung backwards as the boat lurched from a wave. I flew onto my bunk, and the back of my neck, head, and left shoulder slammed full-force into the wooden bookshelf. It almost knocked me unconscious. I lay on the bunk in pain, taking stock of my body, thinking that I was surely injured. After lying still for a few minutes, I realized that I wasn't hurt, and I got up and resumed looking for my phone, which I eventually found wedged between my mattress and the hull. I still had an hour before my watch, so I rested.

When my alarm went off at 11:45, I scarcely wanted to go above. All night the loud slamming and banging noises (which in reality were just coming from ropes and various things hitting the mast), registered in my tired brain as quite ominous warnings that bad things were happening. I felt like my luck had run out and going up on deck for my watch was a bad idea. However, I put on my gear, long pants, a sweater, a rain jacket, and my auto-inflating life vest. To this I attached my handheld and waterproof VHF radio, with which I could call the boat, or another passing ship, should I fall overboard, and my waterproof flashlight. I was beginning to feel safer.

I grabbed my kindle and water bottle, and made my way through the dark and heavily-rocking ship to the stairs and up to the cockpit, where I sat with my back to starboard, my feet braced on the port bench, my left had wrapped around and clutching the jib-sheet, and my right the halyard. I was determined not to have any more bad luck, not alone at night in the cockpit of a rocking sailboat in the middle of the Caribbean Sea.

However, a squall-line was clearly visible and approaching. My bad luck appeared to not have ended. Luckily the boat was equipped with a large bimini (a canvas roof over the cockpit) and a dodger, which I erected, as well as a large plastic tarp on the windward side attached to the bimini. I rolled this down and secured it, and then got back into position, hands on ropes, feet braced, ready for the worst. This was the low-point of the trip.

I could hear the wind as it approached, and I tightened

my grip on the lines to which I held. The boat heeled further and accelerated when the wind and the rain reached us, rising and falling as we crossed the increasing waves. The air temperature dropped. Tiny water droplets became omnipresent. I was thankful for the autopilot that continued to steer us in the right direction through the black night and the squall as I simply sat still and held tight. However as quickly as the squall came on, it went on its way and the tranquility of the evening was restored.

~~~

When I awoke the next morning, we were sailing around the south coast of Puerto Rico. I was surprised at the size of the mountains, shrouded in clouds and with large white wind turbines at the base. A rainbow made an appearance. Robin and I discussed the locations and meanings of various buoys. Clouds formed and dissipated. It rained briefly. We made it to Fajardo and the Sunbay Marina welcomed us, where we docked, cleaned the boat, and waited for the customs officials.

When they arrived, they were pleasant, but took away all of our fresh fruit. I was surprised that they were wearing United States Customs and Border Patrol uniforms, and I was further surprised that I was checking back into the United States. After they left, Robin took down the customary yellow flag and replaced it with an American flag. Of course, Puerto Rico is an American territory and none of this should have surprised me.

We now had access to showers, laundry facilities, dry land, a town, neighbors to talk to, and more SCUBA-diving opportunities.

~~~

The first day in Puerto Rico I spent with Robin and Linc

touring about in a rental car, going to a rainforest, hiking to a waterfall, followed by a drive to Old San Juan, which was strangely reminiscent of my hometown, St Augustine, Florida. It was rather amazing how similar the two places are, both with a fort of similar construction and design overlooking the entrance to the bay and harbor, cobblestone streets, and many shops for tourists. This was all fun, but I was ready for more adventure, and after much research on my iPhone, I located a dive-shop and scheduled a SCUBA dive for the next day.

The only dive I could get on was set up for a group that turned out to be a wedding party from the mainland of the United States, many of whom were from Florida. I was the only SCUBA-diver besides the divemaster. We all boarded a nice dive-boat with a large open deck and a smaller upper deck. We motored for about a half hour to a beach on Isla Vieques, where I snorkeled and then paddled around on a stand-up paddleboard while the other gringos played on the sand and frolicked about in the water. They were of all ages, all related or soon to be via the wedding, and they were having a lot of fun.

This was not the diving adventure I had anticipated, but I was in a positive frame-of-mind and I made the best of it. Next we went to a concrete pier in dark blue water for their snorkeling part of the journey, and my SCUBA-diving part. I'm sure this was not the snorkeling experience that the rest of the folks on-board were expecting.

I had no wetsuit, so I wore my jacket into the water (completely inappropriate, but it helped keep me warm), which was about 40' deep. The divemaster, Juan, and I descended into the dark water and explored the area under the pier. Right away he pointed out a sea-turtle, with its head up in some rocks apparently looking for something to eat. It backed out, took a leisurely look at us, and calmly swam away. Creatures of all sorts swam about or lived attached to something under the pier, including lobster, sponges, a school of spadefish, more turtles, damselfish, wrasse, and grey angelfish. At one point I turned around and saw a man standing on the bottom looking up. He blew air out of his mouth, which formed a ring as it rose, through which he swam on his way back to the surface - a totally unexpected free-diver. After the dive, I went ahead and signed up to dive again the next day, which turned out to be quite a different experience.

Juan was kind enough to give me a ride back to the marina, during which he practiced his English and I my Spanish. I learned that in addition to being a divemaster, he also had a captain's license and studied marine biology, as I did in college. He also told me that in Puerto Rico everyone takes English class starting in the first grade.

~~~

The boat the next morning was full to capacity with 30 SCUBA-divers, all of whom were Puerto Ricans, and no English was spoken on the boat. Luckily I was assigned a friendly dive-buddy, a doctor named David. David interpreted the important parts of the dive briefings to me, which I tried hard to follow, but although I can communicate in Spanish, it's quite a different challenge to understand a Spanish-speaker speaking Spanish to other Spanish-speakers. The words all flowed together and the ones I knew get lost in the mix. Diving, however, is fairly simple and as long as one follows the group and returns to the surface when they do, or before running out of air, there is not much else about each individual dive one needs to know.

David and I were both photographers, he with a still-camera with a flash attached to an arm, and me taking video with my GoPro on a stick with a flashlight. We made a good pair, although I think he was worried about me, as I didn't have a dive-watch, dive-computer, or a wetsuit. Also I was again diving with a jacket on, the kind you might wear jogging, but not in the water. I assured him I had advanced certification and about 50 dives under my belt, but he still kept a close watch on me.

After descending to the bottom, I noticed David motioning to me and pointing to something. I swam to him and looked inside the sponge he was pointing at and was surprised to see a tiny alien-looking crab looking back at us and holding its little claws out on its very skinny arms, defending his territory from us. Soon I was pointing out a boxfish to David. We continued on like this, both looking for interesting things to show each other.

We did two dives that day, and although I was a bit cold and wished I had a wetsuit, I enjoyed them both. We saw a lot more coral than I expected, the water had good visibility, and many fish were visible on the reefs. I had a good time poking around with my camera and flashlight, sticking it into caves and looking for interesting fish, and the act of breathing underwater never gets old.

David and I hit it off well, and we talked quite a bit after the dives. He also was kind enough to give me a ride back to the marina. He practiced his English, and I practiced my Spanish. This is how it is everywhere I've been in Latin America. It's kind of a funny way to have a conversation, in two languages, and it seems like it's going to be awkward at first, but everyone does it. Conversations are slow, with long pauses between sentences, questions and answers, and sometimes the conversations lack meaning or relevance, but the purpose of practicing each other's language is achieved, and it feels like an accomplishment. We also end up with new friends this way. After David dropped me off, the last thing he said was "You have a friend for life!"

Before leaving home, I had made plans to sail with another person on a boat about three hours away from our marina, and Robin agreed to drive me there. It didn't look very far on the map, but it took over four hours to actually get there. The drive was beautiful, through the mountains along the south coast, with many spectacular views of the bright blue and calm Caribbean Sea. During our time sailing, Robin warned me that before crewing on other people's boats one should use an abundance of caution, interview the skipper, and ask lots of questions about the boat, the plans, the skipper's customs and habits etc. The point was that you should not assume every boat was one you should get on.

His point was made clear by a neighboring boat at the marina in Fajardo. It was a good-looking yacht about 45 feet long with classic nautical lines. I think it was a CSY 44. SCUBA tanks were visible on deck, and the skipper was a young American man with his wife and two of her friends aboard. The boat showed some signs of neglect, like rusty bolts on the chain-plates. Robin told me they were soon sailing for Florida, and I mentioned that I might be interested in crewing with them, since I had to go back to Florida soon. He replied that another crew would be welcome, as it would give them "shorter watches and more time to drink beer", at which point I lost interest.

They left a couple days later without me, heading north into a 2-meter north swell generated by a nor'easter (a winter storm rolling off the east coast of America). This meant they would have strong headwinds and very rough seas to contend with. About a week later, after I was gone, Robin informed me that they returned to the marina at night with the deck of the boat cleared. They had hit rough weather, had to take everything off the deck to prevent it from being washed overboard and had to turn around. I'm very glad I was not on that boat; the conditions must have been terrible.

Robin and I eventually found the marina and the skipper of the boat that I had planned on joining. But all was not right. Warning flags were going off in my head, something was not as it should be, and the rising swell heading for Puerto Rico was on my mind.

The boat was not ready to sail, and in the previous days via emails I had made comments about being willing to help out with chores on the vessel, which was moored out-of-sight.

I asked Robin to sit with us before leaving me so I could ask some questions to the skipper. If I stayed, not only would I miss potentially excellent surf, but I would be stuck on a small sailboat and working on it (without pay) for the remainder of my trip. On top of that, the boat was moored, and thus not at a dock. I would not have access to land, or an easy way off the boat. I might have agreed to this if we could at least take the boat out for daysails, but the skipper informed me that the boat would not be ready to sail for a few more weeks.

I couldn't stay. I apologized and got back in the car with Robin, and we drove all the way back to Fajardo.

The next morning, I took over rental of the car, packed up, said goodbye, and headed off toward the west coast of the island in search of surf. Through much communication with friends back in Florida via the magic of the modern phone, I determined that I should go to the town of Rincon and surf a spot called Marias. The next phase of my adventure was on!

~~~

Rincon was easy to find. It is a small surfing destination on the west side of the island, and after much driving around, stopping at various hotels and beaches, I found a place to stay and a surfboard to rent. The small hotel had an attached restaurant and surf shop, all staffed by beautiful young women. What could be better? The place was called The Beach House, and sat on a promontory overlooking Marias and a lighthouse. In the distance was an island I later found out was called Desecheo, and was uninhabited due to the presence of unexploded ordinance from the US military's target practice. From the hotel, I watched the sun set over the water with Desecheo awash in its colors. The setting was perfect!

Puerto Rican iguana

I secured a room and rented a surfboard - a 6' 5" swallowtail with very little rocker (the fore/aft curvature of the bottom). This was not the ideal board for the overhead and powerful surf there, but it was pretty good for a rental board, and my philosophy on surfboards is like my philosophy on guitars or pizza: they're all good. Each surfboard is going to be good at something and each individual board just takes getting used to.

I walked down the hill with my rental board, wearing booties (neoprene foot-coverings) because I had heard that Puerto Rico and this area in particular was rocky and full of sea-urchins, which I did not want to step on. The beach was a thin strip of sand with reef at the water's edge. Palm trees separated the sand from a dirt parking lot full of cars. Many spectators lined the beach, and the waves were big, with 10-12 foot faces breaking on a right point-break.

The lineup was crowded. I studied the break while

stretching on the sand and tried to figure out where to get in the water and paddle out. On the north side of the break were big rocks emerging from the water. I spotted a local stretching and waxing his board, so I asked him where the best place to paddle out was. He was friendly and told me about the spot, where to surf, and where and how to paddle out. He wore a watch and was timing the interval between sets of waves, and he told me his name was Zumi. I waited until he was ready and then I paddled out behind Zumi. We had to walk across rocks with visible sea-urchins, jump into the deeper water, and paddle across a current and into the powerful waves. My little board was good at duck-diving, and I made it out without too much trouble. After taking in the scene and studying the lineup a bit, I caught a handful of great waves. My first day in Rincon was a total success, and I was stoked!

The pretty girl who rented me the board had told me where to get out of the water, and I took her advice, which worked. Getting out of the water around rocks and reef can be very dangerous, as the waves are pushing you towards the shore. First there is the danger of running into a rock head-first while riding on your belly after your last wave. Rocks can hide underwater, only to emerge as the wave you are on sucks up the water in front of it, but this didn't happen.

This did happen to me, many years ago, in Costa Rica at Playa Negra. I had planned my exit carefully, and after my last wave, which was solid 12 feet on the face, I lay on my belly to ride the whitewater in. When you do this, the whitewater first engulfs you as you lay down, then spits you back out in front of the wave. As I was spit out, a huge emergent rock, like a small island, passed by me on my left, completely unexpected. I had finished my wave and straightened out early to avoid another two big rocks at the end of the wave, which should have been far to my right, but I had not seen the rock in the middle of the bay. It must have been hiding underwater while I was on the beach making my exit-plan. If I had straightened out any sooner I would have hit this rock head-on and probably broken my neck, or worse.

Anyway, after getting close to the beach, it is then necessary to get off the board before its fins hit the rocks. At this point you have to put your feet down on the rocks or reef, supporting some of your weight with your hands on the board, and navigate the rocks without letting a shorebreak wave slam you into them. This is when wearing booties is greatly appreciated.

I smiled as I stepped out of the water and onto the sand, unhurt and without the spines of sea urchins in my feet. I continued to smile as I walked across the dirt parking lot and up the paved road to the hotel, where I cleaned up, put on some nice clothes and ate a fabulous dinner in the restaurant while watching the sun set over the water with Isla Desecheo in its foreground.

Each morning for the next three days I woke one hour before first light and made sure I was the first person in the water, so I could get a few waves before the crowd showed up. I would set my alarm for five am, get up, eat some pineapple and a banana, and stretch in the dark. I would put on a jacket and walk down the hill in the dark to the beach, where I would stretch until it became light enough that I had the nerve to paddle out, well before the actual sunrise.

With no other surfers in the water it can be difficult to figure out where to sit and wait for waves. One must read the water, watch where the incoming waves stand up, where they break, and estimate where the bigger ones will break. Once a good position is estimated, lines of sight to structures on the land can be established, like putting a tall tree between two mountains behind it, or in my case here, a blue roof under an orange roof, as there were houses on the hill behind me. On a reef break, a bearing like this is very consistent, and over time will only slightly change with wave size, as the swell increases or decreases, or with a different swell direction. Bearings are much less consistent over time at somewhere like a sandbar in Florida, where the location may only be good for a matter of hours, because the sandbars are constantly changing shape as the water moves across them. Usually there is also a current moving parallel to the beach in one direction or another, and sometimes, with an offshore breeze, slightly out to sea.

Sometimes the current near the beach moves in a direction opposite than the current in the lineup (where the surfers are sitting on their boards waiting for waves). Keeping an eye on landmarks and bearings is thus an essential part of keeping one's position. Holding your position is much easier in the presence of other people, but they can all drift out of position as a group, all thinking they are in the right place because everyone else has not moved relative to them.

Surfers often have a group mentality, and like to surf in packs. I prefer to surf alone without having to compete for waves; the solitude and communion with nature are a large part of my attraction to surfing, although it can be nice to have one or two other surfers in the water just to make it easier to find the right place to sit and wait for waves. We also sometimes cheer each other on as we paddle into good waves, and congratulate each other on good rides after paddling back out, which adds to the fun.

~~~

I was in contact via text with my friend Eddie back in Florida during this part of my trip. He was watching the weather and surf reports and giving me advice on where to surf, including details about currents and reefs. Eddie is academic about things like this, and is a great source of information when on a surf trip to somewhere he has been. He was part of a four-man crew with whom I travelled on my first trip to Costa Rica. Eddie expertly guided us to various surf-spots, always noting swell, weather, tide and predicting the size of the crowd.

Eddie, on my second day in Puerto Rico, suggested that I surf Tres Palmas, a well-known big-wave spot only about a mile from my hotel. The conditions were right for Tres Palmas to be fun, he texted. The reef at Tres Palmas holds waves up to enormous sizes that would be bigger than I can handle, but this day was predicted to be big enough for the spot to work, but not too big for me. So I decided to go for it!

A one-lane dirt road led down to the beach, at the end of which was a small palm-thatch concession stand, shaded by palm trees, selling food and drink, and renting snorkeling gear. A sign denoted the area as the Reserva Marina Tres Palmas. This is a protected coral-reef habitat where elkhorn coral allegedly still thrives. I'd like to return someday and dive on this reef to see how the endangered elkhorn coral is doing.

Tres Palmas

The sandy beach was narrow, shaded by various trees, and separated from the water by rocky reef in the intertidal zone. An old set of concrete steps sat in the area where the water met the land, leading to nowhere, completely out-of-place.

Small waves crashed on the rocky shore, and about a quarter mile across the blue water was a reef on which large waves broke, peeling from right to left as viewed from the beach, terminating in deep water. We call this a right point-break, because from the surfer's perspective the wave breaks from left to right, and starts at the same place, the point, every time, because of the reef underwater.

Two surfers on the point at Tres Palmas were visible from land, but none were on the beach for me to quiz about the details of surfing this spot. I had to determine for myself where to enter the water, which was far from obvious. I chose a rocky shelf in shallow water that appeared to drop off vertically.

Slowly and carefully I crept into the water, taking small steps, shuffling my feet so as not to step into a hole or onto a sea-urchin. As each wave receded, I viewed the reef in front of me, planning my next step. As waves came in I stood still and waited. As they receded again I moved slowly forward, repeating these steps until I felt that I was on the edge of the submerged bluff.

Here I waited, watching the water in front of me for any boils that might denote a submerged chunk of reef. When I felt that the water in front of me was deep, I waited for a wave to come in, and after it washed in I jumped into the water just as it was beginning to wash back out, hoping not to hit anything but water, and thus began a long paddle-out to the reef.

The entire paddle was across deep water, so there were no breaking waves to battle on my way out. The sun was shining and the water was a brilliant dark blue. Pelicans were diving in the shallow water near the beach. When I finally got all the way out, after taking a rest half-way, the two surfers on the point showed me where the lineup was. I looked back to shore and noted three trees in the foreground with a valley directly behind them, which I noted as "three trees in the valley." Perhaps this is where the name "Tres Palmas" came from. This was my bearing and would tell me where to sit in the parallel-to-the-beach orientation.

The two other surfers were on boards specially made for big waves, about eight-feet-long with rounded pin-tails. One man was bald and tattooed, and both looked tough. My board was way out-of-place here. The longer board allows the surfer to paddle faster, covering more ground and getting into big waves easier. The rounded-pin tail allows the board to be stable at high speed, and the rocker lessens the board's chances of nose-diving while dropping into a vertical wave. My shorter board was designed for quick maneuverability on small waves, the flat rocker is for keeping speed when a wave starts losing power. Waves losing power was not an issue here.

The waves were about ten to twelve feet on the face when they started to break, and they broke top-to-bottom, as opposed to crumbling down the face. All this I understood and led to a bit of anxiety on my part. I'm not accustomed to surfing over coral reef, or in waves this big and powerful. Hitting the reef on a wipeout was what I was nervous about. However, I sat in the lineup, giving space and right-of-way to the other two surfers who were already there, and I studied the break.

When the first set came, one of the surfers caught a wave and disappeared, and I never saw him again. I spoke briefly with the other surfer, the bald one, about how chilly it was, and he commented that it was smart of me to be wearing a neoprene shirt. The nor'easter that produced these waves, the same one that forced the sailboat to clear its deck and return to Fajardo, was also sending a chilly sea-breeze to Rincon. Soon he caught a wave, and I never saw him again either.

I was alone, outside at an unfamiliar point-break, one with a reputation for being big and powerful, and I was undergunned. My senses sharpened and a wry smile formed on my face. The adventure-level was high. I studied the next set of waves, not trying to catch one, just watching them as they rolled through, stood up, and broke. I noted what they looked like, where they began to rise and steepen, where the largest wave of the set began to break, how steep the wave face was when it broke, and so on. My confidence increased.

Soon I felt like I could catch one, and I paddled into what I felt was the takeoff-spot, and again took note of the landmarks on the shore: three trees in the valley, slightly on the right side of the valley now that I was deeper on the point.

A set came. I let the first two waves of the set go, waiting for the bigger ones. This wasn't just so that I could catch a bigger wave; it's not a good idea to go for the first waves of a set, as they are typically smaller than the others and if you wipeout early you are sure to take the rest of the set on the head, or you might miss the wave, and again take the next one on the head. But also the first wave of a set is never the biggest one, and I wanted a big one!

The third wave of the set was indeed bigger than the first two, and I liked its shape. I paddled into its path, seeking the spot where instincts told me it would start to break, then I paddled directly towards the beach, as hard as I could.

I felt my feet, then the back of my board, begin to rise. The wave picked me up, high above the surface of the ocean, and I began to accelerate; I knew I had it. The feeling I had right at this moment must be similar to the feeling a hunter gets when he knows the prey he has been hunting is in his sights and is as good as dead. I knew I was going to catch this wave and make the drop, and it felt like great success and achievement with immanent reward.

Right before the crest of the wave got to my feet, and I was looking down into the trough of the wave, I stood up and dropped in, instinctively throwing my arms up into the air in the victory pose as I flew down the face, accelerating both from the drop and from the forward motion of the wave. As I reached the bottom of the wave, I crouched low and turned my head and shoulders right, looking down the wave and leaning into it, slightly weighting my back foot. As a result, the board turned to the right and I pushed through the turn with my legs, shooting us back up onto the face of the overhead wave.

I accelerated even more as I cruised down the line, gracefully (in my mind anyway) carving up and down the face of the big blue wave, which had travelled all the way from the North Atlantic to the place where the Caribbean Sea meets the great ocean, hitting the coast of Puerto Rico and bending around this coral reef and finally breaking right where I had been waiting for it. As I rode the wave, it eventually got smaller as it lost energy to the reef, then hit deep water and turned back into a non-breaking roller, and I pulled off the back, safely into the channel, and paddled back out, smiling big!

I got six more waves at Tres Palmas, and rode my last one in as far as I could, but I still had a long paddle back to the beach, during which I saw some dolphin, always a welcome sight. Rumor has it that when dolphin are around, sharks are not around. But I was not worried about sharks here; the water was clear and they would see me and identify me as "not a fish" and move on. Murky water is much more dangerous, but in reality, worrying about sharks does a surfer no good anyway.

However, now I was faced with the challenge of getting out of the water, and first locating the best place to do this. I had watched the other two surfers as best I could, but the shore was just too far away for me to see where they got out.

Most of the power of the waves had been sapped by the reef outside, where I had been surfing, but the remnants of theses waves were crashing onto the reef at the beach, and I had to pick a spot to exit the water. I studied the beach as I paddled towards it, looking for a "keyhole", that is, a slot in the coral where I could walk out of the water without getting dashed upon the reef.

There was no keyhole, so I selected a deeper spot just to

the right of the ledge I had used to get in the water, as this area was a little bit protected. This was not a life-threatening situation, but I certainly could have gotten hurt and/or damaged my surfboard if I choose poorly. When I was close, I timed the waves and paddled for shore, got off my board, put my feet in front of me, hands on the board to support my weight, and let the waves push me up onto the rocks. I had my neoprene booties on so my feet didn't get cut, and I was able to walk out of the water unscathed. As my feet hit the dry sand, a great feeling of elation came over me that lasted the rest of the day. I had done it! All of my training had come into play: years of surfing, my recent ocean-swimming, freediving, jogging, clean living - all of this had allowed me to surf this spot without worry of getting killed, and all was right in the world.

I was smiling big and feeling fantastic for the rest of the day. I ate a dinner of sashimi tuna at the Beach House while the sun set in the background over the Caribbean Sea. A musician played Bob Marley songs for the dinner crowd. While eating dinner, I asked the pretty waitress to take my picture. I told her this might be the happiest day of my life. The emotion I was experiencing was pure joy, the joy of surfing big waves, the joy of beating alcohol and marijuana, the joy of visiting an exotic new place, the joy of freedom, peace, and deep serenity.

Dry Tortugas to Miami
January, 2017

It is 7:00 am on Jan 17, 2017. The air is warm, the sun is shining, and the wind has finally settled down to a manageable strength. I am standing on the bow of *Sobrius* with one hand on the headstay, looking across the bright blue water of the harbor and the small beach of Garden Key, facing the wind. A fishing boat and a catamaran sit to my right, and behind me is another sailboat. Nobody else stirs in the early morning. It feels like a good day to continue my journey home.

Under bright blue skies, I sit on the foredeck and with gloved hands and pull on the anchor rode. *Sobrius* inches forward as I take in the rode and coil it in the anchor locker beneath me. I pull up both anchors. When the second anchor releases its grip from the seafloor, *Sobrius* begins to slowly drift downwind. I quickly stow the second anchor and walk back to the cockpit.

The motor is already running and warmed up, and I put us in forward gear and steer us around the sailboat behind us and toward the channel leading out of the harbor. Careful not to run into any reef, I steer us out and around Fort Jefferson, towards the great blue sea. The #3 jib is on deck, ready to hoist, and one reef is set in the main, also ready to hoist. I feel tension and fear about this leg of the journey. The incessant howling of the wind in the harbor has probably spooked me a bit. But we must get to St Augustine, and there's only one way to do that: sail. I must rise above my fear and do what must be done.

As we pass the final buoy in the channel, I set the autopilot and go forward to the mast to hoist the sails. Clipped in to the jackline, I rest my back against a shroud, uncleat the main halyard, and begin pulling the sail up. But the first batten catches on the lazyjacks and stops my progress.

I go back to the cockpit and free the mainsheet so the sail can swing behind the wind. Back at the mast I ease the tension on the lazyjacks and raise the main, winching it tight. I move to the other side of the mast and raise the jib, cleat it off and return to the cockpit, where I kill the engine, and the sounds of the wind in the sails and the water moving across the hull bring *Sobrius* to life.

~~~

Fort Jefferson passes to starboard, followed by a green buoy. We pass the final red buoy to port. We are back in the Gulf of Mexico, or perhaps this is the Straits of Florida, or both. Regardless, the three-day leg to Miami has begun.

hoisting the sails leaving Ft Jefferson

It seems like hours have passed, but Fort Jefferson is still in the background and seemingly no smaller. Progress is slow. The wind has gotten lighter. I probably should have left yesterday. Now I need to increase sail area. I climb onto the coachroof and crouch back to the mast, drop the halyard about a foot, take out the reef, and raise the sail completely.

I go below and retrieve the genoa and for the next half hour I take down the jib and replace it with my largest headsail. I use the method from Andrew Evan's book *Singlehanded Sailing, Thoughts, Tips and Techniques & Tactics*. I've read this book cover-to-cover twice and gone through it a third time taking notes. His descriptions of singlehand techniques are thorough and excellent. The headsail change is done while sailing at full speed (which is fairly slow today) on a close reach. *Sobrius* rocks and sways very little, especially compared to when I did this while hove-to on the second day. Today the seas are calm and the wind is light. Instead of reducing sail, I am increasing sail, trying to get us going faster. The work goes smoothly and after twenty minutes I am finished and the genoa, the same one that I tore on my second sea trial, is up and pulling us slowly forward.

But the wind continues to decrease and eventually there is none. I find myself tacking about in a vain search for the wind when hear someone talking to me.

"Sailing vessel *Sobrius*, sailing vessel *Sobrius*, this is the United States Coast Guard, United States Coast Guard" I hear on my handheld VHF radio.

"This is sailing vessel *Sobrius*"

"I see that you have been going in circles for the last hour. What are your intentions?"

"I've been trying to find the wind, but I think I'm going to start the engine and head south into the Gulf Stream current. I'm en route to Miami."

"Thank you. Be advised that we are going to pass you to the west."

"OK, thanks."

I think they were curious about what I was up to, and I certainly hadn't realized that I had been tacking around trying to find the wind for an hour. Was the Coast Guard exaggerating? I don't know; I take everything literally.

I start the motor and we head south, in search of the Gulf Stream current, which is always there. It will carry us to Miami regardless of the lack of wind. The red and white Coast Guard ship passes to the west, and continues on south and out of sight.

I start the engine and lower the sails while it warms up. The wind has completely died and they would only slow us down if I left them up as we motor south. I'm attracted to the open ocean, and I don't want to be anywhere near the Florida Keys while sailing at night. I'd rather be out in deep water where there is nothing to run into, no reefs, no boats, no lobster traps.

The sun sets, we motor on, and I get some sleep, in twenty-minute increments.

~~~

The sun rises turning the sky red, orange, magenta, yellow, even green in some places. It is magnificent. Waking up on a sailboat at sea with no land in sight is one of my favorite things, and being alone makes it even better.

Some do not understand why I wanted to do this trip alone, or why I am interested in becoming a singlehand sailor at all. But I love it. I love the peace, the serenity, the tranquility. I need not adhere to someone else's schedule or whims. I go where I want to go, when I want to go, planned or spontaneous, without having to confer or consider someone else. No one is chattering in my ear; the only sounds come from nature. I commune with nature, I meditate, I think. I plan.

I never experience the anxiety of waiting for my watch to end, because I'm always on watch. I need not worry about someone else's safety. If I had crew I would have felt the need to purchase a proper life-raft, an EPIRB, and probably even more safety gear, because how does a skipper know what is enough when the life of his crew is his responsibility? No crew means no stress. No crew means self-reliance. No crew means ultimate peace and serenity. This is what I want. There are plenty of people with which to interact in my other life, on land. For now, it's just me and *Sobrius*, and the instruments are our only connection to the outside world.

The chartplotter shows that we are closer to Cuba than to Florida, and I wonder how close is too close. We are in the Gulf Stream now and should be getting 2-3 knots of push from the current. But the wind has also returned and we sail along at 4 knots. The engine is off, and the silence is fantastic. I hear no cars, no airplanes, no radio, no television, no people, just the sounds of the air, the water, and my little ship moving through them. The air smells of nothing and my sinuses are gloriously clear. There is no dust at sea, nor is there any pollen or mold spores or air pollution of any sort. I love it here. The smell of nothing is like the sound of silence, golden, serene, paradisiacal.

As the sun continues to rise, the wind freshens to around ten knots, and we are sailing at 4-5 knots. The sky and the water are both bright blue, brilliantly reflecting each other. White fluffy clouds decorate the sky while small waves texture the ocean. The sun is bright, *Sobrius* is heeled about ten degrees and leaving a small wake. She is a fairy dancing to the music of the Gods. She moves with the gentle gracefulness of the 44-year-old French ballerina that she is, masterful, slow in the light wind, translating emotion with every movement. Today the ocean loves us, and we love the ocean. The sailing is perfect, just what I had hoped for while waiting out the weather in the harbor next to Fort Jefferson. I feel joy in my heart, like my chest is expanding and my body is getting lighter. I see beauty all around me. I am at peace; I have found what I seek.

This is why I wanted to become a sailor. I am one with nature in my own private playground. The conditions are perfect. The experience is like taking a drink of cool pure water when one is hot and thirsty, like a deep breath of fresh air after holding your breath, like making love with a beautiful woman. The wind is music, and *Sobrius* is a grand piano. The ocean is an endless plain, across which I ride on a galloping winged unicorn.

~~~

I could not have stayed so long at anchor in the Dry Tortugas if I had a schedule to which I must adhere. Thankfully my life is not so rigid, and I have designed it, albeit in a somewhat haphazard way, to be flexible. My dream of becoming a rock-star, which has guided my life for the past twenty years, allows for no "regular job" with its two weeks of vacation and one week of sick days per year. Being a gigging musician requires one to be able to miss work whenever one needs to, and very few professions allow this sort of behavior. This is why I have been in construction for so long. As long as a carpenter is a good worker and shows up when he says he will, and gives a week or two of notice before missing a day or a week or a month, there is no problem. I also have no wife and no children, not even a dog or a cat or a girlfriend. I had a dog for thirteen years, but he passed away last year.

I had always told myself that when Uncle Henry (my dog) died that I would do some serious travelling. As sad as his death was, it was also an opportunity to spend more time away from home, travelling, adventuring. I rent out rooms in my house, so there is always a bit of income from this. It is financially risky to not have a regular job, with no guaranteed income, and no guaranteed work throughout the year, but this is how I like it. I am free to do as I please, and my various employers and clients are free to hire me or not. Freedom comes at the expense of financial stability, and financial stability comes at the expense of freedom. It is up to us to choose. I choose freedom. I choose to make my own choice. One should never do anything just because everyone else is doing it. Yet this is how most people make their decisions, and thus they fall into the same traps as everybody else. Fear is here for us to face, and adventure waits on the other side.

~~~

As we sail along in the big empty-looking Straits of Florida, *Sobrius* and I are one. I can feel the sea as it moves past the rudder, transmitting its signals up through the rudder-post, to the tiller and into my arm. I steer without thinking, looking ahead at the water and the sky, moving along towards our next destination, about a day away. I am not paying too much attention to navigation, but I know we are headed in the right general direction. What I want is good sailing, and I have that in abundance. I could program waypoints into the chartplotter, and it would constantly calculate the proper course and relay the information to me, but this is the least of my concern, I am simply happy to be out here on this enormous, seemingly endless, body of water sailing my little ship. I am here and it is now, and here and now are good; that is all that matters. My dream is reality.

my favorite day of the journey, closer to Cuba than Florida

Occasionally I take a moment to look at the AIS to see if any other ships are within its 24 –nautical-mile range but out of my field of view. Sometimes enormous cruise ships or container ships are picked up by the AIS, and sometimes they become visible. One is called the *Slottergracht* and is *168 meters* in length! I didn't know ships got that big. But none ever come close enough to cause me to change course. They show up and they disappear. We are in different worlds, on the same sea.

But the surface of the sea is dotted with little purple sailing vessels, bulbous and translucent, drifting downwind like a fleet of old square-riggers. They are not wooden ships, neither steel nor fiberglass. They are biological. We pass hundreds of them, and we pass very close; neither I nor they alter course when we will clearly collide.

Portuguese man-o-war they are, little purple sailing colonies that make ships out of their own bodies. These odd creatures are commonly thought of as jellyfish, but they are actually colonies of siphonophores, hydras. Each tentacle is a different animal. But at the same time all the tentacles of a colony are genetically-identical clones. While their genetics are identical, their forms are different, and they are all specialized for a specific function and each serves the colony as a part of a whole. Their life-form lies somewhere between that of individual and group.

The longest tentacles are individuals specialized in capturing prey (small fish). The shorter tentacles are individuals that digest and share the nutrients. Others function only in reproduction. The "sail" is an individual that has inflated itself with its own carbon dioxide.

Nature is strange; life is diverse. I'm glad not to be swimming among them. Their tentacles are very long, sometimes exceeding twenty feet, and not only sting but also stick to their prey. I always move far away from these things if I see them while I'm surfing. But today they are decorations on the water: living purple jewelry moving with the wind.

Ahead and to port is a flock of birds is feeding on a moving school of fish. The birds fly low and fast, dipping their beaks into the ocean, snatching their lunch. The fish swim fast, near the surface, perhaps chased from below as well as above. The whole moving feast approaches from port and moves across to starboard as we pass. The birds take no notice of us, and I'm sure the fish they chase take none either.

It is noon and we are sailing at 5.8 knots, just cruising along, and I haven't a care in the world. The day consists of just me and my boat, the sea and the sky, the birds and the sea creatures. I am at peace. I am hand-steering my sailboat. I am in my element, deep in nature and very far from land, euphoric. The fruits of the sea are bestowed on us all day in a cornucopia of serenity. I cannot be more thankful; I must be the luckiest man in the world!

~~~

Nature is my first love, and the deeper I get into nature the more I feel her. On the open ocean, with no land in sight, is to be incredibly deep in nature, totally immersed, left alone by society, dealt with indifferently by the wind and the seas, occasionally visited be dolphin or birds, alone with my mind, meditative, contemplative, beholden to no one, facing my own karma, cleansing it. I think perhaps nature is an agent of karma - the law of cause and effect – exacting payments for past transgressions, dispensing reward for good deeds, allowing passage for some, denial for others, still yet the ultimate price and everything in between. Facing raw nature on a regular basis cleanses one of bad karma, preventing it from building up, reminding one to keep a store of good and to accrue no bad. This is one of the ways nature is good for the soul, perhaps why nature and nurture are such similar words, likely from the same root. This is also why those who dwell here are humble people, and perhaps why some with less understanding become superstitious of her. I am not superstitious. I believe good luck comes from good preparation, focus, determination, tenacity, organization, karma. Bad luck comes from lack of these things.

~~~

My second night at sea since leaving Fort Jefferson is about to begin. The sun is descending on the western horizon behind us. It's been a peaceful afternoon and I've been sleeping for the past two hours, 20 minutes at a time. But now I must stay awake, because a huge cruise-ship, colorful lights all over, shares the edge of the water with the sun. As I gaze at the floating behemoth I ponder what it must be like onboard. If they could see, many would be wondering what it was like on my little ship. While it would be convenient to criticize those passengers, I think I will not. They are out on their own versions of adventure. Being out on the water in a boat is always a good time, and if cruise ship is how they all want to do it, then cruise ship it shall be.

~~~

The horizon all around us is pink and purple, blue-grey clouds are scattered above. With the sunset, the air has cooled from hot to pleasant, the water from intense bright and deep blues to a slate-grey speckled with black.

Night falls and the light from the Florida Keys becomes visible beyond the horizon – vaguely bright areas in the otherwise dark sky, stretching from west to east. Red flashing buoys outside the reefs around the keys illuminate the same line – distant warnings to the big ships that are an almost constant presence on the horizon. I try to decipher their lights, but few resemble the textbook examples.

I look for the red or green bow lights, which should tell me whether I am looking at the port side (red) or starboard (green) or neither if the boat is facing away from me. One enormous and brilliantly-lit ship shows a red light. But the red light turns green. Is the ship turning towards me? But then it flashes white – perhaps they are signaling me, do they want me to change course? Now the light is blue. Blue, I think, "what is this, the police?" No, it can't be. I haven't slept enough, why would I think police? The sequence continues – red, green, white, blue. Why would this be? There is so much to learn, and this seems like it must be important information, this pattern of lights.

I get out the binoculars, only to discover that the lights are coming from a party on the top of another cruise ship. My AIS confirms that it is indeed a cruise ship and we are not on a collision course with the floating revelers. I hold my course and laugh at my paranoia. Why would I still fear the police? I am sober now, neither my blood nor my ship carries any drugs.

~~~

The wind has been steadily decreasing since dusk. The sails are beginning to flap about, and this is becoming annoying. However, the sea is calm and the moon is out, illuminating the white sails as they alternately sag as the wind slows and fill as the wind puffs. They make a snapping sound when they suddenly fill with air; the sound is punctuated with the pinging of the rigging as it becomes taut. The blocks add their rattle as the sheets pull and then release them. Then the sails sag and all is silent, until the song is repeated moments later. The chorus is like a barking dog when you are doing your best to fall asleep. You lay there hoping during each interval between barks that the dog won't bark anymore, but it does, and you become more and more annoyed. Somehow this is extremely frustrating and I now decide to take the mainsail all the way in and make its sheet tight. This holds the sail firmly in place along the centerline of *Sobrius*, and the chorus is denied participation by the mainsail section.

However the wind becomes more variable as it dies, and this makes having the sails up pointless. I go through the procedures of taking both of them down, which is easy on a stable deck over the glassy sea, illuminated by the reflection of the sun on the moon.

I start the motor and we continue on towards Miami.

Later in the night – another ship on the horizon – and the AIS alarm goes off; we are on a collision course. Fortunately the AIS is now accessible from the cockpit since I moved it while in the Dry Tortugas. It confirms that the ship is a towing vessel, and these have right-of-way over sailboats as they are constricted by their towing. They also need to be given wide berth because the towing lines between the tug and the barge are often extremely long, so passing behind them is dangerous.

The towing line can cut a small boat like mine in two, whether we hit it directly, or if we pass over the cable when it is slack and then it becomes taut while we are above it, cutting us in two from below. Our closest point of approach (CPA), according to the AIS, is 0.2 mile in 17 minutes. I alter course to starboard, and the CPA drops to 0.0 – I've turned the wrong way and moved more into its path. I alter course to port, but the CPA fails to rise, and we are still going to collide, in about 13 minutes. Perhaps the tug has turned to starboard, and we are like two people doing the dance of trying to get out of each other's way on the sidewalk, but instead turn into each other's path. I alter course more to port as the lights on the ship grow, rising higher above the horizon, coming at me. My mind is tired. The CPA rises, indicating that we will no longer collide. This is what I am doing tonight: motoring north with the sails sheeted tight so they don't annoyingly flap around, and avoiding ships.

Eventually the horizon is clear of ships, the AIS further confirms none are within 24 nautical miles, and I take two consecutive 20-minute naps. I am awake now and I feel better. The night is dark, the stars are out, and the red flashing buoys marking the reefs around the keys are visible about 10 miles to the west. I find the faint glow over the Keys, which are about 20 miles away, to be comforting. Tomorrow I will be eating a hamburger in Miami.

~~~

The sun rises; dark blue and purple sky gives way to hues of orange, yellow and red. Clouds become backlit, bright below and shaded with dark red above, decorating the sky as we continue motoring north. I have been awake most of the night due to the almost constant presence of very large ships. The wind will not return, but the sun always does. Land becomes visible for the first time since leaving Fort Jefferson two days ago, a low line of green on the horizon. The Gulf Stream continues to push us north as it is very close to shore here.

It feels like Biscayne Bay is just ahead, but the chartplotter disagrees, telling me that at this speed (3.5 knots) it is 7 hours north. We motor on.

A large group of sportfishing boats appears on the horizon ahead. The mainland is 3.5 miles to the west and the water is absolutely smooth, glassy; there are no waves and no chop. The boats are all sitting still so I assume they must be anchored out in the clam water, but why are they all here?

Suddenly a plume of dark grey smoke appears behind one of the boats as it comes alive and zips off, and I realize that they are not anchored, they are out doing what sportfishing boats do, they are fishing, clustered in groups, probably chasing the same school of fish.

A flying fish darts out of the water beyond *Sobrius'* bow, flying like a bird just above the surface. Is it flapping its wing-like pectoral fins? I cannot tell – but on it flies – turning left, then right, occasionally boosting its speed by kicking the water with its tail fin. It travels an amazing distance before plunging head-first, torpedo-like, back into the ocean. Flying fish are amazing creatures. They typically fly horizontally about 150 feet, but can sometimes fly up to 400 feet. It is common for them to land on the decks of boats and some sailors, including the late singlehand sailor and author Bernard Moitessier, consider them to be a delicacy. I haven't eaten one, yet.

We motor on, weaving in and out of the sportfishers, scaring more flying fish as we go.

As the sun rises, its intensity increases. Even though it is mid-January I am hot and getting sunburned. I fetch a bucket of cool Atlantic-Ocean water and pour it over myself – instant relief. I dry off and put on a white long-sleeve shirt and a straw hat with a wide brim. *Sobrius* has neither bimini nor dodger, so my choice of clothing is my only defense from the burning sun.

We motor on through the urban seascape. The water here is a brighter blue than it was yesterday, and the lack of wind gives it a smooth texture.

I check the route on the chartplotter and veer closer to shore, seeking a shorter route. I've been staying three or more miles offshore to avoid the reefs closer to shore, but all looks clear on the chartplotter, and I am ready to be at my next destination, the Dinner Key Marina. I move forward, out of the cockpit and into the shade of the mainsail on deck while the tillerpilot steers us. The tillerpilot does a great job of steering, but it does not communicate with the chartplotter or the depth gauge. The shade is cool and the water is clear. I can see the bottom and I gaze at the plants and shells as they go by. The bottom is too close!

Quickly I return to the cockpit and ease the throttle. My depth gauge reads six feet, and my draft is four-foot-seven-inches. I check the chartplotter and zoom in, which clearly tells me that *Sobrius* is surrounded by shallow reef and we will surely run aground if we continue forward at all. I pull the tiller hard to port and turn 90 degrees to starboard, away from land.

Rule #1: stay as far from shore as practicable. Rule #2: never navigate with the chartplotter zoomed out, it omits details like shallow reefs when zoomed out. Rule #3: stay focused, especially when tired and sleep-deprived.

I am now safely back in 85 feet of water, the chartplotter is zoomed in and shows no obstacles. Triumph Reef, which we were about to crash into, is ahead and to port, well out of our path. I am now fully awake and alert, and disaster is averted, for now.

A bump, *Sobrius* shudders, a grinding noise, a vibration, another bump – we have hit something!

I look behind and see a plume of brown dirt rise in our wake; I check the depth gauge – still 85 feet. What have I hit? I pull on the tiller and head further out. Damn this land and its reefs, boats and submerged obstacles! Sailing is so much easier far out to sea.

We motor on, heading for the 110-foot tower marking Fowley Rocks, where we will turn west into Biscayne Bay Channel. I stay far out in deep water, peering about with the binoculars. I still don't know what we hit earlier, but *Sobrius* is not taking on water and continues sailing as if nothing happened.

We pass floating matts of sargassum – brown floating seaweed. A small yellow fish that looks like a moth – the same color as the seaweed – jumps and dives, spreads its fins and comes to a stop as we pass. A ballyhoo springs out of the water and tries to imitate a flying fish. The ballyhoo "tail walks" moving above the surface of the ocean, its head angled oddly towards the bright blue sky, its tail fin flapping madly in the water propelling the cigar-shaped fish away from the perceived danger – the passing of *Sobrius*, a lover of fish and all wildlife, an inanimate sort of wildlife herself.

We motor on, around the Fowley Rocks tower. I find the channel markers with the aid of the binoculars. The chart showed houses on both sides of the channel, so I assumed there would be land under the houses, but there is none. The houses are on stilts, glassy water reflects their bottoms. One on the right is painted a garish yellow and pink and appears to have some large rafters but no roof. Another on the left is blue and grey and is perhaps habitable. A boat of tourists pulls up to the pink and yellow house and they are taking pictures of each other with the house behind them. A sailboat passes to port. It is small, like *Sobrius*, and is a cutter. The hull is off-white and has a red stripe. There is a tan dodger and bimini shading the captain. I wish I had a bimini to shade me from the burning sun. We wave at each other.

I can smell land. It smells like trees and cars and algae on the rocks. I can smell laundry and bacon and burning leaf piles, civilization. It makes me smile.

~~~

A red flashing buoy marked "18" passes to starboard and we are now inside Biscayne Bay; the community of abandoned houses that sit on stilts over the water is behind us. But I realize that I have no idea how much fuel is in *Sobrius'* tank. I visualize pulling into a crowded marina and the engine dying, causing us to drift and crash into expensive boats, and I feel compelled to fill up the tank. I pull out the yellow jerrycan filled with diesel fuel that I bought at a gas station in St Petersburg last week and I top off the tank with the engine still running. I hope this is proper technique and that I am not making a terrible mistake while pouring the fuel into the tank as the engine runs.

We motor on as I search for the entrance to the Dinner Key Marina Channel, peering through the binoculars.

The bay is full of small sailboats: dinghies, catamarans, and odd high-tech racing boats with trapezes. Coaches follow behind in dinghies with outboard motors. They shout orders to the racers through orange bullhorns. Olympic teams train here. The traffic is heavy; today is not like yesterday.

Two catamarans approach, one blue and one red,

racing each other. I change course to avoid them; they have right-of-way because I am under power. They pass very close. They sail away, but now they are turning back towards me. It looks like one will pass behind me but I am on a collision course with the other one. I turn towards them and they pass on either side of me. The coach is waving at me to get out of the way. They are much faster than me, and I'm doing my best to avoid them. I just want to tie off to a mooring and get a hamburger. Still, I have to avoid them one last time before I finally reach the Dinner Key Marina Channel.

I somewhat dread the mooring that I must perform, inexperienced as I am. I'll have to find the mooring ball, drive *Sobrius* between other boats, move to the bow and grab the mooring with the boat-hook. I've only done this once before, and it was under the supervision of an instructor.

I call the marina on my handheld VHF radio, and they assign me to mooring ball #70. I put out my fenders in case I crash into another boat. I consult my iPhone, on which I have uploaded a map of the marina, and I locate mooring #70. The Dinner Key Marina Channel is long, and after 20 minutes of navigating it, we enter the marina. Something tells me I should confirm the mooring assignment. We were having trouble communicating earlier, so I call them again.

"Dinner Key Marina, Dinner Key Marina, sailing vessel *Sobrius*"

"Go ahead captain"

"Confirming that I am assigned mooring ball 70"

"Number 70 is taken sir" they tell me.

"I'm glad I called."

"Please take mooring number 99."

"Number 99, thank you."

We turn left towards the mooring field, leaving the marina behind, and enter another narrow channel with dark green mangroves on both sides, only to be confronted by a group of windsurfers coming in. There is a small motorboat in front of me, also moving out towards the mooring field, and it has to dodge the windsurfers, nearly colliding with one. I follow close behind, feeling tense. We get past all of them, but then a group of racing dinghies and catamarans starts coming at us. Some are zig-zagging through the boats on moorings. I find the scene rather bizarre. They all steer around us like we are no threat at all. I am standing still, tiller in one hand and the tight vertical mainsheet in the other, wearing long pants, a white shirt and a big straw hat. I am piloting a 1972 sailboat. The sailors coming the other way are sitting on the rails of their small high-tech craft, wearing lycra and expensive sunglasses, different worlds passing in the same channel.

Finally, I spot a ball with "99" painted on it. I remain in the channel and pass beyond it, inspecting the area around the mooring, taking note of the boats and the shallow-water buoys nearby, and plan my approach. I turn to starboard and loop back around, enter the mooring field, approach #99 from downwind, ease the throttle to almost neutral, idling forward with a bungee cord around the tiller. I quickly move to the bow, picking up the boat-hook on the way. At the bow I lean out, holding on to the bow pulpit and snag the loop dangling from the floating ball with the boathook. I tie us off, return to the cockpit and kill the engine, sit down, smile and enjoy the sensation of relaxation that overcomes me. It is done!

My second singlehand offshore passage has been successfully completed. All the stress and anxiety I felt moments ago dissipate, replaced with the euphoria of the conclusion of a three-day sail.

As *Sobrius* lies peacefully to mooring ball #99, I mentally review the journey that got me here, the daytime sailing, the night sailing, the big ships, the navigating of channels, avoiding collisions with other boats, catching the mooring ball without the help of crew. It is all finished; mind and body relax. I sit in the cockpit smiling, sinking into my seat, taking in the view: tall buildings in the background connecting Earth with sky, dark green mangroves above blue-green water, and sailboats.

A modern sailboat with a dinghy hanging from davits lies next to me. A couple moves about preparing their clean white vessel for a journey, or perhaps tidying up after one. A large catamaran lies between me and Biscayne Bay, shiny and proud, ready to run somewhere. A dark blue ketch rigged for serious ocean passages, jerrycans lashed to the lifelines, a hard dodger to ward off spray, lines everywhere, looks like it is resting after a long ocean-crossing. A trawler sits in contrast to the sailboats which surround it, looking like a life-size version of a child's bathtub toy. *Sobrius* and I relax.

arrival in Miami

We are in Miami, an urban environment, yet still in the water, still in nature. The city is outside the water, and we are on its edge. This is quite a contrast to Fort Jefferson, yet it is nearly just as tranquil. Sounds are minimal, the view is pleasant, and I am hungry.

I heat a pot of soup, to which I've added a can of tuna,

and eat it with crackers. The sun sets behind Coconut Grove. The sky congratulates me for a job well-done, and then it says goodnight, speaking in colors, speaking in a language deeper than words, speaking directly to the subconscious, the emotions, the soul. I wish that I could communicate so directly as the sky, and I do my best to tell the sky and the water goodnight, goodnight and thank you for allowing a safe passage from the island where I waited patiently for them to tell me that it was time to go.

I retire below and lay in my bunk. *Sobrius* sways gently, hardly perceptible compared to when we are at sea. I close my eyes and sleep until morning, a luxury after sleeping in 20-minute increments for the previous days and nights.

~~~

Breakfast is hot black coffee from the French press, and oatmeal with honey, nuts and dried fruit.

After breakfast I call Cristina, my old friend who lives nearby. We plan a rendezvous. She is a past lover and was my first real girlfriend. We dated in high-school and some of my time in college – long distance. I went to her senior prom when I was a freshman at Florida Institute of Technology. She later went to Harvard. We reconnected a few years ago and fell back in love. She was living in New York City at the time, and I started to make plans to move there to be with her. She is the only woman I ever truly loved, and the only one I ever asked to marry me. Due to circumstances beyond either of our control we were not married and never shall be, yet a deeper connection remains; we were temporary lovers but are destined to be permanent friends.

Cristina is brilliant; Cristina is eccentric; Cristina tells me that I am brilliant, acknowledges my achievements and buoys my soul. I look forward to seeing her as I take the courtesy shuttleboat to shore. I see her as we approach the dock. She is still trim and beautiful with long dark and straight hair, glamorous and proud. We walk to a restaurant on the waterfront and we both order the same thing: cheeseburgers and salads with blue-cheese dressing. We have much to talk about. We discuss the future, the present, life, sailing, philosophy – but neither of us brings up our bizarre past. We are the best of friends, but lovers no more.

In fact my heart no longer cares to fall in love. Love of nature, love of mankind, love of family - these things exist in me, and shall never die, yet the romantic love for a woman no longer seems possible. Cristina was my last try. My heart put everything on the line for that one, and while I briefly experienced true love for the first time, the fuel that feeds that internal and magnificent fire burned bright, and burned out, perhaps never to be replenished.

Cristina invites me to her and her mother's house for the night. I quickly accept her offer. I haven't used a proper bathroom in over a week and a hot shower would be a luxury. The little luxuries seem much bigger after ten days on a small sailboat. Everything seems new and wonderful, even just talking to someone.

~~~

The storm that I am in Miami to avoid comes on slowly, and I discover with a phone call to the Dinner Key Marina that the shuttleboat does not run when the wind is over 15 knots. For the next three days I have no access to *Sobrius*, who is condemned to lie alone on mooring ball #99 for the duration of the storm, which is forecast to have 40-knot winds. I hope that I properly closed her up and I hope that I left all the lines taut.

I stay at Cristina and her mother's house and for the next 5 days I sleep on a comfortable and still couch, take hot showers, brush my teeth while looking in the mirror, and use a real toilet. They cook me hot food and I tell them about my adventures – surfing, diving, sailing, playing in the band.

Cristina takes me to posh social functions: an office-building party, a restaurant opening – where I attempt Latin dancing – smiling at those around me and stepping on her feet in the process. We visit a museum displaying architecture that her grandfather designed, get Mexican take-out, see live music on the roof of a building in Miami Beach, go to a party for a football game that nobody is watching – instead talking to each other as intelligent people should.

at a restaurant opening with Cristina

She takes me to meet Frank on his MacGregor 65 – Ace.
David, an American, and Sophie, a French woman, are aboard
the long sleek sailboat and tell us how he proposed to her after
meeting her only three days prior. Frank invites Cristina and
me to crew on Ace in the race to Cuba in March. I want to go

but it will be a two-week commitment and I really need to get back to work. I haven't worked in over two months now. The financial risk I am already taking weighs on me, but of course, I am committed to *Sobrius* and the journey. I thank Frank but tell him that it is very unlikely that I'll be able to race.

~~~

Finally, after four days, I can access *Sobrius* and I replace the lost propeller zinc, this time using a lock washer that I hope will hold the part firmly to the propeller. The shackle on the boom topping-lift is broken. The mainsheet was left loose and apparently the boom thrashed about in the storm until the sheet wrapped around the winches. I learn.

I call the shuttleboat and get a ride back to shore and start walking into the city in search of a chandlery where I can buy a replacement shackle for the boom topping lift. After walking for a couple miles, I find it and buy a shackle and a pair of sunglasses, which I wear on the walk back to the marina. These will be my souvenir from Miami, and I wear them knowing they will remind me of my time here for as long as I own them.

~~~

I almost leave on Wednesday, but the wind is too light for sailing this morning, and I want to leave in the morning, to get the high-traffic part of south-Florida behind me in the safety of daylight. So I stay another day. I want to attend Cristina's sailing-book-club meeting tonight anyway. She comes out to visit me and see *Sobrius*, arriving on the shuttleboat. She loves my boat. *Sobrius* approves. Cristina is beautiful.

We chat for two hours sitting in the small cockpit, and the time passes swiftly. We talk about sailing, books, Miami, and the possibility of her and a friend sailing with me to Palm

Beach on my way home. The shuttleboat runs on the hour, but the first hour together passes without us noticing, and I call the shuttleboat when the second hour is nearly up. Soon she is stepping off *Sobrius* and onto the shuttleboat while I stay aboard. I watch as she fades into the distance.

Later the shuttleboat fetches me for its last run of the day. I walk through Coconut Grove for three hours, stopping at a café and a taqueria before heading to the Coconut Grove Yacht Club. While sitting in a chair by the water waiting for the meeting, two children approach me and warn me not to get too close to the water because a crocodile is in there somewhere. The children are curious about me and I enjoy interacting with them, not having any of my own.

Later, at Cristina's "Page Sailors" book-club meeting, we discuss Ernest Hemmingway's "The Old Man and the Sea." Her friends are all intelligent and interesting. I reconnect with Chiz, David, Sophie, Frank, and make new connections with others.

After the meeting, Cristina drives me to her house, where we eat pasta that her mother has made. I walk Bebe, their dog, who looks like a small version of my late dog, Uncle Henry. Cristina's friend, another beautiful woman, informs Cristina that she has hurt her foot and can't sail to Palm Beach on *Sobrius*. Cristina is still interested, but I am not confident that this is a good idea. I am still a novice and am wary of pulling into an unfamiliar port and trying to find a dock where I can drop off Cristina. I worry about the timing, the tides, docking… It all seems like too many unknowns and too much responsibility. Sailing alone with no clear schedule seems so much easier to me, at least at this point. So I talk her out of it, but I feel like I have let her down. I vow to return sometime to take her sailing, and I hope I will live up to this vow.

That night, I sleep soundly on the couch provided for me on these rest days in Miami, recovering from the first two thirds of my journey and preparing for the final leg.

In the morning, she drives me to the Dinner Key Marina, where, in the past, residents of Coconut Grove would take their boats into the bay to avoid the mosquitos while they ate dinner aboard their craft. On the way out, the shuttleboat captain takes us to a rock where the resident crocodile, the one the children warned me about the night before, regularly suns itself in the mornings, but the crocodile is not there. Cristina rides with me to *Sobrius* and we say our goodbyes – a parting of two old friends – like the sun and the moon crossing each other's paths, going their separate ways.

St Augustine to The Bahamas and Back
May 2016

      We must take good opportunities when they come our way, because they will not always be available. Sometimes great adventures are right behind an answer of "yes", and a continuation of meaningless existence behind the easier answer of "no". We must all develop the skill to recognize good opportunities and take them when they arise. We also must be prepared when they come up, otherwise there will either be no offer, or no ability to participate. It has been said that good luck happens when preparation and opportunity come together, but another necessary ingredient is the ability to recognize and embrace good opportunity.

      After returning from my Okefenokee adventure, I scheduled a return trip to explore the northern half of the swamp. I had seen a log entry on a sign-in sheet at one of the camping platforms that mentioned seeing a meteor shower. When I got home, I researched meteor-shower dates and found one that coincided with a new moon. I then called the Okefenokee Ranger Station and scheduled another trip.

      However, after returning from St Lucia and Puerto Rico, I was invited to sail to the Bahamas with Eddie and Liam. Eddie was the friend who had suggested surfing Tres Palmas in Puerto Rico. Liam was his friend who didn't know much about sailing, but had recently bought a Hunter Passage 420, *Monkey's Uncle*, and wanted to go to The Bahamas.

      The 420 is a big comfortable center-cockpit sloop, 43 feet long with a beam of nearly 14 feet and a 5-foot draft. It took me a while decide, but I eventually determined that watching the meteor shower while sailing across the Gulf Stream on the way to The Bahamas would be even better than watching it from a platform in the swamp. I was also eager to freedive on some Bahamian coral reef.

This all happened six months before I bought *Sobrius*. At this point I was fully chasing the dream of becoming a sailor, trying to get experience when I could, and ravenously reading books about sailing. The idea of sailing to the Bahamas while the three of us figured things out along the way seemed like a great adventure to me. Eddie was knowledgeable about the boat and its systems and had crewed on maybe a dozen sailboat deliveries, but was not exactly a veteran sailor. So we were essentially three novices with different skill sets sailing to the Bahamas, with more confidence and bravado than experience.

At about 10:30 pm on Friday May 5th, 2016, Liam, Eddie and I finally finished off our extensive last-minute preparations: replacing a through-hull fitting, wiring a new GPS unit, replacing a steaming light, tying the dinghy and an assortment of surfboards, kiteboards and SUP's (stand up paddleboards) to the foredeck, rigging a jack-line, stowing all of our food and gear, installing two locker-doors that I had repaired in my woodshop the night before, a trip to the surf-shop, grocery store, the grocery store again, west Marine, and Eddie's house.

The day reminded me of a recurring dream I have in which I am trying to go surfing, I get to the beach, see the waves in front of me, then realize that my wallet is in my pocket, so I have to go back to my truck, then I can't find my keys... and it goes on and on from one frustrating task to another, and I never get to surf.

But at 10:30 pm we finally cast off the dock-lines from Fish Island Marina in St Augustine Florida, and hailed the drawbridge, requesting an 11:00 opening. As we passed under the Bridge of Lions, some drunk revelers on the drawbridge cheered at us, and we waved back. We raised the mainsail in the dark, then motor-sailed out through the St Augustine Inlet.

Excited to be sailing, I donned my life vest and a

headlight and made my way to the bow. I clipped my tether to the jackline to prevent falling overboard in the dark. From this vantage point I watched for the unlighted buoys that mark the somewhat treacherous channel as we made our way out into the Atlantic Ocean. I stood at the bow with my arms wrapped around the roller-furled headsail as we pounded through the waves in the inlet, my headlight panning back and forth, a small beam of light weakly cutting through the black of the night. The brown water pushed the bow skyward, then let it crash back down, splashing my bare feet and soaking the lower portion of my jeans.

Eddie, a barrel-chested and confident man, the most experienced sailor of our trio of novices, steered while holding a powerful spotlight and also searched for buoys: green squares would reflect back from the right, and red pointed buoys from the left. The inlet is long and has shallow sandbars on both sides, so we waited until we reached the red and white safe-water buoy at the end of the inlet channel before turning south.

Since my watch during the sail from St Lucia to Puerto Rico was 12:00 am to 3:00 am, I volunteered to take the same watch on this trip, although watches were decided to be four hour each, so mine was 12:00 to 4:00. Eddie and Liam went below to get some sleep while I took the helm, happy to be sailing again and excited about the prospects of another unique adventure. The lights of Florida's coast kept me company, three miles to starboard, as peace came over me in the dark and quiet night on the water.

~~~

For a moment I thought that the sun was rising in the southern sky, at one in the morning. A bright orange light appeared on the horizon, then rose into the black sky barely lit by the new moon. The light was the same color as the sun, only smaller and rising faster. What a magical way to begin our journey, with a small sun rising on its own schedule and location! Yet sun it was not, and space-ship it was.

Cape Canaveral was just beyond the dark horizon, and the light was being produced by a Space X rocket, hauling a satellite into orbit. I had read about the scheduled rocket launch but was expecting it for the following evening, as it was scheduled for 1:21 am, May 6, and we had departed St Augustine the evening of May 5th, but of course, it was now early in the morning on May 6th.

After deploying its payload into the sky, the rocket safely returned to Earth, landing on a floating barge in the ocean, and a dim light shown on the eastern horizon as it decelerated for a successful touchdown, only the second rocket ever to return to earth without being destroyed in the process. In addition to the rocket launch, I also had the Aquarid meteor shower to view during my late-night watch. This was the meteor shower I had planned to watch while canoeing and camping in the Okefenokee. Our trip to the Bahamas was off to a good start!

the first morning coffee aboard Monkey's Uncle

The following morning greeted me with blue skies and bright sunshine. Liam was laying down in the cockpit, relaxing on his sailboat, blonde dreadlocks splayed about, fully enjoying his vessel and taking advantage of the newly-installed autopilot. Liam is a true adventurer who spends his time between Maui and St. Augustine, and an experienced big-wave surfer, kitesurfer, skydiver, base-jumper and wing-suit flyer. He was a very fit and health-conscious character with a pescatarian and organic diet, a gentle voice, and a small moustache that developed over the trip. It takes a brave man to buy a sailboat without having been a sailor first. At this point he was all-in, having spent weeks of time, countless money and supreme effort into preparing *Monkey's Uncle* for its voyage to the Abacos.

After motor-sailing all night and morning, the winds finally picked up to 15 to 20 knots from the WSW as we rounded the shallow waters of Cape Canaveral, dodging its numerous sandbars with the help of the highly-detailed display of the GPS unit, a color-screen chart of our area. A little animated icon representing our sailboat pointed in the actual direction that our vessel moved, showing our position over the depth contours of the ocean and relative position to land, including the channel leading into Cape Canaveral and its buoys. The unit was adjustable at the touch of a fingertip on the screen, a true marvel of modern technology. A large container ship crossed our path ahead. An oddly out-of-place sternwheeler moved in the opposite direction, passing us to starboard. Small powerboats zipped out to sea while others returned to port, travelling at right angles to our path.

We shut off the engine as we rounded the cape and pointed *Monkey's Uncle* more south. The boat heeled over on a close reach and cut through the small swell, silently propelled at 7-9 knots, impressively fast for such a comfortable cruiser.

My shift came up at noon, and I shut off the autopilot so I could steer by hand, as I prefer, and to save battery power. Eddie grilled up sausage patties on a gas grill clamped to the stern pulpit behind the center-cockpit. The aroma of the cooking sausage made my mouth water, and I realized just how hungry I was. We ate these on bread I got at the farmer's market topped with my homemade salsa, and it was a hearty and delicious meal. Later in the day I ate one of the bananas that I had brought. Many sailors simply will not allow bananas on a boat, due to an old superstition, but we were not superstitious, or perhaps too foolish to know of the dangers of bananas.

~~~

As we sailed past Melbourne, where I studied Biology at Florida Institute of Technology, fins emerged from the water and rolled back down on the port side of *Monkey's Uncle*. We all broke out our cameras and made our way to the bow, snapping photos and taking video as the four spotted dolphin rode our bow-wake, playing, rolling and jockeying each other for position, spraying us and our cameras with their wet dolphin-breath.

We dropped sail after a brilliant orange and magenta sunset and soon turned due east into the channel leading to Ft Pierce. I was concerned about entering a strange inlet at night, but Eddie was confident and I was third-in-command in a three-person crew. As Eddie steered us through the inlet I scanned the dark water for buoys while standing at the bow with a spotlight, although for the most part the channel was lit up like a Christmas tree and the passage into the Ft Pierce Marina was an easy one. Eddie pulled us up alongside fuel dock #2 and we tied off and got a full night's sleep in preparation for our crossing of the Gulf Stream the next day, about which I felt a bit of apprehension. The Gulf Stream is a strong ocean current and has a reputation for becoming extremely rough when the wind blows against it.

~~~

A farmer's market at the marina was in full-swing the next morning, complete with a live band, fresh fruits and vegetables, bread, coffee, muffins, mushroom tea and various prepared foods. Vendors displayed their goods in a beautiful waterfront setting with palm trees and cobblestones. Under the blue and cloudless sky, I sat on a wooden bench and called my parents for a nice chat. My father used to be a sailor and vicariously enjoys my journeys on the ocean, and I enjoy sharing my experiences with him.

Back at the sailboat, while checking the oil, Liam noticed three inches of water under the engine. This led to a one-half-day delay of our departure as Eddie diagnosed a water leak in the cooling hoses, found replacements requiring visiting two marine supply stores, and fixed the problem. I grilled sausages while he worked, at one point dropping a fuel canister into the water and borrowing a neighbor's boat hook to retrieve it.

We pulled out of the marina around 4 pm, at which time my father called to ask why we hadn't left yet. He had been watching our lack of progress on our SPOT internet page. The SPOT is a small electronic device that sends a satellite signal containing our location to a relay station. This allows our progress to be monitored by anyone who has access to our SPOT internet page. It also acts an emergency beacon, sending out an SOS signal when needed.

We were lucky to be blessed with calm seas as we crossed the Gulf Stream, considering how rough the seas can be there. We alternated between sailing and motor-sailing as the stars and the occasional meteor lit up the sky. But the heavens did not have the monopoly on the evening's light shows; the waters of the Gulf Stream had their own, with a three-dimensional bioluminescent display in our wake that extended across the surface of the ocean and down a fathom or so. Little green lights danced to the rhythm of the water's movement, and we even saw a large floating luminescent jellyfish looking like a small UFO that had landed on the sea. Perhaps it was a UFO; who can be sure?

~~~

Our first morning in The Bahamas, on the Little

Bahama Bank, offered calm, light green water under a misty horizon blending into the clear blue sky. A dazzling sun lit up everything, including the sandy bottom, which was dotted with soft corals and occasional patches of vegetation which were clearly visible and slowly passing under *Monkey's Uncle*. No land was in sight. I wanted to swim, and convinced the others to stop the boat for a moment. There was no wind this morning, so *Monkey's Uncle* drifted to a stop after Eddie cut the engine. I jumped off the bow and swam briefly in the magical, cool, and serene setting. However, thoughts of pelagic tiger sharks patrolling the area converted serenity to fear, and I got out of the water after only swimming from bow to stern. Swimming in the ocean where no land is in sight has a feeling of real danger to it. Somehow it seems like the wildlife is much more of a threat here. It must be an instinctive response to not seeing land, the opposite of "home-field-advantage".

Later, someone suggested tow-surfing behind the sailboat on my longboard. Naturally I thought this was a fabulous idea, and untied my board as Eddie secured a rope to the stern and tied a loop in it for us to hold onto. Carefully Eddie held the nose of my surfboard as the tail dragged in the water and I climbed aboard on my belly. He let go and I let the rope pass through my hands until I was holding onto the loop at the end and stood up. It was while riding my board behind the boat, no land in sight, that I realized I was on the right vacation. I fell once while trying to step onto the board from the moving boat while holding a cup of coffee in one hand. Luckily the coffee cup had a closing lid, which was closed, and thus did not spill or get too much sea-water inside. Eddie took some video as I sipped slightly salty coffee while wake-surfing.

We all took turns surfing across the Little Bahama Bank, and Liam put together his hydrofoil board and rode it, briefly lifting out of the water and hovering a foot or two above the water's surface, supported by an underwater wing attached to the board by a thin carbon-fiber keel.

Liam foil-boarding across the Little Bahama Bank

As we neared Great Sale Cay, the first island of The Bahamas we would encounter, three large and fast trawlers passed us, the first of many to come. On these trawlers were people who wanted to get to their destination quickly. On *Monkey's Uncle* were three novice sailors enjoying the journey.

Soon we were able to turn more south and catch some wind. I cranked on the large winch and hoisted the mainsail while Eddie unfurled the big genoa and then shut off the engine. We all remained silent as we listened to the sounds of the wind and the water moving past our vessel, captivated by the near silence.

Turning off the engine is among the best of events that can happen on a sailboat. I was always advocating for sailing over motorsailing. But on a sailboat with crew, one must compromise, and I didn't always get my way, as sometimes the others felt that we were not moving above a minimum-acceptable speed and thus would start the engine. I believe this furthered my curiosity about singlehand sailing.

~~~

After sailing for most of the day we anchored at Umbrella Cay (pronounced "key") in the afternoon. This is a small and uninhabited island, beautiful and wild, surrounded by nature and submerged wilderness. Calm blue water gives way to yellow sand with a hint of pink, followed by a low line of green and grey-green trees and shrubs, topped by the vast blue sky. This is nearly a silent place, the only sounds were a very faint lapping of water and the distant cooing of cormorants on the beach, their simple conversations blended into a low-pitched hum.

Immediately after dropping anchor the three of us readied our toys. I got my snorkeling gear, my GoPro camera, my new grappling anchor with 120' rode (anchor line), a new leash for my 12' surfboard, my dive knife, weightbelt and neoprene shirt. I put on my black leather Australian hat and mounted my surfboard, now to be used as a kayak to transport me to the reef. Eddie was already out on his paddleboard with a mask and snorkel aboard. Liam was still on the sailboat applying copious amounts of sunscreen as we impatiently paddled upwind towards the cut connecting the Sea of Abaco to the Atlantic Ocean.

As I paddled towards the north end of the island I crossed an area of shallow water and white sand. The water was absolutely clear and I could see the details of individual shells on the bottom. A dark shape swam towards me, about four feet long, with big pectoral fins. It was a shark, the first I saw on this trip. But it was only a harmless nurse shark and quickly moved away as I paddled by on the waveless and shallow water.

After passing through the cut on the end of the island I

dropped anchor over a patch of sand surrounded by coral and geared up. I tied the anchor to the surfboard leash, put my hat in the backpack, and lashed it and the paddle to the surfboard with a bungee cord. I put on my snorkeling gear and looked around. I was between two small uninhabited islands which were themselves between a sea and an ocean. Below me was the unknown, and the adventure-level was high. A feeling of euphoria came over me as I eased into the water and looked down through my mask, wondering what wildlife was around me and feeling a bit of anxiety about the possibility of sharks, but none were in view.

~~~

While there are no sharks to be seen, the area is absolutely teeming with fish. A bluehead wrasse and his harem of yellow females mill about a small coral-head; squirrelfish hide under a ledge; a large grey snapper swims warily away from me, lucky that we have not yet cleared customs or I would have a spear with me. Hogfish and blue-striped grunts go about their business. A lone Nassau grouper hides in a cave while an entire school of very large rainbow parrotfish move in and out of the area, as does large ocean triggerfish. Stoplight parrotfish scrape the rocks and coral, a lone barracuda makes a slightly menacing appearance. The invasive exotic lionfish are here, sitting still under a ledge, extending their long poisonous spines when feeling threatened. A sea cucumber sits on the bottom like a living blob mimicking a terrestrial vegetable. There is so much life here that I am nearly overwhelmed. Not just fish, but schools of fish, move in and out of view. I am truly amazed and very happy to be diving in this remote and beautiful place that few humans have seen.

~~~

While I snorkeled and dove, Eddie paddled off to circle the island. Soon Liam showed up on his paddleboard and I joined him for a circumnavigation of Umbrella Cay. The Atlantic side of the island, about 1.5 miles long, is lined with sharp rock bluffs. A battered and lost paddleboard, a harbinger of things to come, sat on the beach, along with washed up plastic bottles and fishing nets. However this bit of refuse, common along the shores here, was not enough to detract significantly from the natural beauty of the island. I thought about the Okefenokee canoe trip I had abandoned in order to come here while paddling my board across the Atlantic-Ocean water with the same paddle I would have been paddling this day from Big Water platform to Floyd's Island, deep in the swamp, and congratulated myself on a decision well-made.

The sunset on Umbrella Cay was so beautiful that I had to capture it on video. Horizontal bands of purple, magenta, orange and yellow topped the calm Sea of Abaco; a bright orange ball of flame descended over the gently-undulating slate-blue water. Cormorants called in the distance, wishing the sun safe passage around the Earth with their primordial and monotone song of single words in a bird-language forever unknown to man.

~~~

The following day we motored down to Green Turtle Cay, a quaint family island with pastel houses where the locals spoke with a strange and lisping British-like accent. Palm trees and docks lined the bayfront at New Plymouth, masts from sailboats moored in Settlement Harbour and Black Sound poked up over the town; a small ferry transported islanders to and from Abaco Island. Liam paddled his SUP to the island with our passports to clear customs. Soon after we got a call on the VHF radio to come to the office to fill out our paperwork. Eddie and I paddled our boards to a small beach by the city dock and walked down a quaint street to an office in a small blue house staffed by a large smiling black woman watching a televangelist rant and rave about how God loved us so much that we should pay him more attention than Instagram, after which he asked for donations and tried to sell a DVD set. We filled out some forms, paid about $100 each, and strolled back out into the sunshine. Why people watch television like that I'll never know. Otherwise New Plymouth was quiet and everywhere I looked could have been the subject of a painting of tropical paradise.

We walked through town on one-lane streets back to our paddleboards and made our way to the sailboat, where we pulled up the anchor and set off for No Name Cay, the next island to the south, in anticipation of a snorkeling adventure in a marine reserve.

As we rounded the southern tip of the island, our plastic owl, aboard to scare off birds who in the past had fouled the deck with their waste, jumped ship. While retrieving the owl, we noticed that Eddie's 12' SUP, which had been tied to the stern, was missing. We spent the next hour looking for it, but to no avail. However this did give us a nice opportunity to sail along and enjoy the raw beauty of the shore of Abaco Island, with its sandy beaches and sharp rocky bluffs, and Eddie took the loss of his SUP well.

This event later made us all realize how hard it would be to find a man overboard, for if we couldn't find a 12' blue and white SUP which we had lost only minutes before initiating a search, we would certainly have difficulty locating a person in the water. This is a common refrain in sailing books, that when a person falls overboard at sea, they are not likely to be found. Safety measures on an offshore sailboat should focus first and foremost on staying aboard.

Our fruitless search for the lost SUP led us close to Manjack Cay, which Eddie knew to have nice reefs accessible by sailboat on its north side, and we decided to go there to dive.

First we had to cross a large area of shallow water over white sand. I stood at the bow and kept lookout as we approached the cut between Manjack and Ambergris Cays. Soon dark brown patches of coral dotted the seascape, menacing in their unknown depths, threatening to ground or sink our vessel. Liam was below while Eddie and I maneuvered the boat between coral heads looking for a safe place to drop anchor. Small waves broke on shallow coral 100 yards further out to sea on a long and exposed reef lying north-south, parallel to the island. We eventually found a strip of sand aligned with the light wind and long enough to set anchor on the upwind side and still have the boat floating over sand in deep water. The water here was about 30' deep and so clear that the bottom was quite visible from the deck of *Monkey's Uncle*, which fueled a great excitement within me. This is exactly what I wanted to do while in The Bahamas: dive and explore coral reef in clear water.

After dropping the two anchors from the bow, I put on my snorkeling gear and jumped in to check that they were properly set.

I looked around for sharks but saw none. Eddie had mentioned that this was a location where tour guides fed the sharks while tourists watched, which any biologist will tell you is never a good idea. When wildlife associate people with food, they lose their fear of humans and are much more likely to attack. I kept a wary eye out for them as I inspected the anchors and dug them further into the sand. I knew "the man" as Eddie called the sharks, would be watching me whether I saw them or not. However the water in The Bahamas is very clear and therefore sharks can see a swimmer from far away, and they generally keep clear of us. It is well-known that sharks generally go out of their way to avoid people, and that if sharks generally wanted to eat people, we wouldn't be able to swim in the ocean at all.

~~~

I swim off to the nearest patch of coral, about 30 yards away from the anchors, impatient and excited to see some coral and fish, sharks or no sharks. The first coral structure I come to is about 20' across and 8' high, in about 30' of water - an ancient craggy mass of dead coral with both soft and hard corals growing on top of the dead along with algae and various other odd life-forms. Brain coal, fire coral and some plate-like corals are still alive, although as I see everywhere most is dead or dying.

Still many colorful fish swim about, most wary of me, an alien in their midst. A school of blue-chromis, slender and bright electric-blue fish about 3 inches long, swim in the clear water above the reef, dining on a fare invisible to me. Yellow wrasse, bright and small, cigar-shaped, school close to a brain coral, watched over by a large male with a blue head. These fish stay in one area and are visited by larger fish from whom the small and slender wrasse pick off parasites, removing them from the scales and even the gills of the larger fish, who sit still and agape like patients at the dentist. This is a behavior I would very much like to get on video, but have yet to do so. I intended on this trip to mount my camera to a tripod or something heavy and stable and set it on the bottom while I went to the surface so I could film the wrasse at work without me around to disturb their cleaning station.

I am reminded of snorkeling in the Dry Tortugas as a child when a school of these little fish mistook the hair on my legs for worms and tried to pick them off of me while I swam past their cleaning station in a forest of elkhorn coral.

A pair of surgeonfish, dark brown and disc-shaped with pouty mouths, swims away from me. Yellow rays of sunlight penetrate the bright blue water. All around me are the most beautiful shades of blue, darker in places, lighter in others. As I swim to the surface, I spin slowly around and around, taking in the blues all about.

I investigate numerous isolated patches of coral, all in

about 25 feet of clear water separated by undulating sand. The occasional lone barracuda patrols the areas in between. Each reef has a similar population of inhabitants, but with unique arrangements.

Eventually I swim to a large reef, part of the barrier-reef structure on the Atlantic side of the islands, that rises to within five feet of the surface of the clear water. A school of blue tang, darker than I have seen elsewhere, swims around, going about some important business known only to them. Some are dark blue, others border on violet. All have bright blue fins. They make an audible "snap" sound as they turn and change direction together. I have never heard this sound before and am mesmerized, as any sound underwater is unusual.

blue tang

A queen angelfish sees me and hides in a crack. I point my camera and flashlight at the odd creature. Its tail, still visible as it hides, is a brilliant yellow and framed by the blue borders on yellow fins above and below. It turns and looks at me, illuminated by my light. We make eye-contact. I am marveling at its beauty, but what does it see? Its body is yellow, its mouth blue. She has black eyes and a blue crown ringed in violet on her forehead above her face. This fish is a work of art, with blue scales fading to yellow, white and black accents, bright blue in places, luscious colors. The species is one of many anecdotal proofs of a great creative force in nature.

She hides deeper in the cave and I swim on, holding my breath, into the school of blue tang.

A shifting school of blues and dark violets keeps a small distance from me as I invade its space. I follow three blue tang under a ledge and there encounter some of my favorite fish. Royal gramma, small and remarkably beautiful with a purple head and yellow body, red-orange in between, live upside down and underneath ledges in pairs or small groups. This extraordinary fish in unique in its beauty, inverted stance, and in that the male broods eggs in his mouth. They largely disregard me as I shine my light on them and stare through my mask.

Patches of green and white algae decorate the reef like little gardens, red polka-dotted coral competes for space with yellow-green lettuce-like algae that sway in the shifting current. A grey snapper with yellow fins approaches me, then turns back into the dark cave from which it came. I swim up to the top of the reef and see a purple sea fan, more blue tang, and a yellow and blue Spanish hogfish.

Two yellow brain coral, round and big, covered in randomly-curving ridges, jut out from the forest of sea fans, soft corals and algae. They really do look like brains. Another queen angelfish looks at me then backs into a dark crevice in the reef. Everywhere are caves and corals and odd unknown life-forms. It's hard to decide where to look next.

I catch only a quick glimpse of a graysby, a member of

the grouper family, green and brown and covered in red spots, as it darts into a cave. Yellow goatfish mill about in the sand around the reef, looking for buried food, using their barbels which protrude like downward-swooping moustaches from their mouths, digging for their next meal.

The most bizarre fish I see on the reef is a lone spotted trunkfish, a white- and brown-spotted member of the aptly-named boxfish family. These fish are oddly rectangular in shape with body-armor of hexagonal plates. They have a small mouth protruding from their face, from which they shoot jets of water attempting to expose worms and various other invertebrates from the bottom of the sea, where they dwell. They have a strange way of swimming, moving their caudal (tail) fin not back and forth but instead with a vertical wave motion called sculling.

Another odd-looking reef-dweller common to the Caribbean is the porcupine fish. One swims slowly by, looking at me with a big red eye. These fish are slow but fearless, as is the boxfish, because they possess an impenetrable two-part defense of both spines and the ability to inflate from their normal loaf-of-bread shape to that of a basketball-with-spikes shape. They do this by quickly swallowing copious amounts of water. These fish are both pelagic (inhabiting open-ocean waters) and reef dweller, yet are entirely pelagic in the early stages of their life. They are predators of shellfish, and are in turn eaten, when young, by larger predators including marlin.

Stoplight parrotfish swim solo along the bottom, noisily munching on algae and coral polyps scraped off the reef. Curiously, most sand in all the tropics, enjoyed by beach-goers and preferred by sailors as an anchoring-medium, is crushed and digested coral excreted through the anus of parrotfish.

~~~

I don't know how long I stayed in this aquatic playground, or how many times I dove. I had to force myself to stay on the surface long enough to recover between dives, before going back down for more. The attraction of the underwater world is powerful, magnetic, like the voice of my mother when I was young; when you hear it, you must go to it.

After many dives, I eventually felt spent, and after my last dive my legs felt numb, and I decided to head back to the boat. One should not push their luck while freediving, and any odd physical symptom should be viewed as a reason to quit while ahead (by this I mean quitting while you are still alive, because the only penalty in freediving is death by drowning after passing out underwater).

Back on the boat, we weighed anchor and Eddie used the GPS to retrace our circuitous route through the coral heads. It was nearing sundown and the angle of the sun was now such that we could neither see underwater nor distinguish between sand bottom (deep water) and coral patches upon which we might run aground.

~~~

The following morning we turned and headed out through the crystal-clear blue water towards Whale Cay Channel and into the Atlantic Ocean. Emergent rocks, jagged and threatening, were visible on both sides of the channel within 100 yards of our fragile craft. I pondered how much easier GPS had made sailing. While we simply followed a dotted line on our monitor screen, earlier sailors would have been frantically taking bearings to landmarks, consulting paper charts, marking their positions with pencils and parallel rulers, and generally staying focused on all aspects of navigation while negotiating such a narrow pass.

As Whale Cay, a rocky island with waves crashing into it, passed on our starboard side, we put out a fishing line from a round hand-reel and continued heading out to sea so that we could set sail, instead of motor, on the next leg of the day's journey. The hand-line is the way most of the world fishes; rods and reels are perhaps reserved for recreational fishermen who enjoy complicated mechanical devices. The hand-line is simplicity itself, consisting of a round plastic hoop around which sturdy fishing line is wound. The lure is tied to the end, perhaps on a steel leader. When trolling behind a boat, all the line is let out, the hoop is tied loosely to the boat, and a rubber band, which breaks when a fish bites, attaches the line to the boat. When the rubber band snaps, we know we have a fish, untie the hoop from the boat, and with gloves on, pull the fish in while winding the line back in onto the plastic hoop. This device made me wonder why fishing rods and reels were even invented.

It wasn't long before the rubber band snapped, the rope caught the hoop, and Liam put on the orange gloves. He easily reeled in a schoolmaster snapper as I took pictures, him stating that the hand line just paid for itself. Now all of us felt like expensive rods and reels were superfluous, at least for casual fishermen like ourselves.

~~~

As we sailed through the shallow water leading to Loggerhead Channel, our depth gauge failed. This is a very necessary piece of equipment and not having it working can cause one to run aground and possibly do great damage to the boat. I knew the glass window, through which it sent out its signal on the bottom of the boat, was fouled, because I saw it while snorkeling that morning.

As we sailed along at 6 knots in the Atlantic, I jokingly said "Put a line out from the bow and one from the stern and I'll clean it while we are underway." Eddie immediately secured lines to the stern and bow, threw them out into the water, and looked at me expectantly. He had taken me seriously and now I had to live up to my word.

I got out my mask, snorkel and fins, found a pot-scrubber in the galley, and made my way to the bow. Eddie slowed the boat, under sail now, to 2 knots, and I jumped in over the port (windward) side near the bow with a scrubber in my right hand and a dock line in my left. Two knots may not sound very fast, but I was immediately being dragged beside the boat and had little control of my orientation.

My first effort at swimming under the hull was ineffective; my angle to the current was wrong and I was being pushed away from the boat instead of under it. My second effort was a little better, and by the third try I had adjusted the angle of my body so the moving water pushed me under the boat. I found the transducer window and scrubbed furiously before letting go of the line and quickly drifting to the stern, where I grabbed the line off the back of the boat and pulled myself to the ladder off the swim platform. I held on to the swim ladder and let myself be dragged behind the boat for a minute while I watched the bottom go by. The underwater scenery was beautiful in clear blue water, which was about 20' deep with sand, grass and various lonely corals, rocks, and conch passing by on the bottom - a brief glimpse at a different world.

With the depth-meter back to life, we sailed southeast past Whale Cay and through Loggerhead Channel, a one-half-mile wide channel between Whale Cay and Loggerhead Cay, and back into the pristine and beautiful Sea of Abaco. The white-sand bottom in this area gave the water a mystical bright turquoise-blue color. The whole sea was glowing like a back-lit sapphire, yet more majestic and awe-inspiring than any mere gem ever was.

We landed a mutton snapper on the hand-line before tacking to port near Marsh Harbour, the third-largest city in the Bahamas. I was a bit worried that the guys would want to stop at Marsh Harbour, and I was relieved when we sailed on by. I don't have anything against Marsh Harbour, but I was not in the Bahamas to visit cities.

We passed astern of a sailboat flying a huge multi-colored spinnaker as we sailed east, following the suggested route on our chartplotter bearing 82 degrees to the pass between Man-O-War Cay and Matt Lowe's Cay, passing just north of Point Set Rock. Elbow Cay was our destination, and after consulting the Abaco Cruising Guide we decided to anchor somewhere near White Sound. We changed course to 162 degrees towards White Sound, again following the suggested route on both our chartplotter and the Abacos Cruising Guide.

Standing on the bow, peering through binoculars like the explorer as which I like to see myself, I located Porgie Rock in the distance, the only obstacle on our charts. It was easy to spot as it was about 40' across and emerging out of the water - definitely something to avoid contact with. The chart also showed a shallow bar extending north and south of the rock.

However, the depth, or lack thereof, turned out to be the real obstacle. While the chart indicated the mean low water was no less than 6', our newly-cleaned depth meter fell to 5', then 4'. I stood on the bowsprit peering into the clear shallow water, trying in vain to determine if the water in front of us was deep enough for *Monkey's Uncle* pass through. Liam was getting worried and asked me to use the binoculars to read the name of a yacht passing through another channel ahead of us to port. I identified it as the Nauticuss, a stately white sloop. Liam then hailed the Nauticuss on the VHF and described our situation. "You are heading for shallows, I'd turn around and use the northern approach" was the reply.

Headstrong and perhaps foolhardy, we pressed on. We were all anxious to get to the anchorage and surf on the side of the island exposed to the Atlantic and its waves. The depth meter dropped to 3.5', and we hoped this was the depth under our keel, as we drew 4' 11", but we were not sure. "At least it's low tide" I remarked "because if we run aground at low tide we can wait for the tide to come in and lift us off the bottom. If we run aground at high tide we're screwed."

We did not run aground, due only to luck and not to seamanship, and proceeded south along the inside channel to Dorros Cove, where we quickly dropped two anchors. I jumped in with my mask, aligned the anchors with the boat and buried them both in the sand. I noticed what appeared to be a 2" cable that was within 2' of our Danforth anchor, another stroke of luck that we didn't snag it.

We had about one hour to sunset and quickly got our surfboards ready. We planned to paddle out through Tilloo Cut and surf the reef next to the inlet. Our first obstacle was crossing Tahiti Beach. Tahiti Beach is a spit of sand and palm trees dividing our cove from Tilloo Cut, as beautiful and picturesque a place as there ever was. The approach was very shallow, I was paddling my board by hand, Eddie was right behind me on an SUP, and Liam was following with an SUP and a shortboard in tow.

Eddie and I picked up our boards as we walked briskly across the white sand of Tahiti Beach, gingerly stepping across sharp rocks on the far side. We got back in the water, again very shallow, and proceeded towards the rocks of Tilloo Cut as the sun approached the horizon. Tilloo Cut was divided from the shallow and sand-bottomed waters around Tahiti Beach by a large rock with shallow coral on both sides. We had to choose which side of this rock to paddle across, and the choice was not obvious. Both had small breaking waves indicating very shallow water, and my board had a 9-inch fin on the back. Of the two entrances to the cut, I chose the left and closer passage, a pass between large, sharp, and craggy rocks with small waves breaking over coral visible in 1-2' of water. I wasn't sure if I was going to be able to paddle across it, and I had to be very careful not to hit the coral with my hands, but I made it across without incident.

Inside Tilloo Cut the water was deep and we paddled hard against the incoming tide and slowly made our way through the unfamiliar cut and towards the Atlantic. Rock walls bordered the cut, which was about 100 yards wide. Eddie had been here 9 years prior, but it was terra-incognita for me and Liam. The adventure-level was high, unknown currents and rocks awaited, and the likelihood of sharks feeding in inlets like this is always high. But as Florida surfers, we were used to the greater danger of sharks in the murky waters of home, while the water was quite clear and on our large boards we did not resemble their normal fare.

Eddie and I paddled, me laying on my belly, he standing upright and using a paddle. We passed a high jagged cliff topped with large and colorful houses on Elbow Cay to our left. To our right was Tilloo Cay, dominated by nature and without houses. Waves broke angrily on a rock where the waters of the cut met those of the Atlantic, producing a short but rideable-looking left. I tried to stay behind this rock and out of the main current as I paddled hard for the ocean and hopefully some surfing action on the outside.

Eddie and I fought the currents and waves and eventually made it out of the cut and into the Atlantic Ocean. As the sky darkened with the coming sunset we caught a few choppy and unorganized waves and wondered where Liam was. Then we saw him standing on a cliff of sharp jagged-looking rock, peering out to sea, shortboard in arm. I didn't think he would make it to the water that way, but he found some wooden boards on the beach and used them to cross the sharp rocks to the water and soon joined us. He had walked across the island instead of paddling through Tilloo Cut. We eventually moved to the inside and caught a few waves off the rock at the end of the cut, then rode the current of the incoming tide effortlessly back towards home, through the cut and across the shallow coral between the big rocks, all while facing another glorious sunset. We walked across the white sand of Tilloo Beach, only about 20 yards wide, and paddled to *Monkey's Uncle*, where we ate dinner in paradise.

~~~

The following morning, after consulting the charts in the cruising guide, I decided to go on a solo mission to freedive on the barrier reef in the deeper water on the ocean-side of Elbow Cay, north of Tilloo Cut. I packed my backpack with my snorkeling gear, camera and anchor, then started paddling with my kayak paddle for Tilloo Cut and the Atlantic Ocean beyond.

Immediately I spotted a dolphin, paddled towards it and readied my video camera. The majestic creature lazily swam under my board, turning on its side, exposing its white belly and looking at me. I held my video camera, attached to a two-foot stick, underwater and filmed the dolphin close-up as it swam under me, beside me, checking me out.

I was so excited and happy to have gotten this video, but sometimes cameras have their own agenda and the video was lost. I think this was because I turned the camera off right after taking the video, thinking that I needed to save the battery, perhaps while the video was still being saved. This is how lessons are learned in the school of hard knocks. Cameras can break your heart.

I then proceeded out against the current, through Tilloo cut, and then turned north, paddling along the coast of Elbow Cay about one half mile offshore, alone with my first love, nature. The water was clear and I was looking for coral. Bright blue-green water indicated sand on the bottom, fuzzy darker water indicated grass, and light brown water indicated rock. I paddled on. I was looking for colors in the water denoting coral on the bottom: the orange of elkhorn or yellow of brain coral near the surface. But after paddling a long way, I eventually dropped anchor about one mile north of Tilloo cut off what I assumed was the Abaco Inn, visible on a rocky bluff with a surf break between my small craft and the shore. I stayed far out enough to lessen the effect of the swells while I dove. The water was about 40' deep. I geared up, and also got my VHF radio out of my dry-bag and hailed the *Monkey's*

Uncle to check in.

"*Monkey's Uncle, Monkey's Uncle*; Pauly Dangerous"

"*Monkey's Uncle* here, go ahead Pauly Dangerous"

"I'm about one mile north of Tilloo Cut and about a mile off what appears to be the Abaco Inn, ready to dive"

"OK Pauly Dangerous, have fun and stay safe!"

"Will do, over"

After putting on my booties, fins, dive-knife, weight belt, mask, and snorkel, I eased into the water, carefully and quietly, so as not to attract any unwanted attention from large predators. I looked all around to make sure a shark wasn't right behind me, but as always, there was nothing to see. I always followed this protocol when entering the water.

~~~

From the surface, the bottom appears featureless, but as I descend, flat rock with shallow ledges underneath come into view. Algae covers the rock along with hydras and soft corals in lonely patches. The water has a green tint and visibility is about 80'. I continue to swim straight down and fish become visible, swimming about, pushed back and forth by the powerful swell even at this depth.

The water is about 50 feet deep, and I pause at the bottom to watch the local residents. I see blue tang, stoplight parrotfish, yellowhead and bluehead wrasse, Spanish hogfish, the fabulous royal gramma, a lone blue parrotfish pooping sand, four-eyed butterflyfish, and audible bluestriped grunts.

I try to set the video camera on the bottom so I can return to the surface and catch the fish in action without me there to disturb them. But the surge from the swell keeps knocking my camera over. In the future, I will need to mount my camera to something heavy in order to get this sort of footage.

While not spectacular in scenery, this dive is a real treat and the adventure-level is high. I am by myself in the open ocean, a mile offshore in unfamiliar waters on a 12' surfboard freediving solo. I feel alive, vibrant, fully conscious. I am doing what I was meant to do: explore, adventure, commune with nature, take risks, overcome fear.

~~~

The following morning, we moved our floating adventure-headquarters north to Hopetown Harbour, where we topped off our fuel and water tanks, then tied to a mooring ball surrounded by a wide variety of sailboats: a stately and sleek Tartan from Brazil, an Island Packet also from St. Augustine, and a brown sailboat registered in Colorado. A huge catamaran sat on the edge of the crowd. A white Beneteau with in-mast furling and a modern design sat still in the light breeze, looking like a greyhound that wanted to run. Our Hunter stood out with the vast array of surfboards lashed to the fore-deck and lifelines. We were all different people with different stories on varied boats, but in the same harbor.

Monkey's Uncle

I was keen to dive the barrier reef off the north tip of Elbow Cay, so I readied my gear and said goodbye to the guys. Instead of taking Eddie's advice and crossing the narrow island on foot (as I did the following day) I opted for the "scenic route" through the harbor and another mile and a half past Anna Cay, a small island completely covered by a single pink house, through Cook's Cove, and to Hopetown Point and the Atlantic beyond.

The wind was blowing against me and so I paddled close to shore and in the lee of docks and boats along the way. I passed a classic Abaco sailing dinghy anchored in Cook's Cove and took some photographs. I passed a local man working on a boat in a driveway and we waved to each other, a great smile on his face, no doubt wondering what I was up to on my strange craft, backpack lashed down in front of me.

The wind and the waves increased as I rounded the point and faced the ocean, and I pressed on for deeper and hopefully calmer waters. Coral was everywhere beneath me, in front of me, behind me. This was a vast reef. I continued until I was about a mile offshore and in about 30-40 feet of water, where I dropped anchor over sand. Swells lifted and dropped my craft; current pulled the anchor rode tight.

~~~

I dive to check the anchor, which has dragged across the sand and is hooked firmly under a rock ledge, however the rode is in contact with coral closer to the surface, and I have to move the anchor to protect both the coral from the rode and the rode from the coral. Losing my board here would make for a long swim back to land and a long walk back to the harbor.

I have to dive down to the anchor, pick it up and then swim up to where it is tangled in the coral. While holding it and all the rode, I untangle the rode from the coral, careful not to break any of the coral, and them swim up-current dragging everything, including my surfboard, to a spot where I can set the anchor in sand and not get the rode tangled in the coral.

After wrestling with the anchor and rode in the current, I rest and catch my breath, then I dive.

Deep craggy coral with caves, ledges, and various tall and curvy structures dominate the scenery. Soft corals, purple and green and blue, dance like prehistoric plants swaying in the current. Fish swim all around. Colors swirl and sway. Purple sea fans rock back and forth with the swell. Yellow brain corals look pensive, while plate corals drape and undulate over structures like Dali's clock. Fish known and unknown show themselves, hide, then peek back out at me. I occasionally look behind me for sharks, but see none. Sponges of various colors along with many species of algae, hydras and tunicates cover the ancient dead coral deep on the reef in a cacophony of myriad colors. A Nassau grouper, grey and white striped, isn't sure whether it is best to watch me or to hide in a cave, so it does a bit of both.

This is a big barrier reef with coral everywhere, like a mountain-range of coral structure stretching endlessly in both directions parallel to the islands, separating them from the Atlantic Ocean. The reef teems with vibrant life. Massive ledges of coral overhang the depths, shading the ancient coral below. Red, green, orange, grey, blue, violet – all the colors are represented here.

I poke my camera with the flashlight strapped below it into every cave and crevice that I can find. What I can't see on the dive I can look at later on the video. I hope to catch strange and surprised cave-dwelling creatures on video. The light not only illuminates the inside of caves, but it also brings out colors otherwise invisible to the eye at depth. Water filters out light and as depth increases and the longer wavelengths go first. Things that would be red appear blue-grey after about ten feet deep. Orange goes away next, followed be yellow and then green. After about sixty feet, everything appears blue-grey. But a flashlight brings all these colors out, and I am glad that I have one.

Parts of the reef resemble a Dr. Seuss forest, with odd plant-like soft corals rising above the reef like menorahs, many-fingered hands or the antennae of moths. Other places are moonscapes, with hard undulating surfaces and strange curved patterns. It all appears otherworldly, and the soft corals and small fish sway back and forth with the swell. Near the surface, the current is stronger and little fish move about four feet in one direction and then four feet in the other, pushed and pulled all day and all night by the swell, originally generated by wind on the surface, which is created by the convective forces caused by uneven heating of the Earth's atmosphere, heat which comes from the sun by the fusion of hydrogen nuclei into helium.

~~~

After many dives, I packed up and started paddling for home, but I could clearly see colorful live reef structures rising from the bottom thirty feet down to nearly the surface as I paddled across the water. The reef was too tempting, and I stopped, anchored, and dove again. There was just so much to see, I couldn't stop. It was all I could do to rest between dives long enough to retain some semblance of safety.

Eventually, I worked my way into shallower water closer to the cut. I pulled up and stowed the anchor, attached the surfboard leash (ten feet long) to my leg with its velcro strap, and drifted across a shallow section of reef. I paused by kicking against the current to watch a school of bluehead wrasse, hoping to see them pick the parasites off another fish. Instead I saw a lizardfish dart off the bottom and snatch a wrasse in its gaping jaw while the others raced briefly away, only to return to the same coral head seconds later, clearly accepting the death of their comrade as a normal occurrence. A barracuda watched me as I watched the wrasse.

The trip back to the harbor and *Monkey's Uncle* was a delightful and easy downwind cruise. I waved again to the man working on the boat, and he waved back, glad, I'm sure, to see that I had returned from whatever I was up to in the ocean. I had so enjoyed the dive-adventure that when I got back to the boat, I immediately began planning another dive for the following day. But this time, I decided, I would not paddle all the way around the island, but instead walk across it. It was very narrow, so narrow, I found out later that day, that I had to laugh at myself for paddling all the way around the day before.

Eddie and Liam, that afternoon, wanted to kiteboard on the Atlantic side of the island, and I agreed to be their photographer. I paddled my board the short distance to the dock as they rowed over in the dinghy. The island is only about 100 yards across at this point, and a short street leads to a sandy beach which looks out to the reef on which I dove earlier in the day.

They set up their kites and zipped back and forth across the shallow water between the beach and the reef while I took pictures and video from the sand. Liam was riding his foiling kiteboard, and he and his board hovered a few feet above the surface of the water as he sped along, pulled by the wind in his kite.

~~~

Videography is a wonderful way of sharing personal adventures with those that can't be there, letting family and friends, strangers too, live vicariously through my adventures. But it can also be heartbreaking, because sometimes technology fools us into thinking it is functioning when in fact it is not.

The first clue I had was the ominous message "SD Card Error" on my GoPro underwater video camera, which I noticed 90% of the way through this day's freediving session on the barrier reef 1/2 mile off of Hopetown. I had paddled my surfboard the short jaunt from our boat to a public dock in the harbor, paddling on my knees with a kayak paddle, black hat and dark sunglasses on, past the wide variety of moored sailboats. I climbed up onto the dock, pulled up my surfboard and crossed the very narrow island to the beach on the Atlantic side. I paddled out another 1/2 mile across alternating patches of bright blue water over sand and dark blue water over coral to the fabled Abaco Barrier Reef, not far from where I dove the previous day.

It was still morning, the sky was blue and cloudless, the swell of the previous day had died, and the wind was light. I was alone in nature, and all was right in the world.

The water depth over sand was 20-30', but coral heads nearly emerged in some places and were quite visible as I paddled around the shallow ones and across the deeper ones. Soon I saw what I was looking for, the elusive elkhorn coral, reaching up from the depths like the massive orange hands of

Neptune himself.

Throughout the Caribbean elkhorn coral has been dying off (as are other species, like staghorn, of which I saw none) to the point of local extinction in many areas, and it was heartwarming to see it alive and well here. Coral worldwide is dying off at an alarming rate, so seeing any alive is a real treat. Elkhorn and staghorn coral are both critically endangered (as I write this in the year 2017) and thus very highly vulnerable to extinction. For the last 10,000 years, these two species of coral have been largely responsible for much of the creation of coral reefs in the Caribbean. I encourage you, reader, to go and see live coral reef while you still can, and do whatever is in your power to protect what we have left.

As its name implies, elkhorn coral resembles the many-lobed and oddly-shaped antlers of elk (the terrestrial mammal that looks like a large deer), and is similar in proportion, yet much larger than an entire elk when the coral is mature. It is a hard coral, but its surface appears soft and fuzzy, made so by the little tentacles of the cnidarians (pronounced with a silent c) that make up the coral, and is dull orange in color. Coral structures are colonies of little members of the jellyfish phylum (Cnidaria) who attach to a structure and build a little shell around themselves, sticking their tentacles out into the water to catch food. Their structures provide shelter for other creatures like fish and lobster and thousands of others. They are considered a keystone species, as they create the primary habitat of many other species, and their removal from an ecosystem could usher in the collapse of the entire ecosystem.

While much of the elkhorn was dead, I found small patches of it alive, and this reef right off Hopetown had the most live elkhorn that I saw on the trip. There was also plenty of fire coral, brain coral, and a yellow plate coral. Soft corals, which look like plants or fans, were abundant on most of the reefs. However algae, a harbinger of reef-death, was dominating almost everywhere. When nutrient levels are too high, algae outcompete coral. High nutrient levels are a result of sewage and fertilizer running off from land. This is perhaps why the water off the beach had more live coral than the waters nearer the cut where I dove the day before, where water from harbors washed out into the ocean.

I dove all over these magnificent reef clusters, rising from 20-50' of water almost to the surface, until I was satiated. However, towards the end of my session, I noticed the "SD Card Error" warning on my camera. I turned it off, then back on again and dove three more times. These last three videos were the only ones I got from here, which is a shame because this was the healthiest reef of the trip. On YouTube can be found a long video of my freedives from this trip, ("Pauly Dangerous Freedives The Bahamas" https://youtu.be/mNU3xPhFiuw).

~~~

Back at the harbor, Liam and I climbed the Hopetown Lighthouse for a look around from way up high. We could see all the boats in the harbor, the pastel-colored houses of Hopetown, the many different shades of blue, green and turquoise of the surrounding waters, a small hidden harbor (a "hurricane hole") within Hopetown Harbor, a dry-dock with boats being stored and repaired, Man-O-War Cay to the north, Tilloo Cay to the south, Lubbers Quarters Cay and Abaco Island to the east. The lighthouse was unstaffed and the intricate and well-oiled machinery consisting of many gears and rods of the lighthouse were in plain view at the top. A pink and white spiral staircase with arched windows looking outside led us up and back down.

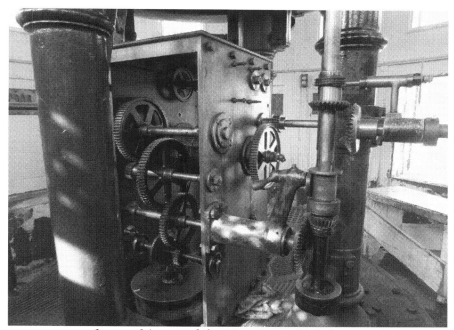

the machinery of the Hopetown Lighthouse

As we walked back out the dock to our paddleboards, a massive tanker was pulling in to the nearby fuel dock. I had to stop and photograph Liam, juxtaposed on his relatively tiny SUP, with the gigantic and archaic steel tanker right behind him.

big ship, little ship

We cast off our mooring and left Hopetown to sail through South Man-O-War Cut and into the Atlantic. The cut was narrow but deep and had breaking waves on both sides, so we decided that we should return the next day for further exploration and maybe a surf.

We dedicated the afternoon to sailing and figuring out the whisker pole. This is a large pole that attaches on one end to the jib-sheet near the clew of the headsail (the lower aft corner) and on the other end to the mast. It holds the headsail out and keeps it stable while sailing downwind. Eddie and I wrestled with the pole, trying to attach it to the headsail without getting hit with it. We made the novice mistake of not attaching a lift-line to the pole, so we had very little control over it. It's best to study techniques like this in a book before attempting to figure them out through trial and error, especially on a large sailboat where the penalties for mistakes are high.

We sailed back in through the same cut, while I rode

sitting on the small seat in the bow pulpit above the anchors and leaning back against the furled headsail, the beauty of The Bahamas completely surrounding me. The white sand, brown rocks and green trees of Man-O-War Cay dominated the scenery. The sun was setting behind us as we sailed back towards Hopetown, casting bright orange and red light over the sky-blue water.

It was dark as we anchored in a small cove just south White Sound in shallow water with no other boats around. That night the sky was clear and the stars were out in full-force, along with Mars shining its slightly red light our way, and the misty trail of the Milky Way cutting across the sky.

~~~

After the brilliant sun rose in the blue sky for yet another day in paradise, we set sail for South Man-O-War Cut, with intentions to surf and dive on the reef we had seen the previous day. On the south edge of the cut, with an incoming tide, we dropped both bow and stern anchors in sand, so as not to swing into the channel and impede traffic. I dove in to set them, but they were both already buried. The water was extremely clear, and we could see a small wave breaking on the reef to the south. We got on our surfboards and paddled over.

Surfing in the clear water was a real treat. The bottom was completely visible and the small waves were transparent; the sky shown through as the waves approached; the colorful coral drifted by underneath as we rode above. I caught a couple waves, but with all the reef around us beckoning, I was anxious to dive, and soon went back to the boat to fetch my dive-gear while Eddie and Liam continued to ride their SUP's on the nearly-invisible waves.

I soon found a nice patch of reef and anchored in the sand next to it. I always drop anchor in the sand so as not to damage the coral. Coral should not be touched, rather it should only be observed.

~~~

The water here is clear, and the coral is healthy, although the patches of reef are dominated by soft corals. A barracuda watches me from a distance of about 30' as I watch the other fish. Blue chromis swim above the reef, royal gramma occupy the underside of ledges, brown doctorfish swim in and out of the coral. As I swim along the bottom and around a corner I see the unmistakable tail fin of a shark, which is laying on the bottom between two large rocks. However this is but a nurse shark, harmless and docile. I take video of it as I slowly swim by, keeping a respectful distance even though I want to put my camera right in its face. I also spot an elusive black grouper which hides before I can get close enough to film it. Perhaps, I think, the grouper has seen too many of its friends speared by humans to allow me to get anywhere near it.

This is a vast fairyland of color and movement hiding beneath the comparatively featureless surface of the ocean. Admission is granted to those who seek it, but very few seek, and I am the only human here. The fish see me, and I see the fish, but they never get to see my world. I have the advantage of getting to visit theirs, and this is a treat of immeasurable value.

I spot a small blue-violet fish swimming erratically within the confines of an orange fire-coral. This is one of my favorite reef-fish: a juvenile yellowtail damselfish. Its bright iridescent blue spots look like stars in a dark night sky. The fire coral in which it swims is the shape of romaine lettuce leaves, separated from the bunch and spaced vertically a few inches apart, creating a labyrinth where small fish can find refuge. Fire coral is hard and orange, but its top edge is white, and it stings like a jellyfish when touched, hence the name. The swell in the water pulls me back and forth as I point my camera at the juvenile damselfish, and I see two of them now. I must be very careful not to brush up against the fire coral as I move with the water. The fish look too fabulous to be real, but real they are, living treasures more wonderful than any human work of art.

As I rise from this magical scene, I pass through a school of yellow wrasse, skinny and shaped like a human's pinky finger. They swim around excitedly, each moving as an individual, all in different directions, yet they all stay within a small territory. Blue tang swim in and out of view, these are a light sky-blue fading to light grey in the center of the body, not the dark blue-violet of the ones I saw off Manjack Cay. A lone Spanish hogfish emerges from the tangled mass of coral, then disappears within. Purple sea fans are all around, singular flat structures like a lady's Japanese fan, but made up of oddly curved lines like veins in an old person's leg. Sea fans are soft corals, and are thus colonies of little cnidarians – jellyfish-like creatures that build a structure around themselves and catch plankton with their very small tentacles.

I am thrilled to find a magnificent elkhorn coral, orange on its underside and white on top, growing like an antler off a mound of ancient and dead coral. Soft corals and sea fans cover the little hill like shrubbery. Yellow wrasse swim all around the elkhorn. I dive deeper, look for royal gramma under ledges, find none and then return to the surface to breathe.

My 12' surfboard is close by, but *Monkey's Uncle* is far away, and appears small on the horizon. But the weather is nice, the sun is shining, and the ocean is calm. I feel quite at home here, and continue to dive. Eddie paddles up on his SUP and joins me for a few dives.

Back underwater, I see a dark shape in the distance; I swim towards it but it moves out of sight before I can identify it. I find an area full of caves and chasms - coral walls undulating vertically and teeming with life surrounding a central sandy area like an arena on the bottom of the sea. A green parrotfish comes to check me out. Its tail has a very bright yellow patch and its fins are decorated with brilliant blue and red accents. It swims into a cave, then comes back out and looks at me again. A lone blue chromis swims over a yellow brain coral that hangs from the side of a wall. I wonder where the rest of its school is; it's probably wondering the same thing.

I shine my flashlight under a big ledge and am greeted by over a dozen royal gramma swimming upside down all within an inch of the coral roof above them. Yellow, red and green coral and algae decorate the background. These fish are so captivatingly beautiful that each time I find them I stay and observe them until I am out of breath and need to return to the surface.

Diving on this reef between elbow Cay and Man-O-War Cay has been a truly wonderful experience. The water is extremely clear, the reef seems endless, the weather is beautiful, and the distance from shore gives the place a feeling of true wilderness. I dive until I am exhausted and completely satiated with the underwater world. It has been a wonderful and priceless adventure and I have a big smile on my face as I paddle about a half mile back to our sailboat.

~~~

Back aboard *Monkey's Uncle* we found ourselves stuck in the inlet, held firmly in place by a strong current and a stern anchor that would not budge. The current was pulling hard on an incoming tide and we could not release the bow anchor until the stern anchor was up, otherwise we would swing into the reef. A normal procedure might be to let out enough rode on the bow anchor to drift right over the stern anchor and then pull it straight up, but the stern anchor was not directly down-current of the bow anchor, so it remained off to port and under tension.

I put the stern-anchor rode on the port jib-winch and

began cranking it in. The tension on the line was high and it even made the boat heel towards the anchor, which was not budging at all. I thought about diving on it to try to set it free, but there was no way to relieve tension on its line and I knew it was buried deep in the sand anyway. All I could think of to do was to winch it in, so I cranked away until the anchor finally gave. When we pulled it aboard we were dismayed to see that its arm was bent almost 90 degrees. We then pulled the bow anchor up with the windlass and returned to Elbow Cay, anchoring at Tilloo Cut in view of the Atlantic.

~~~

The scene could have been a postcard or an advertisement for The Bahamas: Tahiti Beach with its white sand, turquoise water on both sides of the narrow, curved beach, palm trees to the left, bright blue water to the right, brown jagged rocks and the dark blue Atlantic in the background. Small boats were pulled up to the sand and men in trunks and women in bikinis lazed about while dogs and children played in the shallow water and on the sand.

~~~

As dawn broke the next morning and the stars gave way to the all-powerful sun illuminating Tahiti Beach, Tilloo Cut, Elbow Cay and Lubbers Quarters, I packed my dive gear: mask, snorkel, fins, camera, dive light, knife, neoprene shirt, booties, weight belt, anchor, and VHF radio. All this went into my backpack which I lashed to the board in front of me with a bungee cord. I paddled through Tilloo Cut sitting down with my kayak paddle in search of deep water, which, from studying the charts of the area looking for deep water, I knew was one quarter to one half mile offshore, beyond the outskirts of the inlet.

The tide was with me, going out as I was, making my journey to the Atlantic from the Sea of Abaco relaxing one. In the ocean outside the cut and the boundaries of land I paddled against the light morning wind and small waves while small fishing boats passed me, no doubt wondering what I was doing paddling my surfboard with a kayak paddle into the great blue ocean and away from the safety of land.

When I could no longer see the bottom, I dropped the anchor in its closed position to check the depth, which was about 50' and not enough to satisfy my ambition, as I was looking for a deeper dive than I had done so far. I paddled further from land. The next depth check revealed the water to be about 80', and this seemed like plenty, especially since I was alone and about one half mile from shore, on the edge of my comfort-zone. I geared up, but decided not to use my weight belt, as I did not plan on spending any time on the bottom and wanted a speedy and guaranteed trip back to the surface.

I hovered on the surface for a minute or two, breathing through the snorkel. I had been breathing deeply and slowly during the paddle to relax and oxygenate my body, and I paddled slowly to keep my heart-rate down. I had skipped morning coffee for the same reason and I also skipped breakfast so that my body would not be expending energy in digesting food.

~~~

I roll forward, gently push my right leg into the air, kick with my left, and begin my descent into the abyss. I swim down, slowly straight down, deeper, deeper still. I kick gently, pull the snorkel out of my mouth, pinch my nose and blow little puffs of air into my inner ears - equalizing the pressure continuously as I descend. I try not to think, as the brain uses oxygen when thinking.

At about 60' I become negatively buoyant and descend without having to kick, and at roughly 80' I am at the bottom. I look around in a circle, there are no fish here, no reef, just deep clear water. The bottom is composed only of sand and grass; the only features are wavy parallel lines of grass-free sand, about a foot wide and spaced five feet apart. I don't know why these lines are here. Above me the faint glimmer of the sun shines through the surface of the water creating a unique lighting effect seen only underwater, a shimmering produced by the outlines of the waves on the surface. I feel at home, but my lungs are nearly empty and I can't stay long.

Facing the shimmering light, I gently kick for the surface. As I slowly ascended, my mind and body relax, the air in my lungs expands and I became more and more buoyant, reducing the need to kick the higher I go. I feel like I am flying straight upwards through air, but slowly, like a balloon rising. I think in slow motion and use as little energy as possible. A thin black line leads from the anchor on the bottom back to my surfboard on the surface. Its silhouette, tiny against the background of shimmering light, slowly grows and beckons as I ascended towards the air my lungs crave. I blow out nearly all of the air in my lungs right before surfacing, and as my head emerges from the water I fill them with new air in one giant gulp. I am smiling as I climb aboard my surfboard and pull up the anchor.

~~~

I only dove once out in the deep water off Tilloo Cut, as I felt I should quit while I was ahead. Freediving alone in open water in the ocean is creepy and the first rule of freediving is not to do it alone. Blacking out before reaching the surface is a real possibility, and death will soon follow if no one is there to help. The lungs fill with water, the brain is starved for oxygen and drowning occurs within minutes. So after only one dive I pulled up the anchor and paddled downwind for Tilloo cut and the temporary home of *Monkey's Uncle*, feeling satisfied with my morning adventure. I had faced the unknown, the depths of the ocean, and raw nature. I had seen a place few people, if any, had ever seen, that little section of the ocean and its floor. For a moment I lived on the edge and was now coming back from it, feeling completely alive and happy to be so.

As I faced the cut from offshore, Tilloo Cay, with its ragged brown cliffs topped with green shrubs, rose from the water to the left of Tilloo Cut, and Elbow Cay with its own cliffs topped with pastel colored houses sat to the right.

In the distance I could see waves crashing into the rocky shore of Tilloo Cay, eruptions of white between the blue of the Atlantic and the browns and greens of the island. The sun was bright and reflecting off the dark blue water. The tide was still coming out through the cut, and I had to paddle hard to get back inside. But my surfboard gave little resistance and slid across the moving water and I slowly passed through the narrow and rocky inlet, between the large brown and grey rocks over the shallow and colorful coral, then across the sandy one-foot-deep flats to Tahiti Beach, where a man and his dogs were playing in the shallow sky-blue water. I tipped my hat; he waved. I drug my board across the narrow sandbar that is Tahiti Beach, and returned to *Monkey's Uncle*, where the boys welcomed me home with a breakfast of French toast.

~~~

With full stomachs, we paddled to the Abaco Inn via the waters of White Sound, where a friend of Eddie was staying with his wife. On the way out to the island, a powerboat got confused and meandered out of the channel, almost running aground. Eddie stopped to explain to them the channel markers and the rule of "red right return". When returning to port, one should keep the red channel markers to the right (and the green markers to the left).

Eddie's friend's wife saw us from her bungalow and came out to offer us cold bottles of water. I wanted to drink mine quickly and go surfing, so I gulped down about half of the bottle and was instantly rewarded with the sharp pain in the forehead with which we are all familiar. I just wanted to go surfing, but now I had to stand there on the porch and wait for the ice-cream headache to go away before again attempting to finish the bottle of water. The pain subsided and I put the bottle back to my lips. I needed the water, but again was impatient and suffered the consequences an embarrassing second time.

We walked across the island (only about 50 yards) as golf carts carrying vacationers passed by, arriving at the beach on the Atlantic side. A crude and sloping concrete stairway with steps that were too wide for easy walking led us down to the sandy beach on the north side of the Inn, which sat on a rocky bluff. The sun was intense and the cool water beckoned.

We first paddled out about 100 yards to a spot called Rush Reef, which was just barely breaking with waist-high waves in 4' of clear water. The man from the powerboat joined us on a rented SUP while his wife laid in the sand on the beach. She was the only person on the beach and wore a bright red one-piece bathing suit and a big sun hat, lounging and reading a book while we surfed.

After surfing for a while on the outside, we paddled back to the inside (close to the beach) and surfed Japan's, a fast right point breaking just off the sharp rocky bluff and finishing in water only inches deep over reef. I got a few fun waves here, only contacting the reef with my foot once, but not enough to get cut. The scalding-hot pavement on the walk back across the skinny island was worse on my feet. I did not bring my sandals (or my kayak paddle) because I didn't want to leave anything on the beach. I pictured young thieves peeking out of the bushes, ready to steel whatever we left there. But the beach was a lonely place and completely free of thieves. I think my time surfing in Costa Rica, where you cannot leave your sandals on the beach for even a second, influenced my decision to leave my sandals on the boat, which led to my very hot feet.

~~~

Back onboard *Monkey's Uncle* it was time to move again. Liam and Eddie wanted to go to a bar called Nipper's on Great Guana Cay for a Sunday party one of them had heard about. I wanted to sail south to a marine reserve for more nature, solitude and freediving. But I was outvoted and off we went, sailing north on a port tack past Porgie Rock, Hopetown and Man-O-War Cay.

Three hours later we dropped our two anchors in Fisher's Bay among chartered Catamarans and various monohulls. I dove in and set the anchors, making myself feel useful and enjoying, as always, an excuse to get in the water. The bottom was sand covered in grass, which is difficult for anchors to bite through and required me to push both anchors into the sand. The water was about ten feet deep and so we felt quite safe here. A majestic and shiny teal-green schooner pulled into the bay and anchored further out than us, but close enough for all three of us to recognize its beauty. I stared at it through my binoculars and dreamed of someday traveling the world on such a fine sailboat.

Eager to go to the party, Eddie and Liam paddled to a beach bar on their SUP's as I readied my dive gear then paddled off in another direction to a boat ramp. The ramp was quiet and made of stone with old wooden docks on both sides. It led up to a hot, dry, and sandy street, along which I walked in search of the beach on the ocean side. I passed a lonely self-storage facility with a derelict boat outside, then the road ended at a little resort with purple and yellow cottages. I opted to continue through the little resort to try to get to the beach, even though it meant walking across the yard of one of the beach cottages. I tiptoed through the yard, but when I got to the beach I noticed that the cottage I had walked past was boarded up with plywood on all the windows.

I drew an arrow in the sand pointing at the trail I had used and filled the arrow with seaweed so I could find my way back later. I used to do this in caves while spelunking in WV, a world away, denoting the way out of the cave so as not to get lost underground.

Small but powerful waves broke on the sandy shore, and coral was visible right up to the beach. I used a bungee cord to strap my backpack to the surfboard that I had been carrying on my head (the surfboard was too wide to get an arm around it) and I buckled my sandals to the backpack. I pushed the board into the water and through the shore-break, jumped on and started paddling out into the Atlantic. I then noticed one of my sandals was gone and turned to look back at the beach, where I could see it washing back and forth in the skim, and back to the beach I went, glad that nobody was watching. I retrieved my sandal and put my backpack on my back instead of the board and tried again, and after paddling through the waves I took the heavy backpack off and again strapped it to the board.

I paddled out about a quarter mile offshore in search of the barrier reef, visible by the dark color of the water. After paddling for about 20 minutes, I could hear music from the beach and I could see the bar that I assumed was Nipper's on a tall sand bluff a half mile south of where I entered the water. I checked the bottom with quick looks through my mask, and after spotting reef in about 50' of water, I pulled out the anchor, untangled the line, and dropped it over sand.

"Pauly Dangerous, you got your ears on?" I heard from my VHF. I pulled it out of the drybag.

"Loud and clear" I responded.

"We can see you from Nipper's" Eddie said. Loud music was coming through the VHF and was also audible in the air.

"Cool" I said "I'm glad you guys can see me. I've just dropped anchor and am ready to dive. The bar sounds loud!".

"Have fun, we'll be watching".

I put the radio back in the dry-bag and prepared my dive gear. I got in the water quietly and immediately looked all around in a circle to make sure there were no sharks, but as usual there were none. I would have liked to get one on video (besides the nurse shark that I already had) but I really didn't want to see any while swimming. I relaxed, hovered on the surface, breathing deeply and slowly through my snorkel, then swam down towards the dark mass of reef below.

~~~

Like a glimpse into another world, the reef presents a strange and mystical vista few have seen or will see. Dark and ancient coral heads, geriatric, rise from the depths accenting the clear green-tinted water, which becomes slightly darker with depth. My flashlight pierces the blackness of caves formed throughout eons of coral growing upon their deceased ancestors, the living growing on the backs of the dead in a cycle reminiscent of all life. Colorful reef fish decorate the scene with unlikely hues. A lone queen-angelfish, a bright disk of yellow wearing a blue crown of concentric circles on the forehead sees me from a distance as I descend, camera outstretched, but it slips away into a crack in the reef before I can get close enough for a good look. Brilliant royal gramma live out their inverted lives beneath an overhang, sitting still, sprinting to catch an invisible morsel, sitting still again. A school of chub, a grey fish slightly comical in appearance, its face small out of proportion, swims by, looking at me. I can hear a male stoplight parrotfish, brilliant green with a yellow patch in front its tail fin, as it munches on the hard reef, warily observing me with a dark eye.

I look up from the tangled shapes and hues of the reef and observe the surrounding water - vast, empty. I imagine a shark or two just past my vision, keeping their distance from me, the interloper, but I see none.

The reef, in about fifty feet of water, is tall and dark, complete with caves at the bottom and pillars reaching upward like ancient knobby fingers. Strange corals I can't identify dot the mass. I think I see a large barrel-sponge, but closer inspection reveals it to be an unknown hard coral. Patches of blue-grey finger-coral stand out against the dark surroundings. A huge southern stingray sits motionless on the bottom, looking at me with its chondricthian eyes. I can see its long, sharp, and poisoned barb halfway down its whip-like tail.

Stingrays are harmless if left alone, but if stepped on, speared or hassled, they lash out with their tail and either stab or slash the perpetrator with the barb hidden underneath the tail, which breaks off inside the skin and causes a terrible wound made more painful by the poison. It is one of these docile creatures that killed Steve Irwin, "The Crocodile Hunter" as he grabbed hold of one. It stabbed him in the heart.

I satiate myself with the adventure one can only find in

raw nature before returning to the relative safety of my 12-foot surfboard.

~~~

As I paddled towards the beach, two beautiful women in bikinis walked out from Nippers, across the sand towards the water. This was a good opportunity to meet some ladies, I thought to myself. But as I got closer, they both fell down as a small wave hit their feet. They were laughing and stumbling about, drunk and foolish, and immediately were shorn of their attractiveness. This is my new sober life, better in countless ways, but much lonelier too.

Back on the island I met the guys at Nipper's and was glad I didn't drink anymore. The music was too loud and all the ladies were as drunk and foolish as the girls on the beach. Surely I had much more fun on the reef than they did at the bar, and certainly more fun than I would have had not drinking at Nipper's. It wasn't long before I paddled back to the boat and wrote in my notebook as the sun set over the quiet Sea of Abaco with the silhouette of the majestic teal schooner in the foreground.

~~~

As I emerged from the cabin, coffee cup in hand, blue sky glowing from the morning sun, Eddie was reeling in a fish. Excited for the action, I got out my camera, but we laughed as the catch was but a porcupine puffer-fish, inedible and bizarre-looking. It looked at us with its big eyes and spat the hook out of its humanoid mouth on its own, thank goodness - none of us would have wanted to touch the spikey creature.

We weighed anchor and headed north, passing the schooner on the way out; a man, his wife and their daughter sat on the deck drinking coffee and looking dreamily towards the island as we passed. We set sail on a port tack as we approached Loggerhead Channel and passed into the Atlantic.

Earlier we had agreed that we should go through some sailing maneuvers while out in the open water. So after getting a couple miles out and away from land, we all took turns tacking, gybing, and heaving-to. We also did a man-overboard drill, tossing a blue seat-cushion into the water astern and yelling "man overboard!". The helmsman then had to tack and approach the cushion from downwind, getting close to it while heading into the wind to slow down as one of the others retrieved it with a boathook. This was good practice as it not only drilled us all on the proper man-overboard procedure, but also incorporated various boat-handling skills.

We learned a few things during these drills, like the importance of keeping the windward jib-sheet taut during tacking and gybing to keep it from getting snagged by the whisker pole, which was stowed vertically on the mast; the space beneath it was a trap for the line. We also learned that we have to keep all forward hatches shut while sailing to prevent the jib-sheets from catching on them.

After we went through our drills, we set the whisker pole and sailed downwind wing-on-wing (the mainsail on one side of the boat and the headsail on the opposite, so that they are both exposed to the wind coming from behind the boat) toward Green Turtle Cay. I stood at the bow and peered into the water looking for coral heads as we passed through Two-Rocks Channel, craggy brown islets on both sides of us poking out of the water like flat sharp mushrooms. As we passed through the cut from the mighty Atlantic to the Sea of Abaco the water color changed from dark blue to bright turquoise. The water became darker again as we passed over coral, then brilliant sky-blue where the bottom was covered with white sand, and turtle grass gave the water a misty green color. A flock of small white terns hovered over a patch of water, diving to the water's surface and quickly returning to the air, apparently feeding on a school of small fish.

~~~

No Name Cay came into view to the east, an uninhabited island within a land and sea reserve. I wanted to dive on the reef outside No Name Cay, while Eddie and Liam wanted to kitesurf at neighboring Green Turtle Cay.

While we slowly drifted by, the boys dropped me off, then continued to Green Turtle Cay while I paddled my surfboard toward a bay in the middle of the little island, hoping to find a path across to the ocean-side and access to the barrier reef there. The bay was about a quarter mile across and half a mile wide; the entrance was too shallow for sailboats, and no vessels were inside. A wind blew from the southeast, and I turned right and into the wind, paddling close to the mangrove-lined shore where emergent roots reached down into clear water, burying themselves in the sand. I was thankful that there are no saltwater crocodiles in The Bahamas, because this area reminded me of their habitat [further study has enlightened me that crocodiles are sometimes found in The Bahamas, but I was happily ignorant of this while I paddled through the bay].

paddling to No Name Cay

Across the bay a limestone bluff marked the center of the island and I thought there might be a trail there, but I decided to paddle upwind to the far side of the bay first, then drift downwind while looking for a trail. I spotted a cut in the thick tangles of mangroves on the upwind side of the bay, paddled over, and attached the leash of my board to one of the exposed roots. I stepped into the clear shallow water and maneuvered through the mangroves and out onto the island. Old shells and dried chunks of coral dotted the sand in a clearing in the trees. A path led through the low bushes, past an old wooden pallet and a length of old rope 4"-thick, and to a small beach in a cove facing the Atlantic, just what I was looking for!

Small waves broke over shallow coral, visible through the clear water just past the beach. The wind blew at 10-15 knots from the ESE, to my right as I faced the ocean. I was set up for a downwind drift across the barrier reef in a marine reserve, and I expected to see good coral and lots of fish. I went back and retrieved my surfboard.

Sitting down in the sand on this secluded and windswept beach I took off my sandals, exchanged them for booties, strapped my dive-knife to my right calf, bungeed my backpack to my surfboard, and headed out into the mighty Atlantic.

I paddled across bright blue water towards darker water, where I donned my mask and snorkel and slid into the water for an inspection, revealing a featureless bottom covered in turtle-grass. I got back on my board and paddled out towards an area where the water appeared orange, the color of elkhorn coral. Here small waves broke, revealing shallow water and the probability of reef. My next exploratory observation revealed the source of the color: patches of elkhorn coral, orange and fuzzy, but in only about 4' of water, too shallow for snorkeling. I moved to slightly deeper water and got in.

~~~

I drift across the shallow reef with one arm draped across my board and my leash still attached to my right ankle. This arrangement allows me to dive to about 15' while drifting with the current, still attached to my board. Orange and yellow stony corals sit still while sea fans and small fish move back and forth with the rhythm of the swell. I hold on to the board to prevent the sharp coral from contacting my vulnerable skin.

After crossing the reef, the water becomes deeper and invites me in for a few dives. Small red-and-white-striped fish with big black eyes hide underneath ledges, but are revealed by my flashlight. A magnificent juvenile threespot damselfish darts about within the protective confines of a patch of fire coral. The young of this species are bright yellow with a black eyespot on their back near the dorsal fin. Many fish have such a spot, believed to aid in survival by fooling a predator into targeting the false eye instead of the real one. The threespot damselfish changes from bright yellow to drab green as it matures.

After paddling farther downwind, parallel to the island, about 1/8 mile offshore, alone in the ocean wilderness, I cross deeper water and more reef, dark water next to light water, beckoning. I drop my small grappling anchor into water over sand, ready my video camera, and ease into the water.

A wall of ancient coral rises from a sandy bottom 25-feet deep to within 4 feet of the surface. At the bottom, dark caves invite my flashlight to illuminate their interior. A blue parrotfish swims away from my light, while royal gramma go about their business undaunted by the light. As I ascend the reef, a young yellow and blue Spanish hogfish, which become yellow and red with age, cavorts with a small brown doctorfish. The doctorfish is shaped like a blue tang, but is brown. The name comes from the sharp spine by the tail, said to be sharp like a doctor's scalpel, also present on the blue tang. This spine folds forward against the side of the fish and opens like a pocketknife when the fish feels threatened. The blue tang, doctorfish and surgeonfish, all members of the family Acanthuiridea, cause ciguatera, a debilitating disease, and thus can't be eaten. This is probably why they are still common. Thank goodness for ciguatera, otherwise humans would have probably eaten all the reef-fish by now.

Closer to the surface a school of small female yellowhead wrasse move back and forth with the wave action, drifting three feet one way, then three feet the other, continuously dodging coral as they do. I have to mimic this behavior as I video them, also not wanting contact with the sharp reef. Below me I observe two super-male yellowhead wrasse fighting, locking their jaws together in a fish wrestling-match. The supermales are much larger (about 8") and bear different coloration than the females and intermediate males (about 3") of the same species and hold breeding rights to all the females. When a supermale dies, an intermediate male takes its place and becomes a supermale, growing and changing color to suit his new position in the wrasse-society.

After about a dozen dives, I pull up my anchor and paddle toward the cut at the northwest side of the island, between No Name Cay and Pelican Cay. I snorkel again as I drift across shallow water by the inlet. Here most of the coral is bleached, dead or dying. Coral is a symbiotic relationship between single-celled algae and a member of the jellyfish family. The animal builds a calcium carbonate wall around itself (this makes the hard coral structure) and lives attached to the structure with its tentacles protruding to catch its food. The algae live in the coral's body and photosynthesizes its meals. One's waste provides nutrients for the other.

The coral relies on very clean, clear, nutrient-free water for survival. When water conditions deteriorate, the alga is ejected from the coral, which then turns white, thus the term "coral bleaching". Corals are likely to die completely after bleaching, and are often then covered with larger multicellular algae (marine plants). This leads to erosion and the reef is eventually lost forever. The wave energy that the barrier reef once absorbed will then strike the island behind the vanished reef causing the island to erode. The cost of reef-loss is thus dramatic. First goes the color, then the fish, then the reef, then the beaches, the houses, and possibly the entire island and the people.

~~~

As I paddled through the cut between No Name Cay and Green Turtle Cay I could see the large multicolored parachute-like kites of Eddie and Liam as they kite-surfed back and forth across the bay on the southeast side of Green Turtle Cay. I passed a Bahamian man and three young girls fishing from a small boat anchored in the pass between the tiny Pelican Cay and No Name Cay. I waved, and one of the girls waved back, a brief encounter between representatives of two different worlds. I continued paddling against a strong wind that was trying to blow me to my right towards a secluded beach where a couple and a small powerboat dotted the otherwise empty sand. Palm trees danced in the wind, clear water and a rocky bottom passed underneath as I stroked the water with my kayak paddle while sitting on my 12-foot surfboard.

When I got back on *Monkey's Uncle* I pulled out Liam's camera and started taking pictures of them as they whizzed by on their kiteboards.

Green Turtle Cay

We spent the next two nights moored in Black Sound, a harbor with a narrow entrance and a depth marked on the charts as four feet, but in reality, the depth is nine feet. On the way in I spotted a 19' West Wight Potter. This is a very small sailboat that can be trailered and kept in a driveway. I made a mental note to pay it a visit, which I did the following day via my surfboard while Liam and Eddie went to shore.

I paddled alongside the West Wight Potter and yelled "ahoy". A young man appeared, his girlfriend stayed inside. He was a cheerful guy with short curly brown hair a large scar on his abdomen. He told me they were from Oregon and had trailered the boat from there to Miami, then sailed to Bimini. I was impressed and glad to hear that the Gulf Stream could be crossed in such a small boat. Their boat was not even the "blue water" version, which is supposed to be unsinkable and built more strongly, although he told me that they had reinforced their boat for the journey.

~~~

The next morning, after much study of the weather, we cast off the mooring and set out for the Gulf Stream and home via the island of Great Sale, to the east. Foolishly we opted not to top off our fuel and water on the way out, as we thought that we had plenty.

Back in the Sea of Abaco we sailed northwest along the shore of Great Abaco Island while Eddie looked one last time for his lost paddleboard. I scanned the shore with my binoculars and studied each white thing I saw, to no avail. Eddie decided to get on his SUP and paddle downwind closer to the shore. The sky was turning grey behind us. The water got shallower and I steered the boat to the right further from the shore and Eddie, who was becoming harder to see. It was raining in the distance, the horizon disappearing behind a grey mist. Eddie eventually turned from shore and paddled hard towards the boat. The rain got closer, visibly hitting the water making a thin white line where the rain began. He got back onboard before the first rains hit. This was only a brief shower, yet a harbinger of things to come.

After climbing back onboard, Eddie took one look at the instruments and said to me "watch your depth." I looked at the depth gauge and it only read seven feet, way too shallow for comfort. I had been watching Eddie paddle along the shore instead of watching the instruments and we would have run aground if I had continued to steer us straight ahead. I learned another lesson, luckily not the hard way. When at the wheel, don't get distracted. Pay attention to the depth. Many months later I would make the same mistake.

~~~

As we neared Great Sale, the last island we would pass before crossing the mighty and ominous Gulf Stream, we decided to press on instead of anchoring for the night, but the weather had other plans. It was about this time that we ran out of fresh water, and on top of this, the freshwater pump burned itself out while running dry.

Night had fallen and it was raining. Eddie and I were in the cockpit sailing with one reef in the sails. The wind was 15 knots and the rain was becoming heavy. It was Eddie's watch and he was at the helm so I pulled out the tarp we had earlier been experimenting with as a rain catcher. I located a funnel and my life vest and went out on deck. The seas were building and the going was becoming rough. I clipped the carabiner at the end of the tether tied to my life vest to a shroud and opened the port water tank; its opening was on the edge of the deck outside the cockpit. Lightning burst on all sides of us. I struggled in the rain and bucking seas to tie the rain catcher to the shrouds, lifelines and bimini, wishing I had done this before, as now was not the time for trial and error. No matter how I tied it, the rain ran out somewhere besides inside the funnel. After much struggle, I eventually had it in an acceptable if not pretty state and went back to the safety of the cockpit.

However catching water was a fruitless endeavor, as

the water pump was burned out and thus we had no access to the water we were funneling into the water tank. The only water we had left was in five one-gallon containers I had brought and stashed in the "abandon ship box".

~~~

The wind increased to 25 knots, necessitating a second reef in the sails. Eddie steered into the wind; we loosened the leeward jib-sheet, which Eddie tailed while steering (the autopilot was out). I went out on the starboard deck, clipped in, and uncleated the roller furling line as the boat crashed head-on into the waves. Crouching, I moved quickly aft, away from the starboard jib-sheet, which was flailing violently, powered by the thrashing headsail. I pulled with all my might and furled the jib, leaving about one quarter of it out, then cleated off the line, while fending off the starboard jib-sheet with my left forearm protecting my face. Lightning lit up the sky and thunder boomed, wind-driven rain penetrated my inadequate rain gear, and the adventure-level was increasing.

We still had to put another reef in the mainsail, as the boat was heeling excessively and the leeward rail was getting too close to the sea. Back in the cockpit, while Eddie kept the boat facing the increasing wind and waves, I sat on the starboard bench facing the four jamming cleats which held the main halyard, main sheet, second reef line, and spinnaker-pole lift. I handed Eddie the main halyard and opened its cleat, then began winching the second reef line as Eddie tailed (kept tension on) the main halyard as the sail lowered. With the second reef-line tight I left the cockpit and clipped in to a jackline to put in the sail ties.

Carefully I moved to the mast and into the wind and rain, lightning and thunder. *Monkey's Uncle* lurched in the wind-driven waves sending torrents of spray across the deck. My teeth clenched. One-by-one, I pushed six purple sail ties through the second reef points (reinforced holes in the sail aligned horizontally) wrapped them around the partially-furled sail and boom, and tied them with slip-knots, finalizing the second reef. This was sailing, I pondered as I sat wet in the cockpit, doing what needs to be done regardless of the conditions. [In retrospect, I think putting in the sail-ties was both unnecessary and a bit reckless, but at the time it seemed like it had to be done]

We ended up anchoring at Great Sale Cay that night, setting our usual two anchors, although since it was night I did not dive to set them. The rain and wind continued as we dried off, got some food in us, and retired.

~~~

I woke to the sound of the footsteps on the deck above me as I lay in the forward V-berth. I wondered if Eddie was checking the anchors as I had done earlier in the evening. But soon the loud whirring noise of the windlass confirmed that he was in fact pulling up the anchors. Since I slept right near the windlass this was quite loud. I got up, got dressed and went up on deck. It was still dark; the weather had abated and the water was calm. Great Sale Cay was a dark silhouette on smooth black water reflecting the stars. We motored away from the island and out into the sea. I thought I saw the sun rising in the distance, the black of night giving way to light, but it was just the lights of Freeport, and Eddie informed me that it was in fact 2:30 am, which I found disorienting. I made coffee anyway and we had a pleasant and uneventful sail across the Little Bahama Bank. Hours later, the sun did rise in a majestic and awe-inspiring display of color and power as it lit up the clouds, the sky and the sea.

We sailed across the Little Bahama Bank leaving all the islands behind us and entered the deep water of the Atlantic Ocean in the late morning. Around noon we had been out-of-sight of land for a few hours and we stopped to check the oil in the big diesel engine of *Monkey's Uncle*. I felt like I should take the opportunity to dive in the blue and deep (1200') water. I had only dived in water this deep once before, 25 years previous, in Exuma Sound. The experience was quite memorable and is a story I often tell.

I put on my mask, snorkel, fins and dive-knife, but not my weight-belt, and eased into the water from the swim platform on the stern of *Monkey's Uncle*. After looking all around for sharks, of which I expected to see none, I floated and relaxed for a few minutes, making sure I didn't drift too far away from the boat.

~~~

I take one last deep breath and roll forward, stick my legs up in the air, and start my descent, swimming down into the abyss, no bottom visible. Blue, bright blue in all its glory surrounds me. I am entering a different world where anything can come at me, but nothing does, emptiness dominates, nothing below, nothing all around, just bright blue, like being in outer space, the womb, heaven. Looking straight up I can see the bottom of *Monkey's Uncle*, about the size of my outstretched hand, surrounded by the bright surface of the ocean and bobbing gently. But in all other directions the scene is featureless, just bright blue. There is nothing I have ever seen that compares.

I don't know how deep I am, but I stop descending earlier than I might otherwise. With nothing around to use to gauge my depth and motion, it is hard to tell if I am ascending, sitting still, or descending. But I get the earie feeling that I'm sinking ever deeper without knowing it. I know this can't be the case since I would feel the pressure in my inner ears and suction in my mask if I was descending, but I am trying not to think, meditating, conserving energy.

I hover in place for a bit, taking video all the while ("Blue Water Freedive" on YouTube https://youtu.be/fjzVjh3Bgjg), and enjoy the moment, which is magnificent.

~~~

Two short dives were quite enough. While an encounter with a shark is unlikely, it would be potentially dangerous out in the open ocean. While sharks close to shore have plenty to eat, pelagic (ocean-going) sharks are much more opportunistic in their feeding behavior and, I think, should be avoided. We saw one swim by the boat later in the day, its dorsal fin cutting the surface of the ocean, and I was glad I hadn't seen it before we stopped, or else I might not have dove.

me, Eddie and Liam, L to R

We sailed on to the Gulf Stream, northwest from The Bahamas. Curiously, we found ourselves in a current moving from north to south, in the opposite direction that the Gulf Stream flows. This was evident from the difference between our speed-over-ground (calculated by the GPS), 6.5 knots, and our speed across the water (measured by a small paddlewheel under the hull) of 7.5 knots. After consulting the chart, we determined that we were probably in an eddy, a reverse flow of water on the edge of the Gulf Stream created by the resistance from the Little Bahama Bank, the same way a rock or a bend in a river can have a reverse current behind it. I was at the helm, so I altered course to the west and an hour later turned back northwest. Here our GPS speed was now greater than our boat speed, confirming that we were in a northward-moving current, as expected in the mighty Gulf Stream.

The Gulf Stream can be a dangerous place for boats because of the potential conflict of weather and the strong current flowing from south to north. If the wind blows opposite the current, and it often does, large short-period (close together) waves are produced quickly, battering any ship they encounter. In the summer, severe thunderstorms often roll off of Florida and produce high winds, lightning and sometimes waterspouts, like tornadoes over water. The tall aluminum masts of sailboats can obviously be struck by lightning, and this sometimes results in the loss of all electronics on board, or worse.

While we sailed across the Gulf Stream, thunderstorms lit up the horizon in front of us, moving from west to east, left to right from our perspective. We were lucky to have them miss us, since they were huge and moving fast. Our boat was not equipped with radar, which can see thunderstorms and help the crew avoid them.

The final sunset of our journey was magnificent and included a double rainbow in the opposite sky. High clouds produced rays of yellow against a blue sky, turning orange, red, magenta... The three of us watched in awe. None of us spoke for a while as we stared at the sky; our trip was coming to a conclusion, and this was part of the final act, a natural and fleeting work of art in the sky.

We sailed through the night, taking shifts and hand-steering since the autopilot was not working. Thunderstorms lit up the horizon all around us. The storms moved like giant dark patches across the seascape from west to east. Lightning constantly flashed and connected sky to ocean, equalizing the electrical charges between the two and illuminating the dark clouds. While I was at the helm, I tried to steer between the storms, but it was impossible to gauge their speed and distance, so this exercise was futile. But somehow we were lucky enough to have been spared by all of them and instead got a free light show all night long without having to endure a storm.

~~~

As we approached the mainland, the subject of the Crescent Beach Submarine Spring came up in conversation, and we determined to try to find it and maybe dive on it. This is a unique freshwater spring in the ocean and in the past, sailors used this spring to fill their water casks. The spring was in the news recently because Miami wanted access to the water.

We knew the spring was a few miles off Crescent Beach, and I consulted the charts to see if I could find it. Eventually we spotted brown water on the surface and assumed this was it. Eddie convinced Liam and me to dive on it, and we got in the water. Visibility was minimal as the spring seemed to be bellowing out turbid water. I quickly felt very uncomfortable. It is amazing how fast this feeling can come over and dominate the emotions. I waved at Eddie and he brought the boat over and picked me up. There was nothing to see, but at least we tried.

We were almost home when Eddie informed us of an approaching thunderstorm with the potential for 60 mph winds. "Damage to shingles, siding and the potential for downed trees" the robot voice on the weather radio said. Our friend Brian, who saw on Facebook that we were off the coast of St Augustine Beach, texted a warning that a massive and black storm was heading our way. The horizon over Florida indeed turned black, a menacing cloud, dark grey and smooth, curved across the sky from north to south, a rounded front edge bending from top to bottom, approached quickly as Eddie and Liam furled both sails. It was my watch so I put on my life vest and rain jacket, then clipped my tether to the binnacle (a steel post supporting the steering wheel and navigation instruments). We had been heading north along the coast about three miles offshore. I moved us further out until the storm hit, then pointed us into the wind and reduced speed to 2 knots so as not to run up on the beach. The wind picked up to 15 knots, then 20, then maxed out at 37 knots, complete with a blinding rain. I had to put on my reading glasses in order to see, Eddie filmed the event from the safety of the companionway, I gritted my teeth and smiled. The adventure-level was high, peaking once again as we passed the neighborhood in which I lived, our two-week sailing journey coming to a fitting and wet end.

Miami to St Augustine
January, 2017

On the ocean we have ample time to think, meditate, observe, listen, to notice the colors in the sky, the flickering of the stars, the sounds of the wind and the water. We appreciate things we would otherwise overlook, like the texture of the water and the patterns in the way it moves in all three dimensions. We see animals and have ample time to ponder their existence, to attempt to communicate with them telepathically. It doesn't matter if the rest of the world would think this ridiculous, because we are at sea and they are not. We have the time to do as we please, and time is the greatest resource to have, so much of it is claimed by other obligations; it is precious.

Alone at sea as a solo sailor, undistracted by others, I can sort through my past experiences and lessons, appreciate the glory of the present moment, and plan for the future. I re-organize my priorities based on all the knowledge I have gained so far in this life, and I re-define what is good. I appreciate the value of simple things, like breathing clean air, staying afloat, being alive. I appreciate the power of a clean mind, the euphoria of sobriety. I appreciate a dream realized.

The Earth is a school, and the ocean is a classroom, a gymnasium, a playground, and a detention center. Nature is a place to learn and grow. We learn and grow on land among other people as well, but it is the solo experience deep in nature that mankind is currently deprived of and hungers for, knowingly or unknowingly. It is here that we expand our minds and heal our souls. It is here that we reconnect with our ancient past. This is where we used to live. This is where we evolved. It is only in recent human history that we left nature and built civilizations cut off from her. Returning to nature is essential to inner peace and spiritual fulfilment, and the deeper one ventures into nature, the deeper this experience, the greater the reward, and the greater the risk.

~~~

The final leg of my journey home from St Petersburg is about to begin – Miami to St Augustine. I face the upcoming sail with more confidence than the last two legs, and although I feel like I'll be heading into familiar territory, I have a deep respect for the Atlantic Ocean and the Gulf Stream. I also expect it to be cold. It's been warm, hot even, for the past two weeks, but I know the cold lies to the north, it is January, after all.

I've been preparing for the cold since before I bought *Sobrius*, taking cold showers and telling myself that it feels good. I've studied the Wim Hoff breathing method. I've swam in the cold ocean. The ocean is my friend. The cold is the same as heat, only a bit different, the other side of the same coin. This is what I've been telling myself, but it's harder to believe it than it is to say it.

Still I fear the cold. I've packed *Sobrius* with all the cold-weather gear I could come up with, all stashed in one locker – the "warm stuff" locker. I have two black beanies, one says "Yakima", which I got from the bike shop I used to work at, the other has a picture of Barak Obama and was given to me by a redneck who said he couldn't wear it at the NASCAR race. The super-warm "Mad Bomber" hat is in there, from my days as a snow-skier. I used to say that it was impossible to be cold while wearing the Mad Bomber. Also in the warm-stuff locker are two cashmere sweaters, a turtleneck, a silk sweater, neoprene gloves from my days as a mountain-biker, more mountain-bike gloves, various cycling shirts that don't hold water, long underwear, three light jackets, wool socks, ski goggles, more gloves from Home Depot. And most importantly, hanging in the salon is my foul-weather gear: a bright red coat and yellow suspenders, bought at West Marine in St Petersburg. I even have a spare raincoat, a bright yellow one that I bought second-hand at Sailor's Exchange in St. Augustine.

But it is warm in Miami as I prepare *Sobrius* for departure. I speak to her: "We're going home, and I'm going to take care of you. I'm going to do my best to sail you properly. Please hold together, and we'll share many adventures in the future."

I unclip the blue mainsail cover from the mast, roll it up and stash it below. The stern anchor comes out of its locker and fastens to the stern pulpit, ready to act as a brake should I lose power in a channel and drift towards shallow water. Carefully I remove the tillerpilot from its box filled with bubble-wrap. I carry it with both hands and slide its pin into the receiving hole on the starboard rail. I plug its cord into the female receptacle in the cockpit. I open the raw-water intake and close the sink-drain seacock and confirm that the head seacocks are closed. Various power switches are thrown on; instruments come alive. Many small items are stashed. I put on my life-vest, knowing I won't take it off for four days. I turn on the SPOT so family and friends can track me. I start the engine, waiting until I hear its pitch change, telling me it's ready to go.

I move to the bow and take in the scene before untying *Sobrius* from mooring ball # 99. The buildings of Miami stand tall with the green water of Biscayne Bay in the foreground. Sailboats and trawlers surround us, bobbing gently on the surface of the water beneath the clear blue sky. I'll miss this place, but I'm also eager to go home. I reach down and untie the bow-lines from the mooring ball. We barely drift as I return to the cockpit and shift the transmission into forward gear. Steering with the tiller I maneuver around the Hunter and the shiny white catamaran, into the channel and back towards the dark green mangroves and the marina. The busy marina with all its various boats passes to port and we enter the long Dinner Key Marina Channel, heading out towards Biscayne Bay under power and enjoying the warm morning sun.

An hour after untying from the mooring ball, we are out of the channel and in safe water. The wind comes from the south, so we motor-sail into it, looking for the yellow buoy by the entrance of the Biscayne Bay Channel, where abandoned houses perch on stilts hovering above the still water. Only a small fraction of the original houses remains. Hurricane Andrew dispatched with many, dismantling them and scattering their pieces, some across the Bay, some to the Atlantic, destined to indefinitely drift or sink to the bottom, becoming reefs in the end.

We motor on, through the channel and into the vast Atlantic Ocean and its deep water, seeking the current of the Gulf Stream. The wind is light and variable, but the current pushes us north, towards St Augustine, home.

I tie a line to the boom and bring it forward to a block by the bow, centered aft of the anchor locker, bringing the line back to a cleat in the cockpit. I let the boom all the way out to starboard and pull the preventer tight. I let the genoa fly to port and fasten the whisker pole to its sheet, holding it fast. Slowly we drift north, sails wing-on-wing, moving barely faster than the Gulf-Stream current.

One hand on the tiller, I watch the sails, pushing the tiller to port whenever the genoa luffs. When sailing wing-on-wing, I watch the sails, and whenever one luffs I point the tiller at it. This keeps the boat pointed directly downwind and prevents unintentional gybes. The wind is light, so the sails fill with air, then as the wind lightens, we outrun the moving air and the sails deflate, only to snap back into fullness with the next puff of air. The city is far behind us and the only sounds I hear are the swoosh of water moving across the hull and the rattle and whump of the sails deflating and filling, and occasionally the ping of a line against the mast. My nostrils flare and take in the clean air, which is free of any aroma, pure.

leaving Miami in tropical weather

Slowly the wind shifts west, and I take down the whisker pole and move the genoa to starboard, putting us on a beam reach. Sobirus answers the new wind with acceleration. As I steer with the tiller I can feel the air pulling us forward as it rushes through the slot between the two sails. The Atlantic Ocean appears to approve of our presence, providing us with calm waters and favorable winds. The sun is bright and warm; I wear no shirt. The current and the wind push us along faster, 8, 9, even 10 knots (speed over ground). The conditions couldn't be better!

Beyond the stainless-steel stanchions strung with grey synthetic lifeline, long white clouds radiate across the sky like giant still crabs. Blue-grey water rushes past *Sobrius'* hull; undulating black striations denote waves as they propagate through the ocean. We leave a small wake of disturbed water behind us, flat and streaked with white bubbles and sea foam.

White and red line twists around a winch, connected to

a wooden cleat on one end and the clew of the jib on the other. The black mainsheet reaches out at a steep angle to the boom, which hangs over the water, pulling us north. *Sobrius* leans to starboard, and I lean to port, holding the varnished wooden tiller in my right hand. Grey solar panels mounted to the stern rail collect photons sent from our sun, 93 million miles away, and convert them to DC electricity, stored in the three batteries below the starboard quarter berth.

Behind the solar panels, the lifelines and the mainsail, the sky is blue and grey. Dark linear clouds run parallel to our course; bright light behind them shines between the clouds like electric arcs in a battle between light and dark.

Logic tells me that I should sleep while conditions are calm and traffic is light, even though I am not tired and am enjoying the sailing. I set the tillerpilot and go below for a 20-minute nap. This leg of the trip had caused me some apprehension since we will be in colder water and rounding Cape Canaveral, exposed to the mighty Atlantic throughout the entire trip. But I am elated that so far the journey has been peaceful and has been blessed with fine wind and sea conditions. I lay down with a smile on my face and joy in my heart. I am thrilled just by the fact that my little sailboat floats in this vast body of water. *Sobrius* does not leak, and the mast stands tall. The sails pull us forward and ask for nothing in return. Sailing is magical, and I can sleep while *Sobrius* tends to herself.

I wake thinking about food. The seas are calm and cooking shouldn't be a problem. After checking the horizon and the instruments, I pump up the stove, pressurizing the alcohol in the tank inside the stove. Then I get out the denatured alcohol from the locker under the stove and use a straw to transfer an ounce into the depression under the burner on the stove. Before lighting it, I reach across the stove and fetch the small pot into which I empty a can of chili and a can of tuna. I light the alcohol, which preheats the burner. When the flame dies down, I turn the knob which releases vaporized alcohol through the hot burner, which I light with a lighter and begin heating up dinner.

The salon fills with the smell of chili and my mouth waters in anticipation. I take the pot of chili & tuna and a sleeve of crackers to the cockpit and sit with a towel in my lap and the hot pot of dinner on the towel. The tillerpilot keeps us on course as I enjoy my hot meal.

The sky and the sea are blue, the winds are perfect, the temperature is fine, and the skyline of south Florida decorates the horizon. The Atlantic Ocean approves and all is well in the world as I eat chili and gaze at the hazy outlines of buildings in the west. I imagine people in those buildings looking out their windows at the silhouette of my little sailboat out on the vast ocean as I look back at them. The city and the ocean are opposites, juxtaposed with beach in between. I'm happy to be separated from the city, but somehow its view lends me comfort, like the view of the ocean and my sailboat bring comfort to the city-dwellers. Perhaps it is contrast in which we all find comfort as we seek something completely different from our daily lives. My sailboat represents escape, nature, and adventure to them, and their buildings represent comfort, safety, and home to me.

As we sail north towards Cape Canaveral, the coast of Florida fades to the west. Evening falls, the sun sets in its burst of colors, the lights of the coast shine on the horizon before disappearing beneath it. There is no moon, and the stars are magnificent, as many as grains of sand on the beach. The Milky Way stretches across the sky like a cloud, yet it is our galaxy seen on-edge, massive, bigger than our imagination, bigger than our conception. What other worlds might be out there? What other civilizations? What other travelers and explorers might be looking across the galaxy at my planet, at me and my little ship.

South Florida sunset

The night is warm and peaceful with the Gulf Stream current and the friendly breeze both working in our favor. I sleep for three twenty-minute increments and then feel rested and want to sit in the cockpit and steer for a while. Time has little meaning and I am alone in nature, in the dark and starry night on the ocean. It is magical. This is what I came for, this is why I bought a sailboat, this is what it is all about. Moments like this on the ocean make all the hardships of sailing worthwhile. I find myself hoping I will remember this night forever.

~~~

It is morning and we are about 35 nautical miles east of Melbourne, where I went to college at Florida Institute of Technology (FIT) many years ago and fell in love with the ocean through surfing and SCUBA diving. Both sports fostered a deep connection with the ocean and led me to develop skills and knowledge helpful in my sailing. Surfing causes one to develop an understanding of waves, currents, wind, and tides. It also develops balance while standing on a vessel moving across waves on the ocean, a necessary skill while standing on the deck of a sailboat raising a sail or adjusting a line. Sailboats ride waves when sailing downwind, and the control and motion of the boat is similar to that of surfing. Surfing makes one comfortable in the ocean in all kinds of conditions, from tranquil to extremely rough. It helps one develop an intuitive understanding of waves and their motion and habits. It helps me to enjoy my time on the water, regardless of the conditions or the vessel.

As we sail past Melbourne memories flood my conscious mind: sailing small boats in the wide Indian River, learning through trial and error, running aground, kedging off a sandbar, sinking a Sunfish, learning to surf and feeling the irresistible urge to surf every day, SCUBA diving in The Bahamas while taking a summer ecology class, falling in love and then being heartbroken, partying too much and studying too little.

~~~

It is mid-day I need to do a headsail change, as the wind has become too much for the genoa. We are already on a close reach, so there is no question; I will use Andrew Evan's technique. I hank on the smaller sail beneath the genoa, then drop the genoa during a tack, remove it and raise the smaller headsail on the opposite tack. All this is done while sailing fast across the blue-grey water and we lose no ground. I've gotten better at this since the beginning of the voyage; this time it only took fifteen minutes from start to finish. The number two jib is up and we continue to charge north by northeast. I plan to give Cape Canaveral a very wide berth, as shallow sandbars stretch way out to sea around the cape, and shipping traffic near the Canaveral Inlet might be heavy.

Land is fading away and soon the view in all directions is ocean as we approach Cape Canaveral from the south. This cape is the last great milestone of my long journey home. Once around it we will be on the home stretch. But rounding any cape can be a challenge. Capes are known to harbor strong currents as water is deflected around them. If the wind blows against the current then the conditions on the sea can get very rough very quickly.

Right now the wind is blowing from the west, a favorable direction as we can proceed on a beam reach at maximum speed and in relative comfort. The west wind kicks up minimal waves as the fetch (the distance the wind blows over the water) is small where I am. But should the wind shift northward, all this could change for the worse. As for now, all is well and the sailing is fine.

~~~

The temperature is dropping and I put on a long-sleeve shirt. I take off my straw hat, because clouds have covered the sun. The temperature continues to fall. Conditions are changing. I go below and fetch my big red foul-weather jacket, the warmest garment I have.

The waves are building, and the wind is shifting north, to the northwest, against the mighty Gulf-Stream current and against my intended direction of travel. The chartplotter shows that the Cape Canaveral Inlet is directly west of us as we sail northeast. I briefly think about, and quickly dismiss, the idea of going into the inlet and sailing up the Intracoastal Waterway to St Augustine. My mission is to sail home via the ocean and that is what I intend to do.

But my subconscious is wary of the wind shift and I wonder if I am letting my ego make an important decision. The conflict rolls around in my mind; *Sobrius* rises and falls as we sail through the slowly building waves.

My AIS picks up a ship on a close approach and

triggers the alarm, and I check the data on the offending ship. This one is a cruise-liner heading for the inlet. I scan the horizon and find it, a small white lump on the edge where the ocean meets the sky. I guess that altering course to starboard will put me out of its way. Even though sailboats under sail have right-of-way over boats under power, I always get out of the way of big ships. The AIS confirms that starboard was the right way to turn, and the CPA decreases. The big ship appears to sit still as I sail towards it. I wonder if it is moving at all, but my AIS tells me that it is. Yet it continues to appear to sit still. I tack to the northwest and sail away from it and on the new course I can see its motion, and the distance between us increases.

Before getting anywhere near the shoals around the cape, I tack to the northeast. But the waves push me back, hindering my northward progress. I look at the chartplotter and realize that I haven't gotten much past Canaveral Inlet, and the inlet beckons.

"Don't you want to come in and rest? It might get ugly out there tonight."

"No thanks. The ocean it shall be, all the way home."

But somewhere deep in my subconscious lies a worry that I may be letting my ego get the best of me. I know that at the end of the voyage I want to be able to tell my friends and my family that I sailed in the ocean the whole way home, not the Intracoastal Waterway. I want to impress them with my bravery, but I know this is a bad way to make decisions.

I remain stubborn and continue to snub the invitations of the Canaveral Inlet. I want to stay in the ocean; I don't want to go in. My love of adventure causes me to push myself and to try to overcome fear. But the logical side of my mind causes me to consider my inexperience as a sailor, the potential danger of the cape and the worsening conditions. But there is other logic to consider. The inlet channel is miles long and unfamiliar, and the Intracoastal Waterway to which it leads is also terra incognita.

I also have some technical problems to consider. The depth sounder is not working, and the masthead tricolor light is out, which means I will not have an anchor light. I also don't know if places to anchor are available in the Intracoastal, and I would need to anchor in order to sleep tonight and tomorrow night if I were to sail home that way. But without a depth gauge, I am not willing to leave the deep water of the ocean. Out here I don't need it, but in the Intracoastal, I certainly would. Out here, I can sleep while sailing, even if it gets rough (I hope).

I press on, trying to make progress to the north but mostly we just go east, tack, and then go west.

~~~

The chartplotter shows the yellow icon of a weather buoy northeast of us. This is the National Data Buoy Center Station 41009, accessible via the internet and regularly checked by surfers for wave data. I've consulted it dozens of times and wish to see it in person. It doesn't look too far away on the little screen, and we continue tacking against the wind and the building waves. I am hand-steering, pushing the tiller as we go up a wave, pulling on the tiller as we go down the other side, trying to keep the hull in the water so we don't slam in the troughs. The buoy is a nice distraction and a goal which gives me a mission for the rest of the day. It will be another milestone on a long journey home, and old inanimate friend to visit on the ocean. I've seen a photograph of the buoy, on the internet, but there is no way to tell its scale. I am curious to see how big it is; I really have no idea.

As we tack west, I see the inlet on the chartplotter and again it beckons.

"Come on in, it's nice and calm in here."

And again, I must resist its siren song. *Sobrius* and I press on instead, now trying to reach the yellow buoy. We tack to starboard and sail east for an hour. We tack to port and sail west.

The waves continue to build and the conditions worsen. The inlet continues to beckon, the yellow buoy mocks. I keep one hand on the tiller and one on a cleat, both feet are pressed to the backrest opposite my seat. *Sobrius* is heeling 10, then 15, then 20 degrees; white spray flies off the bow when breaking waves hit us. I turn my head when I see the flying water coming, taking it to the back of the head, to the face when I don't see it in time to move.

The sky on the horizon is dark grey, changing to a lighter grey with distance from the horizon, patches of light grey and white poke through. The sea is a dark blueish-grey. There are wavelets on top of waves and the waves are very close together. The waves are relentless, colliding with *Sobrius'* bow every few seconds, hour after hour, all day, all night. The boat rises, the boat falls. I'm wearing my red foul-weather coat, my lifejacket, doubly clipped in to the padeye on the floor and to a padeye on the bulkhead, black and white fingerless gloves from Home Depot, my yellow foul-weather suspenders, and red Nike shoes that don't soak up water. The air is cold but not freezing.

The bow crashes into wave after wave, sending white spray flying off to port, blown by the wind, sometimes blowing into my face.

"How tough are you?"

I continue steering through the waves. "I'm OK with this but I'd rather the wind and the seas decrease a bit."

I get no response. The original question hangs in the salt air. The inlet beckons, the yellow buoy mocks. Northward progress is slow.

Another ship triggers the alarm on the AIS. This one is a towing vessel. I scan the horizon and eventually make out a cube. It grows larger, and its odd cube shape reminds me of the Borg spaceship on Star Trek. It is an anomaly on the ocean. Ships aren't supposed to be cubes – rectangles maybe – but not cubes. I alter course to port, intending to give it very wide berth. I hope to see my old friend the yellow buoy, but its position relative to me has been very slow to change. The waves continue to increase and they make my progress even slower.

"Canaveral Inlet is now behind you, but you could turn back, sail downwind to the inlet and go in for the night."

"No. I want nothing of the Intracoastal, its bridges, its traffic, its channel markers. I want to sail in the ocean. I will complete this journey without using the intracoastal waterway."

"How tough are you?"

"I'm not that tough, but I'm going to continue around the cape."

The tugboat comes into view. It's pulling a huge barge loaded with shipping containers – train cars stacked 8-high in long rows above the sides of the vessel. As the angle between us changes, the cube becomes a rectangle, then, like a maritime shapeshifter, it becomes a cube again. An hour later as it recedes into the distance, still a cube.

It is 3:30 pm and we are almost past the yellow buoy, according to the chartplotter, and I tack us towards it, but I don't see it. We are about 22 miles east of Cape Canaveral and just north of its point. Many obstacles surround the Cape, so prudence dictates that we stay as far away from it as possible.

rounding Cape Canaveral

~~~

The wind has been increasing since yesterday, and I have already taken down the genoa and replaced it with a smaller headsail, yet the wind continues to strengthen. The waves are building too. The night is black. I know I should reduce sail again, but I hesitate. I don't want to work on the foredeck in these conditions; I'd much rather stay in the cockpit where I am safe and relatively comfortable.

I check the inclinometer beneath the compass. It's hovering around 20 degrees. I recently read that 20 degrees of heel should be seen as a sign that it is indeed time to reduce sail, and it would be foolhardy not to do so. But the night is black, the seas are up, and *Sobrius* charges ahead, up one wave and down the next. The wind is blowing out of the northwest, against the current, and this is a condition that sailors are often warned about. When current and wind are in opposition, steep and short-period (close-together) seas build up and become dangerous, especially to small craft. Like a lover, the Atlantic was caressing us earlier today, but is punishing us now.

Even though it is nighttime, the seas are rough, and the air is cold, I must reduce sail. I go over the steps in my head – go below, turn on the deck light, get the working jib out, clip in to the jackine, carry the sail forward, lower the jib-halyard, move to the bow, unroll the new sail on the windward side, remove the existing tack, tack and hank on the new sail below the existing sail, remove the lazy sheet from the existing sail and tie it on to the clew of the new sail, move to the mast, hit the auto-tack button on the tillerpilot's remote control, drop the jib as it comes across the deck, pull on the downhaul, move to the bow, remove the halyard from the old sail and attach it to the new sail, unhank the old sail and roll it under the jackline, move back to the mast, pull on the jib-halyard and raise the new sail, move to the cockpit and trim the new sail, go back to the bow and roll up the old sail and bag it, tie the lazy sheet to the new sail (this step requires leaning out over the side of the boat and, with both hands, tying the sheet to the clew of the working sail), then stash the old sail below and take a break. These are the steps and I start with step one. Just step one, I tell myself. Then I do step two, and of course all the rest; telling myself to just do step one is an easier way to get started.

I work hard, staying clipped in all the time, usually with one tether clipped to a jackline and the other one clipped to a shroud or the other jackline. The decklight, shining down from halfway up the mast, illuminates the front half of *Sobrius*, but beyond this little sphere of light is blackness; I can't see the waves as we crash through them. As I straddle the bow, my legs hang over either side of *Sobrius* and dip into the dark water over and over again as we charge forward. My fingers wrestle with the bronze hanks as I attach the smaller sail to the headstay while cold salty water sprays me in the face.

When the new sail is hanked onto the headstay, I scoot backwards, then carefully stand up and grab ahold of a shroud and make my way to the clew of the working sail. I lean out over the water and untie the sheet lazy sheet from the clew of the working sail. Later, I have to do this again as I tie the lazy sheet to the new sail. It is exhilarating, and scary. Falling in the water would be a long slow death, unless I could swim many miles to shore in the dark, which would not be likely. I do all I can to stay on deck, and in order to remain conscious of the danger, I try to imagine the edge of the boat is a tall cliff.

When the job is done, about 45 minutes later, I sit in the cockpit and breathe deeply. I feel like I have skirted death for nearly an hour and I am very happy to be back in the relative safety and comfort of the cockpit. However, now I have to go reef the main, a similar but much easier task.

I go through the steps of reefing the main, first in my head, then on deck. Standing at the mast and balancing like a surfer I release lines, tension lines, untangle lines, brace myself in different positions, and reduce the size of the mainsail. The reef is much faster than the headsail change, and now sail area is greatly less than it was an hour ago. *Sobrius* heels less, and the motion is calmer, but far from calm.

My stomach is slightly upset as I sit in the cockpit after the headsail change and the mainsail reef. But I appreciate the relative safety and comfort of the cockpit. I appreciate that I am sitting down and not working on the deck anymore. I appreciate that my little ship floats and has so far taken the seas without complaint. I take the tiller in hand and remove the tillerpilot, strapping it to the rail with the shock-cord I installed for this purpose – to keep it aboard in rough conditions.

On this dark night and in these increasingly-angry waters the motion of *Sobrius* is somewhat like riding in the back of a windowless cargo van on a very bad road. She moves in all directions with only a limited amount of predictability. The swell has some regularity, so the up and down motion is mostly regular, but there are constant random motions thrown in, lurching to one side or the other, falling off the back of a wave, the jerk to port when hit by whitewater.

The body of a sailor cannot relax, but instead is constantly working to maintain balance. To relax would be to fall out of my seat and bang around on the cockpit floor. Sometimes sailing is an all-day-all-night athletic event, and now is one of those times. My left arm holds tight to the tiller, pushes and pulls with the passing of each wave. My right hand holds fast to the cockpit rail, the right arm tense, holding me in place. My feet and legs brace against the opposite cockpit bench, pressing my back firmly to the bench on which I sit. My head is turned to the right, staring into the black of the night. My eyes don't see much more than the deck of my boat, but looking in this direction helps maintain orientation. The night is still black, without stars or moon, and the spray is cold. I can no longer see the water before it hits me in the face. I must simply take it; luckily it's not too cold and my foul-weather gear is adequate.

While the conditions are not quite miserable, they certainly are very uncomfortable, and I try to relate the night to past experiences. I tell myself that it certainly is not as cold as some of the snow-skiing I did as a child, and steering the boat is not as hard as riding a bicycle up a mountain on a muddy trail in the woods. I get a bit of comfort from these thoughts.

~~~

"How tough are you?"

"Not as tough as you. But I'm willing to give tonight a go. Really, I have no choice, do I?"

"No, you wanted to be a sailor and you are in it now. I could easily throw much more at you than this. I'm happy to have you out here, but now you must pass this test. I'd have really been disappointed if you'd gone in to Canaveral Inlet earlier."

"Me too. I want to be an ocean-sailor. I want to

complete the journey as I told everyone I would: St Petersburg to St Augustine via the ocean, not the Intracoastal."

"As you should, but there is a fine line between bravery and hubris."

"How does one know the difference?"

"Perhaps there is none."

"Perhaps a little hubris is not such a bad thing."

"Humans are a mix of emotions and motivations. Those whom I know well have a very particular balance of hubris, fear, bravery, compassion, need for adventure, respect, love of beauty, love of tranquility, the ability to appreciate chaos and function in it. Keep doing what you're doing, you are learning my ways."

"I will, it's easy to continue when there's no choice. I guess that's why I'm out here."

~~~

As I sail on through the darkness with the collar of my coat turned up, protecting my neck from the wind and the lower part of my face from the spray, I think about karma and hope mine is all clean. I feel reduced to relying on it to get me through the night.

Nature is an agent of karma. Isolation from nature allows bad karma to build, preventing the isolated from learning from the consequences of their actions, from the laws of cause and effect. Exposure to raw nature is a constant opportunity to cleanse oneself of negative karma, and conversely to benefit from good karma, cause and effect, action/reaction. Good deeds bring about good actions and have positive effects on one's life. Bad deeds bring about bad actions and thus yield negative effects on one's life. Exposure to nature brings about these effects, because nature is an agent of karma. What you owe will be paid, what you deserve will be served. This is one reason why those who live lives exposed to the raw power of nature are generally humble, calm, peaceful, well-balanced, and happy people.

On this day at sea I am relying on my store of good karma to keep my boat afloat and moving in the direction of home. All I can do is steer us through the waves, and I resign myself to whatever fate is in store for me. I sail with the confidence that comes from a life well-lived. I have no control over the weather and I keep telling myself that *Sobrius* has been floating for over 44 years. She will not sink. But still, part of my mind fears this.

The worst fear comes from not knowing what to do in a bad situation. Conversely, fear is more easily controlled when one has done all that can be done both to prepare for and to react to the situation at hand. Once this is achieved, fear no longer serves a purpose and can more easily be dismissed.

~~~

Sobrius rises through a wave, and then there is a feeling of weightlessness, followed by a jarring crash as the flat part of the hull forward of the keel slams into the trough between two waves. The noise is frightening. *Sobrius* is almost as old as me, and I really don't know how much of this she can take.

I consider the possibility of disaster. If she were to break apart and sink to the bottom, I would only have my 12' surfboard (assuming I could get it out in time) and a kayak paddle to get to shore, which is probably 30 miles away, and the wind is blowing away from shore, the water is cold, and the night is black. I would probably survive, but it would be a very bad situation. I must stop thinking negative thoughts. Negative thoughts bring negative actions and negative results. Positive thoughts bring positive actions and positive results. I am here to sail and I am indeed sailing, so all is as it should be. I am here to gain experience, and this is indeed valuable experience, so all is as it should be.

For mental support, I recall some of the harder rides from my days as a mountain-biker. There were times when, deep in the woods, cold, wet and exhausted, with no way out but to continue pedaling, pushing, or carrying my bike, I had to dig for the fortitude to continue. I try to channel the endurance I learned on these rides.

I think back to the first time we did Turkey Pen in the Pisgah National Forest. I had planned a 25-mile loop, and my analysis of the topographical map led me to believe, and to tell the other two guys, that the ride would end with an eight-mile downhill, dropping about 2500 vertical feet, which I anticipated with delight. After riding hard all day, we eventually got to the last mountain-top of the ride and enjoyed the tranquil view of the surrounding mountains and green valleys of the national forest from a rock outcropping before continuing to the big final downhill.

"Here we are" I said, "eight miles of downhill!"

But it wasn't long before we came to a short and steep climb. I was surprised by this, and we all pushed our bikes to the top and silently started down the trail. But it happened again soon after, and this one was not short, rather it was long and steep. I was shocked that these two uphills had escaped my attention while planning the route; I prided myself on my map-reading ability.

If I had studied the maps better, I would have seen that there were actually ten steep uphills along the "eight-mile downhill". And as the ride progressed, I became more dismayed and fatigued at each one. There came a time in this ride when I didn't think I could continue. My friend Doug looked back at me while we were pushing our bikes up a steep muddy climb and I said to him "I'm not sure how much longer I can go on." But in situations like that, there is no quitting. There is no short-cut, no bail-out, one simply must keep riding in order to get out of the woods. There is no other way out.

Remembering this and other long rides gives me strength. It calls up endurance within me and I will myself to be strong and brave. At least now I am seated and don't have to pedal and push a bike up a mountain. I just need to sit here and steer. But it is my eyes and my mind that are becoming weak. Sleep was minimal last night, and it seems unlikely that I will get much, if any, tonight.

~~~

My left hand grips the wooden tiller which my left arm has been pulling and pushing for hours now. We are around the Cape and I am trying to get us closer to shore. The wind is coming out of the northwest, and the waves should be smaller closer to shore, as the fetch will be less. But the mainland is 30 miles away and it will take hours to get close enough to make a difference.

I steer by feel, pushing and pulling on the tiller as we rise and fall through the seas. I try to determine if the seas are decreasing and we make progress west, but there is no change. The conditions are simply black, rough, cold, and windy. The muscles in my torso constantly flex and relax, flex and relax, reacting to the constant motion of the ship. My head bobs, my eyes narrow, my thoughts fade.

My left arm works like a robot, and occasionally my right arm lends support, two hands on the tiller. I stare into the blackness ahead, illuminated green by the starboard bow-light. But then the green disappears; the light has gone out. Only the red light on the port bow remains. Darkness gains ground. The familiar green glow reflecting off the water to the right of the bow is now gone, like a friend who moves away, like a dog you must bury. The light had given me a small bit of confidence and reassurance that all was well. Now it is gone, and with it a bit of my peace-of-mind. The masthead tricolor light is out too and has been since Miami. I think the storm must have damaged it. The failing lights remind me that at any time any part of the boat could fail without warning.

We carry on with a red light on the port bow and a

white light on the stern. Any vessel approaching from starboard would see nothing. But there is nothing that I can do about it now. There is nothing to do but steer.

My face and hands feel that the air is getting colder, but the rest of me is warm and dry inside my foul-weather gear. My eyes see less and less as the night gets darker and darker. Fear tries to gain ground, and I try to rise to the challenge. I've never been in a position like this, in a small sailboat by myself in the ocean with the wind blowing counter to the Gulf Stream. I am being tested. I must have faith in both myself and *Sobrius*. I must have faith in *Sobrius'* ability to remain afloat, that the mast will stay put, that the tiller will continue to steer, that the hull will continue to resist the impact of the waves, that we will not collide with some unseen object in the water and sink. I must have faith in my ability to control the boat, to stay aboard, and to navigate us home. If all else fails, I can paddle my surfboard to shore, whatever the distance. I could even swim it if I had to. My ocean-swimming mantra is "How far can I swim? As far as I need to."

Conscious thought must overcome fear. I can do this and *Sobrius* will continue to sail. She has been across the Atlantic three times (or so I was told by the seller) and this is nothing to her. She's been floating since 1972, and will continue to float. It's just that I am unaccustomed to conditions like these, and there is only myself aboard to sail, navigate, change sails, make decisions.

Conscious thought gets more difficult with the fatigue that comes from sailing for two days straight. I must think slowly, and I must analyze my decisions carefully. Disaster comes from mistakes, and mistakes come from fatigue. The fatigued person can avoid mistakes by thinking more slowly, more carefully, and with more analysis. I only need to sit here in the cockpit and steer, and I need to be clipped in both to the big stainless-steel padeye on the cockpit floor and one of the two bolted to the cabin bulkhead. Nothing bad can come from sitting and steering, doubly clipped in.

Sobrius continues to charge through the waves on a close reach, moving up, down, left, right, but always forward. She feels like an animal underneath me, like a horse running across a field of undulating terrain. Sailing in the dark like this feels like running through a forest at night, bumping into branches and stepping on unknown things, some hard, some squishy, but running without pause like a dog chasing a rabbit. There is no stopping, no short-cut home, no off-switch, and no easy-button. There is only wind, water, sailboat and me. We can stop when we get home, but not before, and home is still over a day away.

In the black night and the relentless seas, my little boat charges on, unafraid, doing what she was made to do, while I steer her, less confident than she. It is she who takes me for a ride tonight.

But my eyes are getting heavier.

~~~

"You've got nowhere to go but forward now."

To the south are shoals and sandbars around the cape. To the west the Gulf Stream and heavier seas. To the north is home, but the wind is coming from the north so I must proceed west, towards the beach and hopefully calmer water.

I want to continue to hand-steer so we don't slam into the troughs between waves, I tell myself, not trusting the tillerpilot to the job. Besides, below-deck is relative chaos. The motion of *Sobrius* is such that maneuvering below-deck is difficult and hazardous. But I really need some rest; my mind is getting weak. I must go below, but I don't want to.

"Sleep, give the tillerpilot a try, let's see how it does in these conditions."

I want to sleep, and I analyze my decision. The tillerpilot is the best one on the market. It is supposed to be able to handle rough conditions. Brian, the guy who built it, told me he used his in ten-foot seas with no problem. The seas here are much smaller than that, it's just that they are unorganized, breaking, and short-period, that is, close together. The tillerpilot should be able to handle it, and I am so tired that I might start making mistakes. It only makes sense to get some sleep. The decision is made, I'll go below and get twenty minutes.

I remove the arm of the tillerpilot from its shock-cord harness and attach it to the post on the tiller. I reach to the control-head by the companionway and turn it on, then adjust the gain to maximum so it can provide the best stability possible. We are north of the Cape and its sandbars and heading WNW towards land and hopefully calmer water. But the seas are working against progress, trying to push us back out to sea. I am exhausted. I hope the tillerpilot is up to the job - we will soon find out.

~~~

Carefully I work my way below, holding on all the time. I step over the #2 jib, rolled and bagged, laying at the base of the steps. *Sobrius* swings wildly in all directions, unpredictable, making it very difficult to maneuver below. Cold and wet, I lay down on the port bunk, fully dressed, life-vest on, the green light on the SPOT clipped to the life-vest blinking. Immediately I feel my core relax, as it hasn't been able to do all day, since the last time I was laying down in my bunk. The muscles in my torso all loosen up, and the feeling is one of great relief. I set the 22-minute countdown timer on my wristwatch and close my eyes. My body lies effortlessly in the narrow bunk and I am glad I decided to lie down.

However, the noise inside *Sobrius* is much greater than the noise in the cockpit. Whitewater bangs into the hull, the tools below my berth rattle, the bulkheads creak, lines bang into the mast – Ping! Ping! Ping! Then BANG! the worst noise – the bow slams. I taste fear. Slamming is scary enough when sitting in the cockpit, but down inside the boat the noise is much greater, like being inside a kick-drum.

It sounds like *Sobrius* will break apart, and I know this will go on all night, assuming we stay afloat. Yet I must sleep – it is the best and only thing for me to do right now. I close my eyes and ask God to get us through the night. I rarely talk to God anymore, but it seems like the right thing to do considering the circumstances. I feel better laying down; I no longer have to exert energy to keep my balance and I have given up control of the ship to the tillerpilot. I begin to relax and try to fall asleep.

I speak to *Sobrius* "Hold together old girl. I'll take care of you. Just hold together tonight."

But the mighty Atlantic hears my plea "This is nothing, I can dish out far worse!"

"Yes, I know, I believe you, but please, not tonight."

It's now 3:50 am, and the alarm on my watch vibrates and then beeps before I fall asleep. I sit up, grab the handrail above my head and slowly work my way through the rocking and shifting cabin to the companionway steps. Has twenty-two minutes already passed? I check the chartplotter for position, direction and speed – all good, and the AIS – no other ships detected. I slide open the hatch and peer around outside. Wind and water, both cold, assault my face. *Sobrius* charges ahead winding about like a python chasing a monkey in a tree. No ships in sight, I duck back inside and hold on tight to a handrail on the ceiling with one hand while the other slides the hatch closed.

"Hold together old girl, I'll take good care of you. We'll go on many great adventures. We just need to get home."

I go back to sleep, fully-dressed in damp foul-weather gear, boots, life-vest, the SPOT flashing. The noise is chaotic, as is the motion, yet I sleep this time. But the alarm goes off and I get up quickly. Something doesn't feel right, surely twenty minutes has not passed. I look at my watch, and indeed something is different. It's counting down from eight minutes. I madly press buttons trying to figure out what's wrong with it, but this only adds to the chaos in the cold, wet, dark, and bucking ship. I can't figure it out, and I give up, resigning myself to eight-minute sleeps. Whatever.

I grab hold of the handrail on the ceiling and pull myself up carefully, stepping over the surfboard/life-raft/dinghy and the 5-gallon jerrycans of water. I put on glasses, check the instruments, the helm, the horizon, and lay back down for another 8-minute rest inside a bucking bronco. Really it's only a 6 or 7 minute rest, since the timer started over as soon as the alarm went off.

I lay in my bunk fully-dressed and damp, the green light on my SPOT flashing, neoprene boots keeping my feet warm, and cross my arms over my chest in coffin-pose. I don't know why I like this position, but it's how I've been sleeping. Perhaps if I symbolically resign myself to possible death, then it becomes one less thing to worry about. I don't fear death, but I do fear being cold. I accept that death is inevitable, and to live on its edge is supreme. Contrast brings appreciation, and the edge of death is the ultimate contrast to living in the comfort and safety of modern society. I sleep for a glorious six minutes, and another. I can't tell how many times I sleep, they blur into each other.

Sobrius rises and falls, rolls to port and rolls to starboard, moves in all possible directions as the sails pull us upwind through the black and unseen seas. My friend John says that the sails actually suck the boat forward, an example of Bernoulli's principle. I think about this as I drift off to sleep. The Pelagic tillerpilot I installed over a day and a half back in St. Petersburg steers us well, if noisily. I am quite impressed with it. I shut my eyes and sleep comes quickly, as does the alarm.

I don't know how many times I lay down to rest, getting up every eight minutes to check the horizon, but eventually I see lights, single white lights on the western horizon, possibly buoys marking the shoals north of Cape Canaveral, possibly ships, or maybe towers on land.

Regardless of what they are, I can no longer allow myself the relative luxury of eight-minute sleeps. Now I have to stay in the cockpit, that is the rule. If I can see lights, then I don't sleep. I can't find them on the chartplotter, and I'm not willing to consult the paper chart in these conditions, so it's impossible to be sure what they are or how far away they are.

I climb into the dark cockpit and clip a tether to the padeye on the floor under the traveler. I turn off the tillerpilot and detach it from the tiller, pivoting the stainless-steel robot-arm and attaching it to the rail with its loop of shock cord. I'm back in action, staring into the blackness of the night, getting sprayed in the face by the mighty Atlantic, steering into invisible waves, steering off their backs by feel, aiming for calmer waters closer to shore, still many miles and many hours away. The adventure-level is high, very high, and I feel unreasonably rested and alert. I am sailing again, and happy to be doing so.

We sail on, cold and tired, but determined. There is no other choice. I stare at the white lights. The chartplotter does not know what they are. I imagine that they could be a lot closer than I assume. At any second they could turn into a fleet of big ships about to run me down, or the beach could rise up between us and them, or they could be marking shoals that could surprise me and bring us to a grinding halt, crushed by the surf, should I look away for a moment. No, I must be vigilant and stare at them. Staring contest, all night long, me vs the lights. They don't blink, nor do they move, but the sense of possible danger helps me stay awake and alert. I know I must think longer and harder about everything, and make decisions more slowly and carefully. The "three a.m. effect" that Andrew Evans warns about in his book about singlehanding looms, and I do not want to become its next victim.

~~~

Black gives way to grey as the eastern sky slowly illuminates behind us. Never have I felt so glad to see a grey sky. The white lights fade away, the waves become visible, and I turn my head to dodge the spray which I took blindly in the face all night. While the light brings a great improvement in moral, the waves, the wind, and the cold are relentless and take their toll on my body and psyche.

Ponce Inlet lies ahead, and now I hear its siren-song.

sailing towards calmer seas

"Come on in, rest up, get a cheeseburger, how about a warm hotel room with a soft, dry bed and a hot shower?"

We sail on, but I can smell the cheeseburger –meat, cheese, bread, warmth, sustenance.

"How tough are you?"

"I'm not so tough."

"Do you want to take a break? Do you want to go in?"

"No, no."

~~~

I sail my little ship through the morning and the cold,

in the wind, through the waves – up the face, down the back, plow into the next face – tiller to port, tiller to starboard. The air is getting colder. I put a black beanie on my head and relish in the increased warmth it brings, like a cat caressing my head, like the embrace of a lover. I don't need anything else. The clothes I wear and the boat in which I sit, the ocean on which we float and the wind that propels us. There is nothing else.

But Ponce Inlet beckons with its succulent hamburgers and dry hotel rooms, heated, clean, motionless. I can feel the warm shower and the soft and still bed. I can see buildings – or are they trees? Grey relief on the horizon. Grey waves, grey sky.

"How tough are you?"

"I'm not so tough."

Midway through the morning I notice that the waves are no longer sending cold spray into my cold face, and we no longer slam off one wave into the trough behind it. I smile at the realization. My prediction was correct, the decreased fetch produces smaller waves, and the conditions are dramatically better. However, now we are out of the warm Gulf Stream and the temperature has plummeted since yesterday. I now know that it is January, it feels like winter out on the water.

The waves have subsided, and so has the wind, yet still my progress is slow. We tack and we tack, sailing into the northwest wind. The city of Port Orange comes into view. Ponce Inlet shows on the chartplotter. I don't even know if sailboats can navigate this inlet, yet still it beckons. In fact it beckons all day, as progress to windward is slow. We tack away from the inlet, we tack back towards the inlet, away, towards, away, towards. Perhaps *Sobrius* and I are in an eddy of the Gulf Stream, a reverse current flowing south next to the main current which flows north, caused by the current passing around Cape Canaveral, further pushed by the north wind. Regardless, I don't want to go back out into the Gulf Stream today.

"Come on in. How tough are you?"

I need a weather report, so I get out my handheld VHF and find one. I always keep one of my two handheld radios in the cockpit while the other is on its charger. I hear the robot voice tell me that there is a small-craft-advisory for the Gulf Stream, but the wind should shift to the west later today, which would put us on a beam-reach to St Augustine, perfect.

I will not go into the inlet, we are too close to give up now. Besides, my starboard bow light, mast tricolor lights, and depth sounder are all out of commission. Navigating the Intracoastal without the lights and the depth sounder would not be safe, and I don't know where I would anchor for the coming night anyway. We stay in my old friend the mighty Atlantic. Respect.

The Atlantic approves.

"Stay another day and night, you can be home tomorrow. It'll be nice, don't give up now."

"Thank you, I think we shall continue."

Movement in the water to starboard catches my attention – fins break the surface and roll. Dolphin swim up for a visit and then disappear. Two seagulls fly by. I see a white oval about 18 inches across approaching *Sobrius*, just beneath the surface. Behind the white oval is a large flat animal, gliding through the water without any perceptible movement. A manta ray it is; its wings protrude through the surface like shark fins – the huge white mouth open and taking in food. The bizarre creature swims by *Sobrius*, I scramble to get video but I don't get my phone out in time. It glides effortlessly around the stern and out of view, swimming and eating, living its manta-ray life. This area seems to be teeming with wildlife.

The wind continues to decrease and the waves follow suit. It is still cold, probably in the forties, but I am relaxed, glad to be comfortable and not fighting the waves anymore. I have plenty of warm clothes, and the warm-stuff locker is my savior this morning. Another manta ray swims by, or perhaps it is the same one.

the final day of sailing

I check my phone and I see a message from Cristina in Miami. She and Frank have been following my progress, and Cristina has forwarded a message from Frank. He suggests I go inland through Ponce Inlet to avoid northwest winds. I switch on my VHF and listen to the weather forecast again; Ponce Inlet is still in view, and I think of hamburgers and hotel rooms, warm showers and soft beds, hot coffee.

The forecast is the same as it was earlier – west winds this afternoon and tonight with cold temperatures dropping into the thirties. *Sobrius* continues to slowly tack upwind, making slow northwest progress. More dolphin visit, and they make me smile.

Mid-day my patience for tacking wears out and I start the engine. There is no logic to this decision, as it may put me in St Augustine before dawn; we are only 60 nautical miles south of home. Yet I don't want to be here anymore. Perhaps it is the beckoning of Ponce Inlet that I need to be free of, and we can lie hove-to off St Augustine Inlet and wait for dawn should we arrive before first light. I further justify the decision by noting that the sky has been cloudy for the past two days, and the batteries might need to be charged. But it might just be the perception of warmth that the running engine brings that I crave. I've been cold for at least 24 hours now. We motor north and Ponce Inlet disappears off the chartplotter, no longer beckoning.

An hour later I pull back on the throttle and put us in neutral. The wind vane on top of the mast is pointing west. Finally, the wind has shifted in our favor. I kill the engine and trim the sails for a beam reach, quickly accelerating to six knots as the sun drops toward the horizon.

We sail along in the calm waters three miles off the beach. I can hear the distant roar of racecars as we pass what must be Daytona Beach. I'm starting to feel like we are back in my neighborhood; the buildings along the coast start to look like home. After 2 ½ weeks and nearly 1000 nautical miles, it is somewhat disorienting to be here in the little sailboat that I bought on the other coast of Florida. I wonder how long it's been since *Sobrius* last sailed in the Atlantic.

The sun sets in a quick explosion of color, fades to grey-blue, purple, then black. There are no ships around. The cold wind is blowing from the shore, and I feel it is safe to get some sleep. I'm glad to be below and out of the cold. I'm thankful that the sea is calm and the motion of *Sobrius* is that of a relaxed vessel gliding across the water like a horse that smells the barn. Tonight below deck is comfortable, not at all like last night.

Twenty minutes later (I fixed the timer) I poke my head up and check the horizon. The air is bitter cold, like it must be in the thirties. I quickly scan for ships and see none, and draw my head back into *Sobrius* like a turtle. I lay down and quickly fall back asleep. I repeat this process two more times before seeing a ship behind us. I creep out of my shell and into the cold cockpit. A container ship is approaching from behind. The AIS sounds its alarm, and I steer east, out of the ship's path miles before it passes us and I shut off the alarm from the cockpit, thankful of my work in moving the AIS to within reach.

Another ship is detected by the AIS, but I can't see it. The instrument says it is "engaged in a diving operation." Who could be diving tonight, I wonder. It should be directly to port, but still I can't find it. Apparently the dive boat has no lights on. Maybe this is on purpose, serving some function that I don't understand. Maybe it's a beacon marking a dive location. But I must assume the signal could be coming from a ship hiding in the dark just ahead. Vigilantly I scan the horizon, both to port and in front of us. The icon of the invisible dive boat moves to aft on the screen of the AIS, and no other ships are visible. I venture back below, welcomed by the relatively warm interior of *Sobrius*. I lay down and cover my legs and feet with a blanket. Peace and serenity overcome me. We are getting close to home.

I sleep and get up to check the horizon and the instruments every 20 minutes until I arise and recognize the 312 bridge, the Bridge of Lions, the Vilano Causeway, and the St. Augustine Lighthouse. I am now truly in home-waters. The beach at 11th St where I surf, where I walk with coffee in the morning, passes by. The state park is clearly distinguishable from its lack of lights. A shrimp boat lies still just outside St Augustine Inlet. I become fully awake.

The familiar setting is disorienting. It's hard for me to believe that I've sailed this little boat all the way around from the other side of Florida. I bought *Sobrius* in St Petersburg, yet somehow we are now just off St Augustine. Two worlds collide. I'm really here.

We sail past the inlet, looking for the safe-water buoy, flashing white in a Morse-A pattern. It hides in the forest of lights from shore. We tack through the west wind, turn 180 degrees, and sail back to the south. I decide a bit of late-night sailing would be fun. It is a beautiful night, with stars and crisp, cold air. The lights of home shine on the horizon.

I can't believe I'm here.

After tacking around in the cold and dark for a pleasant hour, I find the safe-water buoy – I can hear its lonely fog-horn, I can see clearly its slowly flashing dot-dash white light. We pass it to the south and I tack without releasing the jib-sheet. *Sobrius* points just off the wind and we come to a near stop. We are hove-to outside St Augustine Inlet, as planned. The journey is almost over.

I go below and make a hot bowl of soup, but I have no need for a bowl and eat the soup straight from the pot. It warms my body and tastes like success. A powerful feeling of happiness is overcoming all my senses as I come to terms with the fact that I have nearly completed the journey and realized my dream of becoming a singlehand-sailor.

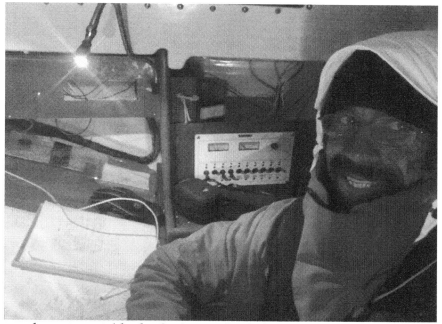

hove-to outside the St Augustine Inlet, waiting for sunrise

~~~

As the sky to the east slowly illuminates from black to

grey, I begin preparing for the end of our journey, packing and organizing. I call the St Augustine City Marina and am elated to be assigned a mooring ball in Salt Run, near the dock, near parking, close to home, and next to the sailboats of friends. This is exactly where I had hoped to get a mooring. I really am the luckiest man in the world.

Sunrise is brilliant, magnificent, bringing light, color, and warmth. I take off my hood and the hat beneath it, shedding layers that I've worn for two days. Clouds on the eastern horizon diffuse and reflect all the colors of sunrise, and the warmth slowly reaches my neck and my blood, circulating throughout my tired but elated self. The realization of being home is coming over me. It's hard to believe, but here we are. I recognize everything: the color of the water, the smell of the air, the buoys, the beaches, the buildings, the bridges. This is where I live, and where *Sobrius* will live. For the last two and a half weeks, this has been my destination, and now I am here.

I drop the jib and bag it. The main is also dropped but left uncovered and ready to hoist in case of an emergency. I pull the stern anchor out of its locker and mount it on the stern pulpit, replacing the yellow life-preserver. I hang the fenders from the lifelines just in case I bump into another sailboat while mooring. Still a novice, and exhausted too, I must be extra careful.

I open the raw-water seacock that supplies the engine with cooling water, put the key in the ignition, turn it on and press the starter button. The Yanmar diesel rumbles to life, its one cylinder banging up and down, reluctantly forcing rackety motion until it warms up and runs a bit more smoothly. We turn into the landbreeze and begin motoring into the inlet, towards home. I must focus on the buoys, I remind myself. I know a shallow sandbar lies to the north, stretching very far out to sea. Another sandbar and then a rock seawall lie to the south. The tide is rising and the current pulls us in.

A large white trawler rushes out to sea, later a sailboat creeps by and the captain and I wave to each other.

As we pass the rock seawall to port, I see the red and green channel markers leading into Salt Run. Between us lies inlet marker #1, and it is not clear whether I should pass this marker to its left or to its right. Why isn't there a red and green buoy marking this intersection like the models in the textbook? I decide to be extra safe and I hail the City Marina on the VHF.

"Keep the green markers on your left" they tell me. They don't understand my question.

"The marker in question is an inlet marker outside the entrance to Salt Run" I try to explain, but they still don't understand my question. The entrance to Salt Run is not, in my opinion, adequately marked. There should be a red and green buoy marking its intersection with the inlet, but there is none, and even though they try, the marina personnel are no help. It's up to me to figure this out, but my mind is tired.

Slowly I approach inlet marker #1. I study the water current – the ripples – reading the water as best I can. Intuition tells me to go between marker #1 and the rock seawall, keeping the inlet channel marker to starboard. I remember there is a shallow sandbar west of the marker, on the other side. It emerges at low tide. I saw a jet-ski stuck there once. My chartplotter agrees and we slowly pass between the rocks and the marker. My depth gauge, which has somehow come back to life, reads 25 feet as we pass. All is well.

The water inside Salt Run is calm, a sense of peace fills me. We are almost to *Sobrius'* new home. The Conch House Marina, where my band I-Vibes plays my favorite gig - Reggae Sunday – passes to starboard. Pilings are still standing at odd angles, damaged last year (2016) by Hurricane Matthew. To port is the tranquil state park with its seagrass, mangroves, and sand dunes. I've surfed on the beach just across those sand dunes many times. I spot my friend John's sailboat *Moonpie* ahead, on which I've sailed many times.

Mooring ball 20 sits waiting for us. I steer *Sobrius* behind *Moonpie* and approach the ball from downwind, like John taught me during a singlehand lesson aboard his boat last year. I put *Sobrius* in neutral and quickly move to the bow, pick up the boathook along the way, and fetch the pennant on mooring ball. I tie us off, and return to the cockpit an accomplished singlehand-sailor. My dream has been realized!

~~~

One thousand nautical miles are behind us as I shut off the engine for the last time on this journey. I turn and look in the direction *Sobrius* points; the black and white striped St Augustine Lighthouse stands tall directly ahead. Above it the sky is grey and undulating; below the water is grey and undulating, on Earth as it is in Heaven, in Heaven as it is on Earth.

I feel an uncontrolled happiness. It's Christmas and I am a child who got just what he wanted. I experience the first kiss of a new lover. Electricity emanates from my skin in an explosion of golden aura. I am awake, I am dreaming, there is no difference. I feel disoriented; it's hard to believe this is real. I am here, in St Augustine, on a boat I purchased on the other coast of Florida two-and-a-half months ago. I have done it! I learned how to sail, bought a sailboat, and sailed her home singlehanded. My whole being is bursting with joy in a chorus of all the joyous emotions as I stand on the deck of my sailboat and look around at the familiar lighthouse, the other sailboats that live here, the green and yellow salt marsh, the houses on the bank, a wooden dock damaged by Hurricane Matthew, a pelican on a piling, looking at me. An osprey flies overhead looking for a fish to catch. These are all my friends. It is all real. I am here and the time is now, and here and now are fantastic.

I think I hear my name in the cold wind. I am so lucky to be here, and the wind is welcoming me home. I hear my name again, and now I think someone must be hailing me from shore. I stand up and look, and I see Jillian, a friend, waving, a one-woman welcoming party, a friend whom I met through the journey of sobriety, welcoming me at the end of my journey on *Sobrius*. My phone dings, alerting me of a text. It's Jillian. She says she saw the picture of me at the navigation table I had previously posted on Facebook, announcing my arrival, so she came to the dock to greet me. She asks if I need anything, and I tell her that I could use a ride home, if she could give me thirty minutes to close up *Sobrius*.

I cover the mainsail with its blue sail cover, remove the jacklines and stow them in the anchor locker, roll up the jib-sheets and stow them in the aft locker, put away the handheld VHF, turn off the power, shut a couple of seacocks, and lock up my little ship. It's cold, and I'm still wearing my foul-weather gear: red jacket, yellow bibs, neoprene shoes. I lower my 12' surfboard into the water and climb aboard with kayak paddle in hand. I turn and look at *Sobrius* as I slowly drift off, wondering if I forgot anything. The dock is only a couple hundred yards away and the water is calm. I casually paddle to the little beach by the lighthouse dock. When I get to shore, Jillian has a hot cup of coffee and a sandwich for me. The coffee tastes like a dream come true, and I devour the sandwich with a smile on my face that doesn't go away for a week.

Singlehand miles: 1242

arrival in St Augustine

Epilogue

When I returned back to my old life after this journey, everything on land seemed glorious and wonderful. I had developed a new appreciation for the common things. My bed, although disappointingly motionless, was big and soft and luxurious. My bathroom seemed incredibly convenient, with running water, a toilet that flushed every time, and a big bathtub with hot water and plenty of soap and shampoo. The laundry room, the kitchen, all the space in my house, the big yard – everything seemed so big and decadent, and still. It's odd that nothing moves on land, while everything moves on the ocean. A sailor is never still, and thus can never totally relax. On land, one is often totally relaxed, and this seemed a luxury to me, although now I see that this is one reason why so many people are out of shape.

The company of people is a blessing that the solo sailor foregoes when at sea. While the tranquility and solitude are wonderful, after this journey I craved talking to other people. I wanted to tell my story to everyone. I wanted to hear what all my friends had been up to as well. Really it is the contrast which is so good. Everything on land and in society is a contrast to a solo sailing journey and this makes both seem more valuable, if both are experienced.

I was lucky enough to find steady work soon after arriving home, and I will soon have all my debts paid off. I plan to work hard all year until spring and then sail to The Bahamas. In the past my attitude towards work has been slack. I've always enjoyed working short days, and taking days off whenever I felt like it. But now I have a new attitude. I've been working hard, putting in forty-hour weeks consistently. I don't want days off spread out randomly. Instead I want to work hard and steadily until it's time to go on another adventure.

I want to focus only on the "prime time" of life, that is, the important activities, like adventure. Sobriety has helped me a lot in this respect. In the past, I was always encouraged to go home early from work by the fact that intoxicants were always waiting for me there. Why not go home and catch a buzz, the little devils in me would say. Sure, why not? Not anymore. Now I work all I can, knowing that I'm on schedule to be able to take a few months off in the spring if I can work steadily for the rest of the year.

For my next adventure, I plan is to sail from Jacksonville, Florida, where *Sobrius* is comfortably docked at The Marina at Ortega Landing, to San Salvador, The Bahamas, where I will clear customs and take a break, and maybe go surfing and SCUBA-diving. Then perhaps I'll explore some of the more remote islands, like Samana Cay, the Plana Cays, and the Jumentos Cays. I'll bask in solitude and do some freediving. I'll look for the fabled blue holes and try to find an octopus to get on video. After getting my fill of the remote "Far Bahamas", I'll cruise through the Exumas, Eluthra, then the Abacos, and on back to Florida. Maybe I'll go visit Cristina again before sailing home to St Augustine. There's sure to be another book in such an adventure.

Acknowledgements

First and foremost, I thank my mother and father, Betsy and Willis Trammell, for supporting this new endeavor of mine. Without their help, I would not have such a fine boat, and this book would be about a much humbler adventure. Without their moral support, I might never have attempted the solo sail around Florida.

Thanks to Dr. Christopher Ruhland, Cristina Vidal, Robin Tooz-Hobson, and my mother for their help editing this book.

Thanks again to Robin Toozs-Hobson for letting me crew on his boat *Sophie Ems* from St Lucia to Puerto Rico.

Thanks to Cristina Vidal and her mother for providing me with a comfortable place to stay while in Miami.

Thanks to Al Lima of Florida West Coast Yachts, the broker who sold me *Sobrius* and helped with many tasks after the sale.

Thanks to Stephen at Marine Supply Warehouse in St Petersburg for supplies and endless advice.

Thanks to Keith Donaldson at Advanced Sails in St Petersburg for repairing my genoa that I tore on my second sea-trial.

Thanks to Salt Creek Marina in St Petersburg for letting me do so much work to my boat there.

Thanks to the St Petersburg Municipal Marina for providing me with a slip and allowing me to work on *Sobrius* while there.

Thanks to The Marina at Ortega Landing in Jacksonville for providing us with a fine place to stay and the beautiful clubhouse in which I wrote most of this book.

Thanks to John Blackford for letting me crew on his sailboat *Moonpie* and for giving me a singlehand lesson.

Thanks to Liam McCormick and Eddie Toy for inviting

me to sail with them on Liam's boat *Monkey's Uncle* to The Bahamas.

Thanks to Sailtime, St Augustine Sailing, and American Sailing Association for teaching me how to sail properly.

Thanks to Jillian Jackson for greeting me with coffee, a sandwich, and a ride home at the end of my journey.

~~~

And finally, thanks to everyone who helped me get and stay sober, so all this could happen.

~~~

Now it's your turn,
go live out *your* dream!

Made in the USA
Coppell, TX
10 December 2019